The Paradox of Transgression in Games

M000006900

The Paradox of Transgression in Games looks at transgressive games as an aesthetic experience, tackling how players respond to game content that shocks, disturbs, and distresses, and how contemporary video games can evoke intense emotional reactions.

The book delves into the commercial success of many controversial video games: although such games may appear shocking for the observing bystander, playing them is experienced as deeply rewarding for the player. Drawing on qualitative player studies and approaches from media aesthetics theory, the book challenges the perception of games as innocent entertainment, and examines the range of emotional, moral, and intellectual experiences of players. As they explore what players consider transgressive, the authors ask whether there is something about the gameplay situation that works to mitigate the sense of transgression, stressing gameplay as an aesthetic experience.

Anchoring the aesthetic game experience both in play studies as well as in aesthetic theory, this book will be an essential resource for scholars and students of game studies, aesthetics, media studies, philosophy of art, and emotions.

Torill Elvira Mortensen, dr.art., is associate professor at the IT University of Copenhagen, Denmark. She holds a PhD from 2003 on text-based games, and much of her research and publications are on the use of games and social media. She is one of the founding members of the journal *Game Studies* and served on the board of the Digital Games Research Association from 2006–2010. She is the author of *Perceiving Play: The Art and Study of Computer Games* (2009), the primary editor of the collection *The Dark Side of Gameplay: Controversial Issues in Playful Environments* (2015), and a Digital Games Research Association (DiGRA) distinguished scholar (2019).

Kristine Jørgensen, PhD, is full professor in media studies at University of Bergen, Norway. She holds a PhD from 2007 on the functionality of sound in video games. She was the project director and principal investigator of the *Games and Transgressive Aesthetics* research project funded by the Research Council of Norway (2015–2019), and is the author of *A Comprehensive Study of Sound in Computer Games* (2009), *Gameworld Interfaces* (2013), and the primary editor of the volume *Transgression in Games and Play* (2019).

Routledge Advances in Game Studies

For more information about this series, please visit: https://www.routledge.com

The Paradox of Transgression in Games

Torill Elvira Mortensen and
Kristine Jørgensen

Routledge
Taylor & Francis Group

LONDON AND NEW YORK

First published 2020
by Routledge
2 Park Square, Milton Park, Abingdon, Oxon OX14 4RN

and by Routledge
605 Third Avenue, New York, NY 10017

First issued in paperback 2022

Routledge is an imprint of the Taylor & Francis Group, an informa business

Publisher's Note
The publisher has gone to great lengths to ensure the quality of this reprint but points out that some imperfections in the original copies may be apparent.

Library of Congress Cataloging-in-Publication Data
A catalog record has been requested for this book

ISBN: 978-1-03-240061-7 (pbk)
ISBN: 978-0-367-41839-7 (hbk)
ISBN: 978-0-367-81647-6 (ebk)

DOI: 10.4324/9780367816476

Typeset in Sabon
by codeMantra

Contents

Illustrations

Figure

Tables

Photo: Copyright Jørn Lavoll, Draum Studio.

Preface

Over the almost three years of planning and writing this book, we have had the opportunity to collaborate in a manner which has been exceptionally rewarding, rich, and educating. Both of us authors have brought our strengths to the table and have uniquely influenced the book. We both come out of media studies, with somewhat different approaches to game analysis, and this book would not have been what you now see without both of our ideas, abilities, and inspirations. The constant sparring process necessary for a work like this has enriched both of our professional lives and offers a better product to the reader than either of us would have created alone.

The book has come into being from a truly collaborative process, where Torill Elvira Mortensen and Kristine Jørgensen both actively contributed to each chapter. Each chapter has been worked through several times by both of us. Its overarching ideas are grounded in the *Games and Transgressive Aesthetics* research project, in which Jørgensen was the principal investigator and project director, and Mortensen was an active partner. The three main ideas relating to the paradox of transgression, the fallacy of play, and the ludic sublime have been worked out in tight dialogue, starting with a workshop in November 2016, where we developed the *Games and Transgressive Aesthetics Manifesto* (Mortensen and Jørgensen 2016). Our further work with this book has spanned intensive writing workshops in Bologna, Italy; Copenhagen, Denmark; and Bergen, Norway.

However, if we were to specify a division of labor in the process, it would be reasonable to state that Mortensen's greatest footprint is on the chapters that deal explicitly with aesthetics and emotion, while Jørgensen's most visibly shows in the chapters that deal with player experiences and the empirical material. In this book, Mortensen has delved into a long history of philosophy on aesthetic appreciation and emotion, and with her rich experience as a researcher focusing on online play and digital media, she has provided analytical insight into how transgressions in games relate to transgressions in culture and society at large. Jørgensen has conducted the empirical studies presented in the book, and with her life-long experience as a player, she has provided a gameplay-sensitive approach to analyzing player experiences with transgressive games.

We are grateful for having had the opportunity to collaborate on this book and hope that our contribution is valuable for a deeper understanding of video game aesthetics.

Acknowledgments

Above all, we would like to thank the participants that were willing to talk about transgressive game experiences. Special thanks to those who were also willing to play such games over extended periods of time and log their experiences. We appreciate what you went through to enable us to better understand video games as an aesthetic medium of expression.

This book springs out of the *Games and Transgressive Aesthetics* project, funded by the Research Council of Norway. Other supporting institutions were University of Bergen, The IT University of Copenhagen, and the Council of Applied Media Research. Thank you for supporting the writing process throughout with time, travel funding, and encouragement for excellent research.

We are also indebted to a number of colleagues. Our warmest thanks go to those who have read longer or shorter parts of our manuscript at different stages of completion: Thank you, Jaakko Stenros, Tomasz Z. Majkowski, Jaroslav Švelch, Holger Pötzsch, Emma Witkowski, Asbjørn Grønstad, and Øyvind Vågnes for truly valuable feedback. We would like to thank everyone involved in the *Games and Transgressive Aesthetics* project in different capacities – as collaborators on publications or as participants in workshops and seminars. We also express our thanks to the research groups we are part of. We thank the Cross-disciplinary Network for Games Research and the Media Aesthetics research group at the University of Bergen. At the IT University of Copenhagen, we particularly want to thank the Culture and Technology (CulT) research group and the Center for Computer Games Research (CCGR) for their contribution. This book would never have been possible without the inspirational and provocative conversations that we have had with all of you. Not least, we sincerely thank Veronica Innocenti and Paolo Noto at the University of Bologna for their time and for facilitating access to the beautiful and rich libraries of this significant university in the initial months of writing on this book.

We also thank Malgorzata Anna Pacholczyk for solid research assistance in collecting empirical data. Thanks to the anonymous reviewers for invaluable feedback and to Suzanne Richardson and the staff at Routledge for a solid and professional publishing process.

Last but not least, without our families, we would never be able to perform as we do. Anchoring us in reality, they are the reasons this book was possible at all.

Kristine thanks Frank and Lasse for fun and games, and for being there. Torill thanks Trygve, Erla, and Hauk – this, like everything, is for you.

Introduction
Exploring transgressions in games

Video games are notorious for excessive violence and stereotypical representations, and have through the late 1990s and up until today consistently pushed the limits of public sensibility. To play such games may appear shocking for the observing bystander, while it is experienced as *fun* for the player engaging with it. A pressing question is *why* players would indulge in excessive and explicit game content; and further, what happens to the sense of transgression in a gameplay situation. Does playing a game somehow remove inhibitions and limitations? Building on play theory, one reason players endure transgressive game content may be that in-game transgressions take place inside a separate space in which the player is generally physically safe from the transgressions and within an explicitly ludic context where the actions taken have a very different meaning from the actions observed. Looking at video games from the context of Bakhtin's carnival offers a second explanation, as sociologists Lauren Langman and Andras Lukacs state that "transgressions not only provide forbidden indulgences, but [also] the very fact of violating the norm and "getting" away with it provides another pleasure" and that "the gratification of 'forbidden desires' whether erotic, exhibitionist, narcissistic, or aggressive is even more pleasurable due to the very transgression of the norm" (Langman and Lukacs 2010, 67). A third, popular explanation of why people tolerate transgressions in games is escapism, from realism and into fiction, from putting the "real" world aside for the virtual, or into play itself. Game scholar Gordon Calleja states that "it would be no exaggeration to say that digital games are considered the epitome of contemporary escapism" (Calleja 2010). Calleja explains this through "the binary illusion", an assumption that the digitally produced exists outside of reality, as if the playing of games can be shut away from the social, cultural, and technological context within which it takes place.

Springing out of the research project *Games and Transgressive Aesthetics* at the University of Bergen between 2015 and 2019, this book takes an aesthetic perspective toward understanding transgressions in games. According to dictionary definitions, to *transgress* means to overstep the boundaries of taste, moral code, social taboos, or law (Collins English

Dictionary 2017). Transgressions include the overstepping of social norms, but also individual sensibilities, and even though something is experienced as individually transgressive or may come down to subjective interpretations, most people would recognize the violation of the norms of a society of which they are part. While a minor part of our discussion will be concerned with the social and political controversies games cause or are part of, the aim of this book is to understand the aesthetic of the provocative nature of games. One hypothesis we want to explore is that games and play are uniquely suited to transgressive aesthetics, and this is why digital games are currently both immensely popular mainstream entertainment and still controversial. To do so, we explore the difference between the profound transgressions that make us reject an expression and aesthetic transgressions, which we are able to contextualize and somehow process due to its aesthetic context. Considering how play tends to mitigate overwhelming experiences and make them manageable, the main question of this book is whether the aesthetic of games renders their transgressions manageable. Engaging with games as media texts and aesthetic artifacts, this book asks: What happens to the sense of play when encountering transgressive game content? How can the ludic context and the sense of transgression interact; in other words, how does the sense of play affect transgressions, and how do transgressions affect the sense of play? Comparing games to avant-garde art and looking at their carnivalesque nature, we critically question the controversies surrounding games. We discuss how games transgress through their inclusion of content that breaks the expectation of target groups, the norms of society, subjective sensibilities and taste, and rules and codes of the game as well as conventions of genre and technology.

Established as a niche field in the 1990s, game studies is flourishing today. It is developing as its own field, sometimes referred to simply as "ludology" – the study of the unique aspects of games, but is also tightly interwoven with other fields. Game studies is concerned with the study of games, players, and the contexts surrounding games and players, and for this reason perspectives spanning fields such as computer science, media studies, sociology, economy, anthropology, and literature studies are examples of areas that have been applied to the study of games. *The Paradox of Transgression in Games* is a product of this multidisciplinary nature of game studies and engages with theories, findings, and ideas from the wide universe of game research. As we specifically study transgression in games – a topic that spans far beyond the games themselves – we need to take advantage of the breadth of the field.

Although we do position this work firmly in the multidisciplinary field of game studies, this does not mean we will not offend. We take advantage of theories already applied in other disciplines, particularly media studies and aesthetics, and we will twist their original meaning in ways that makes sense in the context of transgressive games. Although our aim is to create a better understanding of transgression in games, we also acknowledge that our work will not be the final and absolute work. This means that we will treat certain topics briefly and that we also may ignore other topics. We see this work as an early attempt of illuminating the transgressive aesthetic of video games, and our ambition is to initiate a debate around a topic that we believe is at the core of game aesthetics. We want to present a perspective on how we can think about games and how games are experienced. This is a step toward more varied conversations about how we enjoy, understand, and incorporate games in contemporary culture.

Three main ideas

The book will explore transgressions in games through three ideas: First, we argue against the *fallacy of play*, that is, the erroneous idea that games and play concern that which is non-serious, fun, safe, and with little consequence outside itself. Although we acknowledge that games and play can be understood as taking place inside their own frame of reference, it is important to stress that the boundary between games and the world is never absolute but instead permeable and porous (Salen and Zimmerman 2004, 94). We stress that although the context of games and play may have a mitigating effect on the sense of transgression, games and play can indeed be subversive, unsafe, and concern real-life issues (Csikszentmihaly 1981, 14; Geertz 1973, 432–33; Jørgensen 2014; Linderoth and Mortensen 2015; Malaby 2007, 107; Montola 2010; Schechner 2013, pts. 118–119; Taylor 2006, 151–55; Stenros 2015, 72–76). Thus, we explore games that challenge the fallacy of play by being provocative, uncomfortable, or frustrating, and look at how such content interact with the play activity, which in itself also can be ambiguous by oscillating between different emotional states varying from excitement to frustration.

Following the idea that the aesthetic context of games as well as the playful mindset may contribute to mitigating the discomfort of transgressive game content, our second argument concerns what we see as a *paradox of transgression*. The paradox of transgression is the phenomenon that when something is experienced as an absolute transgression, it cannot be engaged with and that if we are able to engage with it, it cannot be a transgression.

For this reason, we distinguish between *profound transgression* and *transgressive aesthetics*:

> The paradox of transgression is that the profoundly transgressive negates the transgressive aesthetic, while the transgressive aesthetic mitigates the profound transgression.
>
> (Mortensen and Jørgensen 2016)

This means that when the sense of transgression is aestheticized or put in a playful context, it is often experienced as less severe and therefore also bearable. When transgressive practices are integrated into culture, either through the carnival, a rite of passage, as transgressive art in an art gallery, or as media expressions hailed for their edginess, these practices are accepted into a particular cultural context where they are rarely experienced as a profound transgression. They are accepted as *challenging* established norms, but it is also implied that by being accepted, these practices do not go as far as actually *breaking* said norms in this particular context. In other words, context, and audience matter: Splatter films and violent games may cross the line for your grandmother or mother, as the advertisement for the horror game *Dead Space 2* (Visceral Games 2011) suggests (Benedetti 2011), but they do not offer profound transgressions for their fans. Transgressive art and media are for this reason never absolute transgressions, except for audiences outside the target group. Thus, the paradox of transgression reveals the deeply cultural, and subcultural, meaning of transgression relating to the breaking of taboos and crossing of social and cultural boundaries, acts which are examples of deviant behavior at the same time as such acts also contribute to maintaining the established hegemony (Bakhtin 1999; Bataille 1985; Jenks 2003, 2). In an aesthetic context such as games, this means that if the player is able to continue engaging with the aesthetic work, it cannot be a profound transgression because, to count as a profound transgression, the aesthetic work must disturb the user to the extent that they no longer want to engage with it. In other words, profoundly transgressive media content would render a film "unwatchable" (Grønstad 2012, 9–10) or a game "unplayable".

Related to the paradox of transgression is the fact that often when we encounter uncomfortable, repulsive, or taboo content in aesthetic contexts such as games, we do not automatically reject it outright, but may instead accept its presence as part of an aesthetic experience. Although transgressions in games may overwhelm the audience with revulsion, this aesthetic experience can also be acknowledged as awe-inspiring and stunning in all its excess or exaggeration. This is at the core of our third argument, which concerns the *sublime*. Following Immanuel Kant, we encounter the sublime when we have an overwhelming experience of something "larger than ourselves". In game studies, we find this as the *ludic sublime* (Vella 2015), the sense of awe when the play potential of a game overwhelms the player, when the game reveals its mechanisms and meanings and the player glimpses the strategies and possibilities in the game. The ludic sublime concerns the realization that while the game may be overwhelming, it is also something that can be overcome by effort and strategy. We argue that well-designed games indeed can create sublime experiences that go beyond the ludic sublime as defined by Daniel Vella and may overwhelm experiences of discomfort, anger, or fear, leaving the players with strong aesthetic experiences provoked by the entirety of video game play rather than single aspects.

Our three main ideas call for an explanation of what we mean by *aesthetics*. While dictionary entries typically define "aesthetics" as the "formal study of art, especially in relation to the idea of beauty" (Cambridge

Dictionary 2018), there is a broader and more precise notion that aesthetics concerns the meaning, validity, and value judgments relating to works of art (Kirkpatrick 2011, 13; Sharp and Thomas 2019, 4). Aesthetic judgment thus goes beyond the beautiful and may be based on the valuation of other features specific for the work in question. While aesthetics often seems to be associated with visual properties, it concerns those features of a work that appreciators associate with value. Further, the focus on aesthetics as relating to perception and appreciation implies that the sense that we are dealing with something aesthetic emerges from the relationship between a work and the perceiving subject (Aldama and Lindenberger 2016, 42; Shelley 2015; Slater, n.d). For games, this means that they are aesthetic works in so far as they are appreciated by the players, and that the elements that create this sensation are associated with the full spectrum of the medium, spanning game mechanics as well as representational features. Thus, we follow Graeme Kirkpatrick's idea that games are primarily aesthetic objects and that video game aesthetics concerns a particular kind of experience, stressing the ludic elements of this experience (Kirkpatrick 2011, 1–2). We highlight the fact that interaction and play are part of the aesthetics of video games and important for how they move us. When we discuss transgressive aesthetics in games, we are focusing on a perspective that challenges the idea that the aesthetic concerns beauty and appreciation, but instead stresses the concept that meaning also springs out of expressions that approach the point of rejection through emotional and ethical overload; provocation, shock, and occasionally disgust. In games, such transgressive aesthetics is experienced through gameplay as well as through representation, and in this book, we investigate how players make sense of a transgressive game aesthetic.

This book is concerned with the line between *profound transgressions* and *transgressive aesthetics* in games – what it is that makes players cringe and stop playing a game, and what makes players keep playing even when the game is experienced as excessive, provocative, or repulsive. In this sense, our perspective is on the player's side. We are explicitly avoiding a normative view of what kind of content may or may not be appropriate in games; rather, the book is an investigation of research on what players experience as transgressive game content, how players experience transgressive game situations, what they do when confronted with transgressions in games, and what role transgressive experiences have in the play situation.

Background and previous work

Transgression is a well-discussed term in art, philosophy, and the social sciences, and we do not attempt to challenge the previous, established understandings of the term as we apply it to games. While games and play as transgressive experiences are well established, particularly in relation to religious and cultural rituals (Bakhtin 1999; Schechner 2013; Turner

2009), the modern game forms we focus on are still discussed as disgusting and dangerous. Historically, research on the transgressive side of games has followed the tradition of media effects research and has been dominated by psychological effect studies focusing on both whether violent game content makes players violent and excessive use (Ferguson 2010; Gentile and Stone 2005; Kutner and Olson 2008; Nielsen 2016). This perspective has invited discussions more concerned with the potential for corruption of the young and vulnerable (Hern 2013) than with whether games can be understood as aesthetically provocative and transformative. The consequence of the dominance of concern rhetoric in public debates on games is a lack of language for analysis and criticism of the more provocative and extreme structures and content players, reviewers and others engaged with games and play practices will encounter. Provocative, transgressive games remain framed in a language of concern and protection, blocking a deeper understanding of the process of reception, critical reading, and aesthetic appreciation.

With the rise of game studies as a cross-disciplinary field spanning the humanities, social sciences, and computer sciences, there has been an influx of more context-oriented and culturally sensitive research, attentive toward games as cultural products and activities; as social arenas; and as representational, expressive, and computational media. Springing out of these perspectives is research on how players make sense of games and include them in their lives, and how they experience them and interpret them as media texts; it is from this perspective that this book rises. Examples of some works that stress this perspective and act as our inspiration are Graeme Kirkpatrick's work on game aesthetics (Kirkpatrick 2011) and Miguel Sicart's research on how games include ethics and ethical reflection (Sicart 2009, 2013). Others are Doris C. Rusch's design-focused research on how to express human experience in games (Rusch 2009, 2017), Mary Flanagan's work on radical game design for critical games (Flanagan 2013), and Brian Schrank's research on avant-garde video games (Schrank 2014). Of special interest to our perspective is Torill Elvira Mortensen, Jonas Linderoth, and Ashley Brown's edited volume *The Dark Side of Gameplay* (2015) that explores how players engage with the "darker" side of life through games and why taking on the role as criminals and carrying out transgressive acts is fascinating when playing games. This book is also closely related to Kristine Jørgensen and Faltin Karlsen's edited volume *Transgression in Games and Play* (2018), which focuses on transgressive play practices and game experiences in a similar perspective. But by introducing *transgressive aesthetic* to games in this volume, we specifically look at games through a lens designed to create meaning out of expressions which approach the point of rejection through emotional and moral overload, shock, awe, and occasionally disgust.

The context for looking at transgressive games from an aesthetic perspective is the tradition of transgressive art. As a particular genre of postmodernist art, *transgressive art* is an established practice of rebellious art that aims to shock and offend, and to question and subvert conventional moral beliefs (Cashell 2009, 1). It is what "disgusts, discomforts, unnerves, offends as well as art that triggers in us experiences of pain and shame" (Aldama and Lindenberger 2016, 1). Transgressive art is in conflict with social and aesthetic norms and sometimes condemned as a speculative attempt of drawing attention under the alibi of art; at other times, examples of this art form are accused of going so far in its taboo-breaking that it becomes impossible to engage with (Cashell 2009, 1). While transgressive art is in opposition against what is accepted as art within the art discourse itself, it rebels by taking the audience out of their comfort zone and question "all received and ostensibly incontestable values" (Grønstad 2012, 38). This gives it the potential to enable reflection and awareness by forcing the audience to confront issues that tend to evoke unease and discomfort (Julius 2002, 189). We also find the concept of transgressive aesthetics in other discourses outside the narrow sphere of art. Directors such as Lars von Trier and Quentin Tarantino are celebrated artists who base their work on creating discomfort and challenging the norms of both filmmaking and society. Lars von Trier explores the technical limitations of the medium while he describes painful, often depressing topics, and his movie *The House that Jack Built* caused massive walkouts in the festival in Cannes in 2018 (Mumford 2018). Quentin Tarantino creates ultraviolent, satirical works, and his most recent work *Once Upon a Time... in Hollywood* is praised by reviewers for being provocative and confusing, simultaneously (Bradshaw 2019). Both directors explore topics such as drug abuse, nihilism, and sexual experimentation, and aim to transform cinematic creativity, yet still have tremendous success among their audiences – often with topics that we see reflected in video games. Video games have historically been notorious for pushing the limits of public sensibility through its excessive use of violence. Certain indie developers, such as the Newsgaming design collective as well as live-action role-playing games traditions such as the Nordic LARP, have also been exploring uncomfortable and controversial topics, backed by researchers interested in the medium-specific powers of games for communicating meaningful, critical, and thought-provoking representations of sensitive issues.

By talking about games that challenge our values and sensibilities as *transgressive*, we are including such games into this particular aesthetic tradition. While we do not insist that all provocative games should be treated as identical to transgressive art, our purpose here is to show that games are aesthetic media that have expressive potential and power that rival those of other aesthetic forms. Also by pointing out the *aesthetic* aspect, we are stressing that it is the relationship between the game as a work and the player as audience that is central. This "player-response" approach acknowledges the expressive purpose of the designed artifact which a game is, and it underlines the players' awareness of the game as a work created by an artist with an expressive purpose in mind. This expressive purpose may be anything from provocation to entertainment, and allows us to take a broad perspective that includes both the aesthetics of gameplay as well as the fact that sometimes people appreciate fictional tragedies and other uncomfortable entertainment (Bartsch and Oliver 2011; Cupchik 2011; Oliver 2008; Schramm and Wirth 2010; Tamborini et al. 2010; Zillman 1998), including video games (Oliver et al. 2016; Rogers et al. 2017).

If we look at game studies literature, the term *transgression* has been used in connection with deviant or subversive play, that is, play that breaks the rules or the intended design of the game, or that challenges social norms and cultural expectations. Although the idea of play as boundary-breaking and explorative is old (Csikszentmihaly 1981; Schechner 2013; Sutton-Smith 1997), and subversive practices also are well-documented in early research on online play (Dibbel 1993; Taylor and Jakobsson 2003), the word *transgression* as a concept to describe boundary-breaking play was first used by game researcher Espen Aarseth (2007). He argues that understanding this kind of transgressive play is crucial for understanding game culture, because it challenges the idea of an implied player inscribed into the game. Gender studies scholar Jenny Sundén defined transgressive play as "innovation and, possibly, subversion, of finding, exploring and exploiting loopholes in the game fabric" (2009) in her ethnographic studies of how sexuality has been used as a resource for transgressive play in *World of Warcraft* (Blizzard 2004), and learning scientist Yasmin B. Kafai and her colleagues used the concept in their study of gender play of girls in virtual worlds to describe "activities and attitudes that challenge, or transgress, stereotypical notions of how a girl is supposed to look, act and behave" (Kafai et al. 2009). While such practices indeed concern the relationship between a work and the player, we argue that in these studies transgression springs out of the players' norm-breaking and convention-challenging actions, and what the player decides to do with the game rather than out of the game content in itself. Although such transgressive play practices may result from certain kinds of game design, they are examples of *transgressive play practices* rather than *transgressive game content*, which is the focus of this book.

While we *play* the structured and rule-bound games, *play* alone is a free-form and more permeable activity. Philosopher and sociologist Roger Caillois uses the terms *ludus* and *paidia* for the play of games and free-form play, respectively (Caillois 2001). In many languages, *play* denotes the activity itself, while *game* refers to the rule system or even the object. This has caused the verb "gaming" to become common in English-language game studies to distinguish the ludus type of play. Game designers and researchers Katie Salen and Eric Zimmerman define play as "free movement within a more rigid structure" (Salen and Zimmerman 2004), and argue that play is something that occurs both in opposition to and through exploring and experimenting with the rigid structures. However, as play is central for activities relating to games, we cannot keep a strict boundary where we completely exclude transgressive play practices. We will discuss such play practices where relevant and look closer at consequences of having transgressive game content in a playful context. Thus, the book will also explore the interplay between transgressive content and play. An important question is how can play and playfulness affect the sense of transgression? And how may transgressive content affect play and the sense of playfulness? Further, we will also address the question of whether transgressive game content concerns the representational aspects alone or whether game mechanics can also be transgressive. Here we will discuss scholar and game designer Ian Bogost's theory of *procedural rhetorics* that stresses that games are procedural systems that carry meaning and make arguments through rules and game mechanics (Bogost 2007, 44–46).

A player-response perspective on game analysis

While the main concern of this book is transgressive games rather than transgressive play, it is important to stress that from our perspective, it is not really possible to study games without also taking the player into account. Thus, our viewpoint echoes the reader-response theorist Wolfgang Iser's idea that "[c]entral to the Reading of every literary work is the interaction between its structure and its recipient" (Iser 1978, 20).

In game studies, much of the analysis and understanding of games has been carried out through researcher self-play, based on the idea that, in order to understand how a particular game works, the researcher has to experience it themselves (Aarseth 2003; Mäyrä 2008, 165–67; Mortensen 2002). In such studies, the player is either the researcher themselves as an empirical, historical player – however unrepresentative they may be – or an *implied player* (Aarseth 2007; Mortensen 2003) intended by the design of the game. According to Aarseth, there is a divide between humanist research focusing on textual analysis and the sociologically and ethnographically oriented research focusing on empirical players:

> These two camps, one focused on understanding games through playing them, and one focused on observing actual players, represent two quite separate paradigms in terms of their player perspective.
>
> (Aarseth 2007)

We argue that it is a fallacy to claim that game analysis through self-play and observing actual players are two incompatible paradigms. We could point out that the common practice of autoethnography in game studies already muddies the waters if we try to create a strict disciplinary divide, but rather than chasing disciplinary purity, we believe that these two player perspective paradigms must be combined if we are to understand games as interactive media.

Building on Aarseth's own term *real-time hermeneutics,* which is characterized as "analysis practiced as performance, with direct feedback from the system" (Aarseth 2003), Jonne Arjoranta argues that the hermeneutic process of games go beyond the fact that they are works that need interpretation. Instead, there is a real-time hermeneutics at work "concerned with the processes of interpretation that are active when the player plays" (Arjoranta 2015, 59). Thus, understanding the meaning-making process in games is less about individual interpretation and more about looking into how the game is understood as it is being played, including the important fact that the player may change their playstyle and course of action during play based on how their interpretations of the in-game events change in real time.

Transgressive readings

With focus on the fact that the meaning of games comes into being as a real-time process in which the player is an active participant, the concept of real-time hermeneutics allows us to understand the complex interplay between interpretation and gameplay. Following this line of thought, in our research we rely heavily on player data in order to better understand transgressive games. We have conducted qualitative studies involving players because we believe that as interactive media, games are better understood through a multiple player perspective. In other words, since a game changes according to player choices, gameplay style, player skill, and game literacy as well as according to emergent game features, such as artificial intelligence and how different processes are simulated, self-play can only provide a limited perspective of a game, even if one plays in a "transgressive" way that breaks with designer intent, if we follow Aarseth's use of the term. In order to position more clearly how we understand "transgressive play", let us compare this to Stuart Hall's *oppositional reading* (2006, 173). Cultural theorist Stuart Hall describes in his famous essay "Encoding and Decoding in the Television Discourse" how hegemony and corporate power creates particular readings depending on the readers' position, from the dominant position by way of the negotiated to the oppositional. While a hegemonic/dominant reading would follow the encoded message intended by the authors of the text, the oppositional reading deliberately questions the dominant story and looks for other interpretations, and at its best, it crosses the boundaries of our assumptions while revealing and questioning the norms and power structures of society. A *negotiated* reading will thus partly accept the encoded message. However, as researchers, our aim should be to take a step back and look for the whole picture and beyond. We must look for both dominant and oppositional readings not only in our own game analyses but also when we try to understand other players' readings. We must look further than this and look for *transgressive readings,* that is, readings that either break radically (and sometimes also intentionally) with the apparent intention of the text or which break radically with how people normally engage with the text. When neo-Nazis embrace *The Elder Scrolls V: Skyrim* (Bethesda Game Studios 2011) because they are able to identify with the nationalist and xenophobic Nords (Bjørkelo 2017) or when modders of the same game create modifications that enable players to rape non-playing characters (Májkowski 2017), this can be seen as an example of a transgressive reading. Attentive toward a diverse player perspective, in this book, we look at the broad spectrum of readings, from the dominant to the oppositional, while we also pay attention to such transgressive readings.

What we also take from Hall's perspective is the mixed methods approach that is required to understand both sides of the communication process, with a focus on the meaning-making, both as it is presented in the work and in the way users perceive and create meaning. Aarseth argues that since games sometimes allow players to do unexpected things that most likely would have been made impossible by design if the developers had predicted them, it is important to include such transgressive practices "as a counterweight to the implied player position" (Aarseth 2007). While transgressive play practices are indeed important and an interesting method both in game analyses and in studies of historical players, researching these practices through self-play does not provide a multi-faceted perspective of the differences in meaning-making that emerge between players, both those who "counter-play" and those who play as intended by the design of the game.

Further, since most contemporary games are also representational and expressive media, we need to understand how players interact with game mechanisms and how the messages shaped by the game are received and experienced in a gameplay context. Here our own play will only enable a very limited understanding based on the researcher's own cultural and social predispositions. Understanding dominant/hegemonic, negotiated, and oppositional interpretations of a game's message can only be achieved through taking into account multiple player perspectives.

This does not mean that we disagree with the importance of playing as research. On the contrary, we believe that this is essential to an approach taking into consideration multiple player perspective approach. In his paper "Playing Research: Methodological approaches to game analysis", Aarseth writes that there are three ways of gaining knowledge of a game: We can study the design of the game; we can observe others play or read their reports; or we can play the game ourselves. We must experience the game personally to avoid misunderstandings, and observation alone will not allow us to understand the player experience; further, the mental interpretation of rules is invisible for outsiders (Aarseth 2003). What we want to highlight is that combining play as research with other players' perspectives is not only optional, but mandatory for any serious investigation of a game.

Method and data collection

As the purpose of this book is a study of transgressive games and what makes them transgressive, we have played potentially transgressive games and analyzed their game design. But we have also realized our limitations in that matter: What we find uncomfortable, others may enjoy. When others get offended, we may not. This is the nature of transgression – while there are a few things that are likely to offend large groups, for the most part we have different thresholds of transgression. Taking this into consideration, within the *Games and Transgressive Aesthetics* research project we have carried out qualitative research among players to get an insight into how they interpret a selection of games. For an overview of whether players have clear memories of experiences with transgressive content and what kind of attitudes are present, we carried out introductory focus group studies; for a more detailed insight into the actual gameplay experiences with potentially transgressive games, we carried out gameplay journal studies. In addition to the data we have collected for this study, we are also leaning on tangential data collected by other researchers as well as public debates about and reviews of transgressive games.

Focus groups was the method used for an introductory, exploratory study to gain insight into what experiences players have with transgressive game content, their willingness to talk about it, and their attitudes toward such content. We chose focus groups rather than individual interviews in order to offer the participants an arena for deliberation among peers. We also considered the idea that transgressive and controversial topics could potentially be uncomfortable to discuss with a researcher alone and easier with the support of others. Based on their willingness to discuss controversial and uncomfortable content in games, key individuals were recruited from the environments surrounding local game associations in a Norwegian city. These key recruits were individuals who considered video games to be central to their field of interest without necessarily labeling themselves "gamers". At the same time, the selection of key individuals was sensitive toward securing diverse opinions with regards to games and game content. After initial conversations with each of the key individuals, they were given mandate to recruit additional individuals into their group; these new recruits did not have to be people with whom they agreed, but should be individuals they trusted they would be able to have interesting conversations with.

In order to get more information on the lived play experiences, we conducted another study featuring gameplay journals, where players played the games at their own pace and in their own homes while filling in a log detailing what they had been doing in the game that day, whether there were any events that they found particularly noteworthy, and what they felt about those events. Focusing on a combination of games that had provoked public controversy or been discussed in gaming media either as including topics that were taboo or as emotionally difficult, the respondents each chose one of the six games: *This War of Mine* (11 bit studios and War Child 2014), *Hatred* (Destructive Creations 2015), *Alien: Isolation* (Creative Assembly 2014), *Beyond: Two Souls* (Quantic Dream 2013), and *Bloodborne* (From Software 2015). *Grand Theft Auto V* (Rockstar North 2013) was added to the study later in order to cover how an open-world approach to game design would affect the reception of a highly debated game. A factor in our selection of games also concerned a sensitivity toward having diverse genres and in covering games where a potential sense of transgression was created by the representational aspect as well as games where this was created by the game mechanics. We were also attentive toward combining obscure as well as more popular games. Recruitment of participants happened mainly through social media, such as our Twitter accounts, the *Games and Transgressive Aesthetics* project blog, and Facebook page. Also, physical posters were distributed at high schools and schools of higher education in the Bergen area in Norway, but only six of the recruits were living in the area. Having completed their logs, either because they had quit or completed the game, they were subject to a follow-up interview clarifying the journal entries. Among those who completed the study by logging their gameplay and participating in a follow-up interview, there were a total of 30 participants from 13 countries. Five recruits abandoned the journal after zero or one entry, leaving us with a total of 25 participants. All participants who completed one of the studies are listed in Table 0.1.

While the benefit of our approach is that it provides a broad player perspective, it also has drawbacks. Recruiting players to a study of transgressive games is itself challenging. First of all, submitting people to potentially uncomfortable, offensive, or repulsive game content is not ethically straight-forward. As research ethics regulations for obvious reasons demand that participation in research is voluntary, those participating in the study must be willing to submit to content that could potentially create a level of discomfort. This created a problem with the distinction between profound and aesthetic transgression: If somebody is willing to submit themselves to transgression, it is likely that they do not find the transgressions *profound*. This is part of the definition of a profound transgression – it makes the experience unbearable. It is likely that those interested in participating may have expected a sense of discomfort, but not something that crossed the line into becoming unplayable to them. So our methods suffered from an instance of the paradox of transgression: If you are willing to submit to the content, it is not likely to be profoundly transgressive; and if the content is profoundly transgressive, you are not willing to play. Hence, what we in reality subjected the participants to and what we thus in reality studied was *transgressive aesthetics*: It concerns an artistic practice of intentional disturbance (Mortensen and Jørgensen 2016). In this sense, the transgressive experience takes place inside a context that is both fictional, ludic, and stylized or aestheticized, all factors that we argue contribute to mitigate the sense of transgression. Not least, volunteering to participate in the study

Table 0.1 Overview of player respondents

Pseudonym/age	Occupation	Nationality	Study
"Anette" (24)	Unskilled worker	Norway	Focus group 3
"Aron" (35)	Skilled worker	Norway	Focus group 1
"Brian" (19)	Student	Netherlands	*Hatred* gameplay journal
"Bridget" (21)	Student	Great Britain	*GTAV* gameplay journal
"Cole" (34)	Teaching assistant	Canada	*GTAV* gameplay journal
"Danny" (22)	Student	Poland	*Hatred* gameplay journal
"David" (27)	Recent graduate	Hungary	*Alien: Isolation* gameplay journal
"Frank" (29)	Shop assistant	Sweden	*Alien: Isolation* gameplay journal
"Fred" (38)	Researcher	Netherlands	*This War of Mine* gameplay journal
"Greg" (31)	Unskilled worker	Norway	Focus group 3
"Helen" (25)	Student	Finland	*Beyond: Two Souls* gameplay journal
"Henry" (22)	Student	Poland	*Bloodborne* gameplay journal
"James" (25)	Photographer	Indonesia	*Bloodborne* gameplay journal
"Jane" (38)	IT support worker	Poland	*This War of Mine* gameplay journal
"John" (21)	Student	Norway	Focus group 4
"Josh" (23)	Student	Norway	*Bloodborne* gameplay journal
"Karen" (23)	Student	Norway	Focus group 2
"Keith" (29)	Game designer	Poland	*Hatred* gameplay journal
"Kris" (26)	IT consultant	Belgium	*Beyond: Two Souls* gameplay journal
"Leon" (39)	Photographer	Lithuania	*This War of Mine* gameplay journal
"Luke" (29)	Student	Norway	Focus group 2
"Mary" (25)	Game designer	Norway	Focus group 3
"Mel" (26)	Graphic designer	Poland	*Alien: Isolation* gameplay journal
"Nathan" (37)	Unemployed	Norway	*Bloodborne* gameplay journal
"Neil" (25)	Student	Norway	Focus group 4
"Norah" (35)	Distribution associate	Norway	*GTAV* gameplay journal
"Oscar" (36)	Engineer	Norway	Focus group 1
"Paul" (22)	Student	Poland	*Alien: Isolation* gameplay journal
"Penny" (23)	Student	Turkey	*Beyond: Two Souls* gameplay journal
"Peter" (26)	Unemployed	Norway	Focus group 4
"Phil" (30)	Teacher	Poland	*Alien: Isolation* gameplay journal
"Sally" (26)	Consumer market researcher	USA	*GTAV* gameplay journal
"Sarah" (26)	Student	Netherlands	*Bloodborne* gameplay journal
"Shaun" (28)	Unemployed	Norway	Focus group 2
"Stan" (28)	Student	Poland	*This War of Mine* gameplay journal
"Ted" (25)	Unemployed	Norway	Focus group 4
"Theo" (23)	Student	Norway	*Beyond: Two Souls* gameplay journal
"Tony" (36)	Skilled worker	Norway	Focus group 1

may in itself be enough to move any sense of transgression from profound to aesthetic through the new framing.

However, by playing at their own pace in the sanctity of their home, participants could decide for themselves how much they could tackle and when to stop playing, should their sensibilities be challenged. Of course, some volunteers may also be genuinely interested in having profoundly transgressive game experiences, not necessarily due to inherent masochism but because of an interest in games as a medium and in contributing to research in the field. Also, as positive psychology has shown, people often appreciate tragedies and other forms of "uncomfortable entertainment" for any number of reasons, such as, but not limited to, insight into the human condition and relevance to their own lives (Oliver et al. 2016; Tamborini et al. 2010).

Another methodological challenge is researching subjective experiences. While researching other people's experiences, the researcher is twice removed from the experience, limited to interpreting how other individuals describe and interpret their experiences (Smith, Flowers, and Larkin 2009, 35). We are thus limited both by the participants' self-awareness and ability to describe and interpret their own experiences, and the researcher's ability to describe and interpret those accounts again. With respect to the focus group studies, this issue is also amplified by the fact that the participants are discussing and contextualizing their memories of uncomfortable game experiences, which is not the same as describing the memories in themselves. Also, the dynamic of focus group studies often tends to reveal more about attitudes and interpretations than about experiences (Smith, Flowers, and Larkin 2009, 71–73). However, as an introductory study, using focus groups enabled us to get insight into overarching issues related to player attitudes toward uncomfortable experiences as well as their willingness and ability to talk about these. Using gameplay journals, however, we were able to get one step closer to the experiences. While still limited by the participants' ability to express themselves, gameplay journals allowed the participants to write down their experiences and emotions shortly after they occurred. Also, since they filled in their logs after every gameplay session, it is possible to track their description of their experiences over some time. Additionally, as the journals differed a lot in terms of detail, in the follow-up interview the researchers could ask participants to elaborate on issues that were unclear in the logs.

The gameplay journals allowed for an initial, immediate expression of the reaction to transgression, which might have been closer to affect than emotion, as we discuss in Chapter 6. In this context, we define *affect* as the immediate, pre-interpretation reaction to an event or message, while emotion is the interpreted reaction when we have managed to decide what we actually felt (Brennan 2004, 5). In an interview or a conversation with a peer group, the description of the reaction would almost certainly be about the emotion the players felt after interpretation, due to the need to explain it to others. A journal, while still dependent on language and suffering from the same limitations of how we understand and explain emotion, is directed toward the individual, and it is more likely that the players register pre-judgment reactions rather than an emotion filtered for discussions.

However, in terms of getting close to the actual experience, the self-play that Aarseth (2007) is arguing for is valuable. According to play scholar Jaakko Stenros, it is difficult to simply observe the intrinsic motivation behind much play (2015, 63). Even though we are seasoned players, as game scholars, our experiences are colored by an academic discourse, and for this reason we are far from the average player. What playing the games used and discussed in our studies, as well as other transgressive games that have been the subjects of controversy, gives us is an insight into what kinds of discomfort they may evoke. It also gives us a chance to experience the interplay between transgression and playfulness. This has been used as a point of departure for formulating our hypotheses and the research questions we are exploring through additional player studies.

Book overview

Transgression is a moving target and addressing transgressions in games is a complex endeavor. The discussion needs to touch a wide range of topics that have as much to do with art, emotions, and digital media as with games. To cater to the complexity of the topic, this book will illuminate the phenomenon of transgression in games from different angles.

This book is structured in three main sections, which center on transgressive games, transgressive experiences, and transgressive aesthetics. After the present introductory chapter, we move onto the first section, *Transgression in Games*. The three chapters in this section discuss the concept of transgression in context with video games and argue for our first main idea, the paradox of transgression, and in what ways it applies to games. Chapter 1, *Old Term, New Game*, discusses transgression as a concept and grounds it in existing discourses such as sociology and art. With focus on ludic transgressions, the chapter also compares transgression in games to related concepts such as cheating and looks at public controversies over game content and discusses what kind of content that has been looked upon as norm-breaking and why. An important part of the chapter is also concerned with what are considered to be taboos in modern video games. Chapter 2, *Form and Content of Transgressive Games*, concerns the apparatus of video games. Debating whether game mechanics can be understood as a game's *form* if the representational aspects are the *content*, the chapter argues that the sense of transgression can spring out of either or a combination of the two. In the last chapter of the section, Chapter 3, *Transgressive Games: An Overview*, we discuss what makes a game transgressive and what characterizes different forms of transgressive games. Further, with point of departure in the experiences of the player respondents in our study, we present the games that have been central to our empirical studies – why they have been selected and in what ways they can be understood as transgressive. While it is impossible, due to the subjective and contextually dependent nature of transgression, to create a canon of transgressive games, we will discuss what types of transgressive games and game elements players have noted and discussed through our research and that of others, through online discussions, and through game reviews and discussions in the media.

The second part of the book is called *Experiences with Transgressive Games* and consists of three chapters, in which the empirical data is discussed in detail. The section orbits the second main idea of the book, the fallacy of play and how this affects player experiences with uncomfortable and provocative game content. In Chapter 4, *Transgressive Games and the Player-Response Perspective*, we are presenting the player-response perspective in detail and argue for its applicability to understanding transgressive game content. As discussed previously in this chapter, we are of the opinion that this perspective allows us a holistic understanding of how players deal with the complex interplay between cultural norms and cultural forms. Chapter 5, *Transgressive Gameplay Experiences*, is a discussion of play and engagement that looks at how the player respondents in our studies deal with potentially transgressive content in games and how it interacts with their overall sense of engagement in the game. Central for the argument is the idea that play can be serious and uncomfortable, and we show that this is central for understanding how players tackle transgressive content in games. In Chapter 6, *Transgressive Game Content and Emotional Response*, we discuss player responses to transgressive game content with point of departure in the psychology of emotions. With point of departure in the relationship between cognition, emotion, and affect, we look at how the different reactions of our player respondents to specific content. In this chapter, we also discuss the concept of flow and how this mental state is affected by transgressive gameplay experiences.

In the third section, *Games and Transgressive Aesthetics*, we are moving into the domain of aesthetic theory. We are looking at perspectives from the field of aesthetics relevant for understanding transgression in games, culminating in an argument about the ludic sublime and how it helps us understand and explain the role of transgression in games. We explore the notion that aesthetics concerns the perception and appreciation of artistic works, regardless of whether or not they are "beautiful" in the classical sense. Chapter 7, *The Carnivalesque Aesthetics of Games*, presents the most central aesthetic characteristics of transgressive game content and how it relates to other aesthetic discourses. We show how transgressive game aesthetics is linked to a functionalist aesthetic, yet how it is also in concert with pathos rhetoric. Further, the chapter looks at how transgressive game aesthetics relates to Bakhtin's carnival and the literary genre that he calls the Menippean satire. In Chapter 8, *Game Aesthetics and the Sublime*, we develop our final argument concerning the ludic sublime. The chapter starts with a discussion of how games position themselves with respect to ideas of the avant-garde and kitsch before we explore the relationship between games with respect to the idea of sublimity in classical and modern aesthetics. With this theoretical framework as point of departure, we revisit the experiences of our player respondents to formulate a theory of sublime experiences with transgressive aesthetics in games.

In the last chapter, we take a step back and look at the book from an overarching perspective, evaluating our initial hypotheses and summing up our theory of games and transgressive aesthetics. Central to the chapter is a concluding discussion where we sum up what our findings means for understanding transgressive games in contemporary society, including how transgressive games can help us understand the role of games and game culture in contemporary society. Further, the chapter returns to the three concepts we find to be vital to understanding transgressive aesthetics in games: the fallacy of play, the paradox of transgression, and the ludic sublime. The chapter reiterates these ideas and makes a last coherent argument formulating the relationship between them. Here we stress that the existence of transgressive games is in itself an indication of the fallacy of play, as it highlights the fact that games can indeed be uncomfortable and provocative, but also highly serious and have consequence for life outside games. We here revisit the idea that within the state of play, we are frequently more able to process challenges which would be too much in any other contexts. This also connects play to the second idea – that transgression is in itself a paradox in an aesthetic context because once we experience something as aesthetic it stops being profoundly transgressive, and vice versa. However, it is here that the ludic sublime finds its place: As the aesthetics of that which at once is overwhelming and playful; which can grip players due to the sense that the overwhelming can somehow be mastered and controlled. The risk inherent in gameplay – the risk of losing – is at the heart of the ludic sublime. Considering that play is about high stakes and emotional engagement, it comes as no surprise that transgressive aesthetics are at the core of game structures, game experiences, and game content.

References

11 bit studios, and War Child. 2014. *This War of Mine*. 11 bit studios.

Aarseth, Espen. 2003. "Playing Research: Methodological Approaches to Game Analysis." In *Proceedings of Melbourne Digital Arts & Culture* Conference. doi:10.7238/a.v0i7.763.

———. 2007. "I Fought the Law: Transgressive Play and the Implied Player." In *3rd Digital Games Research Association International Conference: "Situated Play", DiGRA 2007*, 130–33. Digital Games Research Association (DIGRA). doi:10.1057/9781137429704.

Aldama, Frederick Luis, and Herbert Lindenberger. 2016. *Aesthetics of Discomfort: Conversations on Disquieting Art*. Ann Arbor: University of Michigan Press. https://muse.jhu.edu/book/44685.

Arjoranta, Jonne. 2015. *Real-Time Hermeneutics. Meaning-Making in Ludo-Narrative Digital Games*. PhD thesis. University of Jyväskylä. https://jyx.jyu.fi/handle/123456789/45647.

Bakhtin, Mikhail. 1999. *Problems of Dostoevsky's Poetics.* Minneapolis, London: University of Minnesota Press.

Bartsch, Anne, and Mary Beth Oliver. 2011. "Making Sense of Entertainment." *Journal of Media Psychology* 23 (1): 12–17. doi:10.1027/1864-1105/a000026.

Bataille, Georges. 1985. *Visions of Excess: Selected Writings, 1927–1939.* Minneapolis: University of Minnesota.

Benedetti, Winda. 2011. "Your Mama Plays 'Dead Space 2.'" Kotaku 2011. http://kotaku.com/5739837/your-mama-plays-dead-space-2.

Bethesda Game Studios. 2011. *The Elder Scrolls V: Skyrim.* Bethesda Softworks LLC.

Bjørkelo, Kristian A. 2017. "They Are Basically Jews with Pointy Ears and Gay Magic." *PhD Seminar on Media, Culture and Participation.*

Blizzard. 2004. *World of Warcraft.* Blizzard Entertainment Inc.

Bogost, Ian. 2007. *Persuasive Games: The Expressive Power of Videogames.* Cambridge: MIT Press.

Bradshaw, Peter. 2019. "Once Upon a Time... in Hollywood Review – Tarantino's Dazzling LA Redemption Song." *The Guardian*, May 21, 2019. www.theguardian.com/film/2019/may/21/once-upon-a-time-in-hollywood-review-tarantino-dazzling-dicaprio-pitt.

Brennan, Teresa. 2004. *The Transmission of Affect.* Cornell University Press.

Caillois, Roger. 2001. *Man, Play and Games.* Urbana: University of Illinois Press; Wantage: University Presses Marketing.

Calleja, Gordon. 2010. "Digital Games and Escapism." *Games and Culture* 5 (4): 335–53. doi:10.1177/1555412009360412.

Cambridge Dictionary. 2018. "Aesthetics." *Cambridge Dictionary Online.* Cambridge University Press. https://dictionary.cambridge.org/dictionary/english/aesthetics.

Cashell, Kieran. 2009. *Aftershock: The Ethics of Contemporary Transgressive Art.* I.B. Tauris.

Collins English Dictionary. 2017. "Transgress Definition and Meaning." *Collins English Dictionary.* HarperCollins Publishers. www.collinsdictionary.com/dictionary/english/transgress.

Creative Assembly. 2014. *Alien: Isolation.* Sega.

Csikszentmihaly, Mihaly. 1981. "Some Paradoxes in the Definition of Play." In *Play in Context, (A(Ssn. for the) A(Nthropological) S(Tudy of) P(Lay) Proc. Ser. ; 5 ; 1979*, edited by Alyce Taylor Cheska, 14–26. West Point, NY: Leisure.

Cupchik, Gerald C. 2011. "The Role of Feeling in the Entertainment=Emotion Formula." *Journal of Media Psychology* 23 (1): 6–11. doi:10.1027/1864-1105/a000025.

Destructive Creations. 2015. *Hatred.* Destructive Creations. www.hatredgame.com/.

Dibbel, Julian. 1993. "A Rape in Cyberspace." *Village Voice* XXXVIII (51). www.ludd.luth.se/mud/aber/articles/village_voice.html.

Ferguson, Christopher J. 2010. "Media Violence Effects and Violent Crime: Good Science or Moral Panic?" In *Violent Crime: Clinical and Social Implications*, edited by Christopher J Ferguson, 37–56. London: Sage Publications, Ltd.

Flanagan, Mary. 2013. *Critical Play: Radical Game Design.* Paperback. Cambridge: MIT Press.

From Software. 2015. *Bloodborne.* Sony Interactive Entertainment.

Geertz, Clifford. 1973. *The Interpretation of Cultures: Selected Essays.* New York: Basic Books.

Gentile, Douglas A., and W. Stone. 2005. "Violent Video Game Effects on Children and Adolescents." *Minerva Pedriatrica* 57 (6): 337–58.

Grønstad, Asbjørn. 2012. *Screening the Unwatchable: Spaces of Negation in Post-Millennial Art Cinema.* New York: Palgrave Macmillan.

Hall, Stuart. 2006. "Encoding/Decoding." In *Media and Cultural Studies: Keyworks,* edited by Meenakshi Gigi Durham and Douglas M. Kellner, 755. Malden, MA: Blackwell.

Hern, Alex. 2013. "Grand Theft Auto 5 under Fire for Graphic Torture Scene." *The Guardian,* September 18, 2013. www.theguardian.com/technology/2013/sep/18/grand-theft-auto-5-under-fire-for-graphic-torture-scene.

Iser, Wolfgang. 1978. *The Act of Reading: A Theory of Aesthetic Response.* London: Routledge and Kegan Paul.

Jenks, Chris. 2003. *Transgressions.* London: Routledge.

Jørgensen, Kristine. 2014. "Devil's Plaything. On the Coundary between Playful and Serious." DiGRA Nordic '14. Proceedings of the 2014 International DiGRA Nordic Conference. 2014. www.digra.org/digital-library/publications/devils-plaything-on-the-boundary-between-playful-and-serious/.

Jørgensen, Kristine, and Faltin Karlsen. 2018. *Transgression in Games and Play.* Cambridge: MIT Press.

Julius, Anthony. 2002. *Transgressions: The Offences of Art.* Chicago, IL: University of Chicago Press.

Kafai, Yasmin, Carrie Heeter, Jill Denner, and Jen Sun. 2009. *Beyond Barbie and Mortal Kombat: New Perspectives on Gender, Gaming, and Computing.* Cambridge: MIT Press.

Kirkpatrick, Graeme. 2011. *Aesthetic Theory and the Video Game.* Manchester: Manchester University Press.

Kutner, Lawrence, and Cheryl K. Olson. 2008. *Grand Theft Childhood: The Surprising Truth about Violent Video Games and What Parents Can Do.* Simon & Schuster.

Langman, Lauren, and Andras Lukacs. 2010. "Capitalism, Contradiction, and the Carnivalesque: Alienated Labor vs. Ludic Play." In *Utopic Dreams and Apocalyptic Fantasies: Critical Approaches to Researching Video Game Play,* edited by J. Talmadge Wright, David G. Embrick, and Andras Lukacs, 59–72. Lanham, ML: Lexington Books.

Linderoth, Jonas, and Torill Elvira Mortensen. 2015. "Dark Play: The Aesthetics of Controversial Playfulness." In *The Dark Side of Game Play: Controversial Issues Un Playful Environments,* edited by Torill Elvira Mortensen, Jonas Linderoth, and Ashley M. L Brown, 3–12. London: Routledge.

Majkowski, Tomasz Z. 2017. "Skyrim Deviants. Pornographic Modding as Carnivalesque Practice." Paper preseented at *Researching the Transgressive Aspects of Gaming and Play Seminar.* Bologna.

Malaby, Thomas M. 2007. "Beyond Play." *Games and Culture* 2 (2): 95–113. doi:10.1177/1555412007299434.

Mäyrä, Frans. 2008. *An Introduction to Game Studies: Games in Culture.* Thousand Oaks, CA: SAGE.

Meades, Alan. 2015. "Boosting, Glitching and Modding Call of Duty: Assertive Dark Play Manifestations, Communities, Pleasures and Organic Resilience." In *The Dark Side of Game Play: Controversial Issues in Playful Environments,* edited by Torill Elvira Mortensen, Jonas Linderoth, and Ashely M.L. Brown, 242–60. New York and London: Routledge. doi:10.4324/9781315738680.

Montola, Markus. 2010. "The Positive Negative Experience in Extreme Role-Playing." In *Nordic DiGRA 2010*. Stockholm: DiGRA. www.digra.org/wp-content/uploads/digital-library/10343.56524.pdf.

Mortensen, Torill Elvira. 2002. "Playing with Players: Potential Methodologies for MUDs." *Game Studies: The International Journal of Computer Game Research* 2 (1). www.gamestudies.org/0102/mortensen/.

———. 2003. "Pleasures of the Player: Flow and Control in Online Games." *Thesis for Dr. Art, University of Bergen.*

Mortensen, Torill Elvira, and Kristine Jørgensen. 2016. "Games and Transgressive Aesthetics: A Manifesto." Games and Transgressive Aesthetics. November 21, 2016. https://gta.b.uib.no/2016/11/21/manifesto/.

Mumford, Gwilym. 2018. "'Vomitive. Pathetic': Lars von Trier Film Prompts Mass Walkouts at Cannes | Film | The Guardian." *The Guardian*, May 15, 2018. www.theguardian.com/film/2018/may/15/vomitive-pathetic-lars-von-trier-film-prompts-mass-walkouts-at-cannes.

Nielsen, Rune Kristian Lundedal. 2016. "Is Game Addiction a Mental Disorder? A Dissertation on the History and Science of the Concept of Internet Gaming Disorder." IT University of Copenhagen.

Oliver, Mary Beth. 2008. "Tender Affective States as Predictors of Entertainment Preference." *Journal of Communication* 58 (1): 40–61. doi:10.1111/j.1460-2466.2007.00373.x.

Oliver, Mary Beth, Nicholas David Bowman, Julia K. Woolley, Ryan Rogers, Brett I. Sherrick, and Mun-Young Chung. 2016. "Video Games as Meaningful Entertainment Experiences." *Psychology of Popular Media Culture* 5 (4): 390–405. doi:10.1037/ppm0000066.

Quantic Dream. 2013. *Beyond: Two Souls*. Sony Interactive Entertainment.

Rockstar North. 2013. *Grand Theft Auto V*. Edited by Rockstar Games. *Grand Theft Auto*. New York: Rockstar Games.

Rogers, Ryan, Julia Woolley, Brett Sherrick, Nicholas David Bowman, and Mary Beth Oliver. 2017. "Fun Versus Meaningful Video Game Experiences: A Qualitative Analysis of User Responses." *The Computer Games Journal* 6 (1–2): 63–79. doi:10.1007/s40869-016-0029-9.

Rusch, Doris C. 2009. "Mechanisms of the Soul – Tackling the Human Condition in Videogames." www.digra.org/wp-content/uploads/digital-library/09287.01371.pdf.

———. 2017. *Making Deep Games: Designing Games with Meaning and Purpose*. Boca Raton, London, New York: Focal Press.

Salen, Katie, and Eric Zimmerman. 2004. *Rules of Play: Game Design Fundamentals*. Cambridge: MIT Press.

Schechner, Richard. 2013. *Performance Studies: An Introduction*. 3rd ed. London: Routledge.

Schramm, Holger, and Werner Wirth. 2010. "Exploring the Paradox of Sad-Film Enjoyment: The Role of Multiple Appraisals and Meta-Appraisals." *Poetics* 38 (3): 319–35. doi:10.1016/j.poetic.2010.03.002.

Schrank, Brian. 2014. *Avant-Garde Videogames: Playing with Technoculture*. Cambridge: MIT Press.

Sharp, John, and David Thomas. 2019. *Fun, Taste, & Games: An Aesthetics of the Idle, Unproductive and Otherwise Playful*. Cambridge: MIT Press.

Shelley, James. 2015. "The Concept of the Aesthetic." In *The Stanford Encyclopedia of Philosophy*, edited by Edward N. Zalta. https://plato.stanford.edu/archives/win2015/entries/aesthetic-concept/.

Sicart, Miguel. 2009. *The Ethics of Computer Games.* Cambridge: MIT Press.

———. 2013. *Beyond Choices.* Cambridge: MIT Press.

Slater, Barry Hartley. n.d. "Aesthetics." *Internet Encyclopedia of Philosophy.* University of Tennessee. https://www.iep.utm.edu/aestheti/.

Smith, Jonathan A., Paul. Flowers, and Michael Larkin. 2009. *Interpretative Phenomenological Analysis: Theory, Method, and Research.* SAGE.

Stenros, Jaakko. 2015. "Playfulness, Play, and Games. A Constructionist Ludology Approach." Tampere: University of Tampere.

Sundén, Jenny. 2009. "Play as Transgression: An Ethnographic Approach to Queer GameCultures."In*ProceedingsofDiGRA2009:BreakingNewGround:Innovation in Games, Play, Practice and Theory.* www.digra.org/digital-library/publications/ play-as-transgression-an-ethnographic-approach-to-queer-game-cultures/.

Sutton-Smith, Brian. 1997. *The Ambiguity of Play.* Cambridge; London: Harvard University Press.

Tamborini, Ron, Nicholas David Bowman, Allison Eden, and Ashley Organ. 2010. "Defining Media Enjoyment as the Satisfaction of Intrinsic Needs." *Journal of Communication* 60 (4): 758–77. doi:10.1111/j.1460-2466.2010.01513.x.

Taylor, T. L. 2006. *Play between Worlds: Exploring Online Game Culture.* Cambridge: MIT Press.

Taylor, T. L., and Mikael Jakobsson. 2003. "The Sopranos Meets EverQuest: Socialization Processes in Massively Multiuser Games." In *Digital Arts & Culture Streaming Wor(l)Ds Conference Proceedings.* http://mjson.se/doc/ sopranos_meets_eq_faf_v3.pdf.

Turner, Victor. 2009. "Liminal to Liminoid, in Play, Flow, and Ritual: An Essay in Comparative Symbology." *Originally Published as "Liminal to Liminoid, in Play, Flow, and Ritual: An Essay in Comparative Symbology,"* Part of the Rice University Studies, 60 (3), Summer 1974 (Houston, TX: Rice University), 53–92 60 (3).

Vella, Daniel. 2015. "No Mastery Without Mystery: Dark Souls and the Ludic Sublime." *Game Studies, the International Journal Computer Game Research* 15 (1). http://gamestudies.org/1501/articles/vella.

Visceral Games. 2011. *Dead Space 2.* Electronic Arts.

Zillman, Dolf. 1998. "Does Tragic Drama Have Redeeming Value?" *Siegener Periodikum Für Internationale Litteraturwissenschaft* 16 (1): 1–11.

Part 1

Transgression in games

1 Old term, new game

Despite reminders that there were video games as early as 1958 (Brookhaven National Library n.d.), the novelty aspect of digital games is connected to the fairly recent emergence of the computer as a personal entertainment tool. But by speaking of digital games as something new, we tend to forget that how they work, what they do, and how we feel about and react to them are not particularly novel. We have been shocked by games and loved it since ancient times. The gladiator fights of ancient Rome led to the death of others (Köhne et al. 2000), and Renaissance party games such as *The Game of Ridiculous Blasphemies (Giuoco delle bestemmie ridiculose)*, a game first described in 1551 (Ringhieri 1551), were designed to shock our sense of propriety. While the gladiator fights, despite their brutal content, were considered acceptable entertainment for the masses similar to sport events today, *Ridiculous Blasphemies*, reconstructed by game scholars Riccardo Fassone and William Huber (2016), was designed to shock the players (through forcing them to listen to and memorize obscenities), then torture them (through tickling and poking) into committing the same blasphemies themselves. Considering this history of brutality, shock, and blasphemy, it should come as no surprise when games lead to acts or concern themselves with topics which are horrifying and shocking or, as we focus on in this book, *transgressive*.

The transgressive

The concept of the *transgressive* is a word often used in the same breath as words such as shocking, taboo, controversial, and subversive. These terms tend to inhabit the same property of meaning: The landscape of issues that disturb, create discomfort, or shake established norms, and to which we react immediately and with affect. They are not synonymous though – *controversy* tends to be used to describe public disputes or disagreements, and *subversion* means to overthrow or turn something on its head. In relation to games, the term *controversial* is commonly used to talk about any public debates that games may stir, ranging from excessive violence and provocative content to legal disputes, and we often find the games that may be characterized as transgressive among the games tagged as controversial. This is why we will look at the term *transgressive* from different angles, and among other things look into what is controversial in the aesthetics of games: What creates discussions, disagreements, or even strife.

In the aesthetic domain, the concept of the *transgressive* is often associated with rebellious and oppositional practices. In the art world, *transgressive art*, for example, is a postmodern art genre that intends to question the definition of art through disturbance and offense (Aldama and Lindenberger 2016; Cashell 2009). One well-known and famous work of transgressive art is American artist Andres Serrano's photograph of an indistinct crucifix tinted in orange, and it may at first glance reflect other depictions of crucifixes in art and may not occur as particularly transgressive. Not before the viewer reads the title of the photograph does a sense of transgression emerge: *Piss Christ* (1987). In the words of lawyer and scholar Anthony Julius: "It has an immediately jarring effect" (Julius 2002, 15). Although urinating is not in itself particularly controversial, realizing that the artwork one was admiring a moment ago really is a photo of a religious symbol submerged in the artist's urine may first create the immediate affective response of shock and disgust. *Piss Christ* is transgressive because it crosses the boundaries between the sacred and the profane: It brings a question of hygiene into the land of the taboo as the excretions move from the realm of the artist's private bodily waste to being applied to symbols of faith.

And it is this potential for movement from one distinctive realm to the other, this possibility for the breaking of boundaries, which makes a work of art transgressive. A transgressive work follows the ideal that boundaries should be broken because they stand for the petrified and stale, and that such breaking of boundaries is something fluid, fresh, and to be admired. The ideal, according to Julius, is that "[w]hen a boundary is broken, one tastes the infinite" (Julius 2002, 20). Since a transgressive aesthetic is unstable, balanced in the borderlands of norms and expectations, the act of transgressing – the transgression – is vital. Hence, in order to understand a *transgressive* aesthetic – an aesthetic that invites or permits transgressions – we need to understand transgressions. To understand how transgressive aesthetics is tightly interwoven with the act of transgression, consider the famous and seminal sculpture *Fountain*, submitted by Marcel Duchamp, signed R. Mutt (1917). By taking an everyday object used for passing bodily fluids and submitting it as art, Duchamp managed to be rejected from an exhibition where all artists who paid the participation fee were supposed to be accepted. The urinal was too transgressive for the committee. However, today, this work is no longer transgressive, but an established part of the canon of art, denoting a turning point for our understanding of modern art. Thus, even though the work of art is no longer a transgression in the art world, it is still characterized under the label transgressive art – the act of transgression defines the transgressive aesthetics. This also means that whether an artwork is transgressive or not is culturally and historically dependent.

We see here that *transgressive* may thus have two slightly different meanings: It may be a simple adjective, a modifier that describes a form of art: It is the art form of transgression – an art form that aims to break with the norms of society. But there is also another implied meaning springing out of the discussion above about context, and which suggest an indecisiveness about whether or not *the transgressive* is something that is relative or absolute. When it is describing an established art form, it is obvious that it is accepted by the art community and thus no longer is an example of a profound transgression. It is instead an example of transgressive aesthetics. Although transgressive aesthetics indeed is designed to challenge and may be provocative for many, its framing mitigates its impact. As indicated briefly in the introductory chapter, it is thus possible to understand transgressive as an approximation or a movement toward a transgression. If we see *transgression* as an absolute overstepping of a boundary – as something profound – the *transgressive* indicates that we remain on the inside of the boundary, but able to identify it and to understand what crossing it means.

In this sense, when we talk about a transgressive game, this can be understood as a framing with similar connotations as transgressive art or transgressive aesthetics – as a designed artifact that includes topics that may challenge, provoke, or disturb some people. Although transgressive games may for some also provoke profound transgressions that overstep their boundaries and make them decide to quit the game out of outrage or distaste, the aesthetic context puts it into a mitigating frame of reference. Similarly, a *transgressive experience* may challenge a person's sensibilities or emotions, but is only an approximation that makes visible the boundary for absolute transgression. In other words, it is not experienced as a profound transgression. Thus, as something absolute, a *transgression* can therefore be attributed to the personal and the subjective, while *transgressive* is a descriptor of a general overarching category of that which aims to shock, but does not state whether or not it is actually able to do so.

Transgression

Following the above discussion, the term *transgression* offers an immediate meaning of something that crosses the limits for what we can accept. The Latin meaning of the noun is the act of walking or crossing over, and in this sense, the original Latin *transgressus* is still clearly recognizable as we consistently understand transgression as meaning overstepping or going, somehow, too far. It is used, in a legal sense, to describe transgression of the law or crime (O'Neill and Seal 2012); it is used in a normative sense as a transgression of the sensibilities of society (Jenks 2003); and in an aesthetic sense to describe offensive art (Cashell 2009 l. 178). Reviewing the historical use of the term transgression, Julius identifies four meanings: The denial of doctrinal truths; the violation of rules, conventions, principles, or taboos; giving serious offense; and the erasure or disordering of conceptual or physical boundaries (Julius 2002, 19). Perhaps the most general use of the term is the way sociologist Chris Jenks defines it (2013, 21): "Transgression is a social process. Transgression is that which transcends boundaries or exceeds limits". He further underlines how transgression is tied to limits, to the point of being utterly dependent on them: "The only way the limitless world is provided with any structure or coherence is through the excesses that transgress that world and thus construct it – the completion that follows and accompanies transgression" (2013, 23).

Tying transgression directly to limits and boundaries opens one of the connections to play and games. Games are defined by rules and limitations, an accepted part of the study of games from cultural historian Johan Huizinga (1955, 11) to philosopher Bernard Suits (Suits 1990, 39) to play theorist Brian Sutton-Smith (Sutton-Smith 1997) and to game designers and scholars Katie Salen and Eric Zimmerman (Salen and Zimmerman 2004) as well as by play that explores, pushes, and occasionally transgresses these limitations. We claim that if rules are vital to games, so are transgressions. Jenks states the relationship between rules and transgressions as "that conduct which breaks rules or exceeds boundaries", and he insists that rules invite transgressions (Jenks 2003). Reflecting Georges Bataille, Jenks states that "[t]ransgression is a deeply reflexive act of denial and affirmation" and suggests that any act of transgression acknowledges and puts emphasis on the convention being transgressed. For this reason, it contributes to upholding existing norms while they are being trespassed (Jenks 2003, 2).

Cheating

Games are made by rules and limitations: The arena, the objects, the environments and their affordances, and the game mechanics are all limitations and rules that can be transgressed, and that sometimes even ask to be transgressed. The presence of rules and their implicit invitation to overstep them are what indelibly ties transgression to games, making transgression a part of play whether limits are actually broken or not. We find the same argument in French sociologist Roger Caillois's discussion about the connection between cheating and play, where he underlines that the cheat depends on the boundaries of play and that for this reason it is in the cheater's interest that these boundaries are maintained (2001). Caillois contrasts this with corruption, which does not acknowledge the rules and limitations. While cheating depends on others following the rules, corruption means not acknowledging or caring about rules at all. In this manner, we can say that transgression reminds more of cheating than of corruption since cheating depends on rules in order to transgress, and transgression confirms the rules. The most important aspect of transgression is the boundary it steps over, not its moral value. It is, as criminologists Maggie O'Neill and Lizzie Seal point out, a rebellion against order rather than shapeless disorder (2012).

It is a paradox that something that is so integral to the idea of what games are about is a transgression. Understanding the common ludic transgression of cheating is vital to understanding the transgressive aesthetics of games. According to Salen and Zimmerman, a cheater is a player who "breaks rules, but only to further the act of winning" (Salen and Zimmerman 2004, 275). Cheating in games happens within very sharply defined limits, as the rules of a game need to be clear and simple enough that players can learn, remember, and start challenging them, without the rules becoming indistinct and causing doubt. In games, it must be easy to recognize the limits. All who have experienced any kind of gameplay are aware of the importance of knowing and enforcing the rules. This is why every box of board games comes with written rulebooks, and video games have rules that are defined by the computer code into something similar to natural law (Lessig 2006) – the game is not complete without the rules. But, as game scholar Mia Consalvo argues in her important work *Cheating: Gaining Advantage in Video Games*, even with the strictly defined rules that come with analog games in general and video games in particular, cheating is contextual and defined by the norms and social rules of the group of players (Consalvo 2007). Take, for instance, the example of exploiting bugs and glitches, which may or may not be considered cheating (Consalvo 2007). Since players of digital games expect the system to take care of rule management, it can be argued that exploiting bugs and weaknesses in the code of a digital game cannot be considered cheating; at the same time, game developers of online games often explicitly define such exploitation as breaking with the end-user license agreements (EULA) and thus also with the rules of the game in a legal sense. Against this backdrop, it is also interesting to consider the tradition among programmers to leave "Easter Eggs" in the code: Surprises and "rewards" for players who try to take advantage of the game in extraordinary, non-conventional ways. This cultural acceptance of taking advantage of the digital environment when possible can make the line between cheating and non-cheating difficult to spot.

The cultural dynamics of transgression

These culturally agreed-upon aspects of where the boundary can be found is also a problem with transgression, as O'Neill and Seal (2012, 4) point out: "[C]rossing boundaries and exceeding limits is not something that groups and individuals perceived as transgressive always want or intend, but is something which occurs when they are seen as 'out of place'". Although cheating, in its most strict form, is an intended act, designed to give the cheater an advantage as long as everybody else follow the rules, breaking game rules can, like other forms of transgression, be accidental, the result of the rules being indeterminate, indistinct, and mutable. In an act of transgression, the "rule" that is broken can be a law, which makes it a criminal act, but it may also be a norm, a habit, tradition, or polite sensibility, and transgressions often happen as a result of simple cultural transpositions. In the case of digital games, of course, it can also be the hacking or modification of a game rule coded into the software system or, as mentioned above, the utilization of an error or bug in the software.

This is the point where transgression becomes extremely hard to pin down. Since the boundaries a transgressor can step over may only be perceived from within a very particular subjective and also cultural perspective, defining transgression will always depend on point of view. There are no objective transgressions, only relative. This is why transgressions so clearly demonstrate where the limits of norms and cultural agreement can be found. By looking at what we react to with shock, fear, or disgust, we can start to uncover the unspoken agreements that rule our culture. This allows us to speak about "the unsayable", to cite Sanford Budick and Wolfgang Iser (1996). In their overwhelming and irresistible presence, transgressions work by making visible that which is so accepted, so ubiquitous, and preeminent that it is not questioned until it is violated. Transgression reveals the unspoken limitations, the norms we never knew about, because it had never occurred to us that they could be broken. Why would somebody urinate on a crucifix, photograph it, and exhibit it as art? Until the act was done, nobody knew the reactions it would provoke. As an example, most of us live in the belief that cancer, while tragic and terrifying, is something that can be talked openly about without the stigma of, for instance, carrying a sexually transmittable disease. At the same time, the reactions to *That Dragon, Cancer* (Numinous Games 2016) show us that the topic of cancer can be so controversial that certain play communities in which members have no problems with violence and sexual contents really struggle (Klepek 2016) with the idea of a game about something as heartbreakingly sad as a young child dying from cancer. This is an interesting reaction to this particular game as games containing violence, racism, and even sexual violence rarely make dedicated gamers experience any kind of transgression, or if they do, the pleasure of playing, often in defiance of what society wants for them, makes up for the sense of discomfort. But the reactions to *That Dragon, Cancer*, demonstrate where the limits go for some of these game communities. The reaction exemplifies that it is too simplistic to claim that these players have become emotionally stunted (Coughlan 2014); rather, they operate according to different expectations, where they expect to be grossed out, scared, titillated, or angry but not heartbreakingly sad.

This ties the discussion of transgressive content in games firmly to the discussions of aesthetics and to discussions of, for instance, genres. By preparing the audience for the experience they are about the have, genres negotiate transgressions, in several cases moving them from the profoundly transgressive to an experience of transgressive aesthetics; that is, from the absolutely unbearable and unplayable to a sense of discomfort that we are able to endure because it happens in a context that we recognize as aesthetic. One of the areas where genre labels have been used actively in order to ensure this is in cinema, and this is why a movie such as John Waters's cult film *Pink Flamingos* (Waters 1972) can be shown without repeatedly drawing outraged and disgusted audiences. Genres prepare audiences for the kind of boundaries a film may break. But this also allows for both playing up to and breaking with the expectation of the audience, which permits producers of transgressive and avant-garde art to find and push at the normative barriers we operate within, to overcome the restrictions of the norms of society.

Norms

Transgressions, being acts of crossing boundaries, are closely connected to a somewhat vague concept describing a powerful mechanism – the mechanism that supports our attempts at agreeing about our respective worlds: *Social norms*. Social norms are informal rules that govern behavior in social groups, and are often seen as something that constrains behavior (Bicchieri, Muldoon, and Sontuoso 2018). According to Chris Jenks, understanding transgressions depends on the distinction between the *normal*, understood as the typical and general social reality that characterizes norm-abiding or normative behavior, and the *pathological*, which is the irregular that implies inherent threats to the social structure (Jenks 2003, 24–25). There are two problems with norms, which flow into the problem of transgression. First, norms are not simple, but "can be formal or informal, personal or collective, descriptive of what most people do, or prescriptive of behavior" (Bicchieri 2005). The reasons we conform to norms are varied and sometimes even depend on conflicting behavior.

Second, while norms are the informal rules that make society function, even in settings where it might have been better for the individual to defy them, they are often not explicitly, consciously, nor deliberately followed. As philosopher and psychologist Cristina Bicchieri states:

> [T]he belief/desire model of choice that is the core of my rational reconstruction of social norms does not commit us to avow that we always engage in conscious deliberation to decide whether to follow a norm. We may follow a norm automatically and thoughtlessly and yet still be able to explain our action in terms of beliefs and desires.
>
> (Bicchieri 2005)

Although Bicchieri is mainly concerned with social and not aesthetic norms, her examples of transgressions are still relevant in our context. We can, for instance, recognize the matter of transgressions carried out for the purpose of helping others (Bicchieri 2005). Examples of such transgressions are stealing bread for the purpose of feeding a starving child or stripping naked in public for the purpose of saving a drowning person. In such cases, the transgression is not connected to any of the negative terms normally used to describe them, but rather to altruism and defiance in order to do good. These acts (stealing, stripping) will still be recognized as transgressions, since they overstep the social norms of the relevant community. What these examples demonstrate is the occasional need for transgressions, since they highlight the norms and make them visible, much like the aesthetic of negativity seen in the discussion of Budick and Iser (1996).

The existence of transgressions confirms the existence of norms, rules, and limits, and Bicchieri explains that by obeying a norm, we expect that others will conform as well, leading to a collective behavior that confirms the norm among those who follow it (Bicchieri 2005, 2). Norms are self-confirming, until the point where they are challenged. At that point, those who find the norms useful will defend them. While norms can be invisible to the people who obey them, they are kept in place by a complex network of self-interest, social consciousness, and peer pressure. Still, we reach decisions on our actions either *deliberatively* by being aware of the decisions we make or *automatically* by acting based on pre-judgment (Bicchieri 2005). Since we are unaware of much of our decision-making processes, most of the time our decisions are automatic, in the sense that we do not ask ourselves how we reached a decision, even if we believe our decision-making process is rational and deliberate. The boundaries we move within, created by the norms we more or less consciously live by, are largely invisible to us.

What makes the normative decisions visible to us is when we experience a transgression of our norms, either on our own part or by others. As the French philosopher Michel Foucault argues, transgressions reveal the limits surrounding us:

> Transgression is an action which involves the limit, that narrow zone of a line where it displays the flash of its passage, but perhaps also its entire trajectory, even its origin: it is likely that transgression has its entire space in the line it crosses. The play of limits and transgression seems to be regulated by a simple obstinacy: Transgression incessantly crosses and recrosses a line which closes up behind it in a wave of extremely short duration, and this it is made to return once more right to the horizon of the uncrossable.
>
> (Foucault 1977, 33–34)

Here, Foucault not only points out that if there are no limits to break, there can be no transgression; he illuminates how limits and transgressions mutually depend on each other: Limits must be crossable, or else they are not limits but natural laws, but at the same time, these limits must be hard to cross, or transgressing them would be pointless.

To return to an example of transgressions in games: The earlier mentioned *Game of Ridiculous Blasphemies*, designed to be norm-breaking, crossed several boundaries, and as far as we can understand from our perspective almost 500 years later, we can identify at least three transgressions. First, each player needed to speak a blasphemous sentence out loud. We can recognize this as a transgression against the norm of how to speak about religion; and for a Christian, this is also a transgression against the word of the Bible. Also, for players to reveal their own dirty imagination would also be experienced as a personal transgression. Next, the target of the round would need to memorize the blasphemous sentences, before all the other players would start to poke or tickle the target in the attempt of upsetting the target as the target would repeat the blasphemous sentences out loud. This involved a transgression against the zone of intimacy that we all are surrounded by and against 16th-century norms about touching members of the opposite sex in mixed company. Last, the target had to repeat the blasphemous sentences of other players; thus again breaking the norms of what is acceptable to say out loud, but also potentially transgressing their own personal sensibilities when being forced to repeat blasphemies first imagined by others. Of course, although the transgressions would take place inside the playful context of a game, issues relating to the social expectations of the involved players and the particular social setting and arena in which the game was played would complicate the game further. At the same time, this game demonstrates how a game mechanic may survive the shifting norms and still be transgressive 500 years later, where a stable work of art such as Duchamp's *Fountain* may not. It is possible to insert modern blasphemy into an old mechanism by picking new and updated profanities for the target to repeat, while it is much harder to remain offended by a static object that has been added to the canon of modernist art.

But a game does not need to be designed for transgression in order to transgress against accepted norms. From more recent days, the game *Playing History: Slave Trade* (Serious Games Interactive 2015) caused massive uproar (Macfarlan 2015). In order to educate users about the cruel and inhuman conditions slaves were transported under, the designers were using Tetris' stacking mechanism to demonstrate how slaves were packed in the holds of slave ships in a game segment that got dubbed "Slave Tetris". What the Danish game company did not consider was that from the perspective of cultures with a more difficult colonial and slave-trading past, this was a breach of a norm the designers had never before encountered. It caused a massive controversy, as the reactions to it outlined a limit for how to deal with slavery in the borderland of entertainment and education. While Simon Egenfeldt-Nielsen, CEO of Serious Games Interactive, claimed that the "Slave Tetris" segment was there in order to create disgust at the inhuman conditions that slaves were forced to endure, the short segment was removed from the game. In the end, the aim of this game was to educate, not to create controversy or be experienced as transgressive.

Game controversies and the transgression of norms

The study of ludic transgressions and playful provocations teaches us the importance of norms, of the expectations of the culture you move within. These expectations change abruptly as we move between cultures and sub-cultures and are often sufficiently durable that they can be used as markers for certain demographics. Nudity or sex is, for instance, more provocative in the US entertainment market than violence, while in the European entertainment market, for either of those to be transgressive, they need to have an additional meaning. This dependence on cultural markers is why games, like most entertainment media, tend to be framed by genres. Each game genre, obeying different conventions that shape the norms for that genre, adheres to different expectations, such as the possibility for showing blood and gore in first person shooters or scantily clad women in fighting games (Lynch et al. 2016). This eases the widespread, often cross-cultural marketing, of games and reduces the outrage that will inevitably follow when expectations are broken in the migration of meaning from one subculture to another.

From our research into how players deal with game content that challenges their sensibilities, we see that players are not easily provoked, and when they are it is rarely by the same things. If there is a common pattern to what is experienced as transgressive in a gameplay context and how, it is that it is very dependent on the players' subjective reading of game and on their expectations from and experience with game genres. One example is how the player respondents recounted their experiences with playing the controversial shooter *Hatred* (Destructive Creations 2015), described as "the most violent game on earth" (Jenkins 2015). Although for some of the player respondents, the initial response was disgust, after a certain time of gameplay, our respondents mainly reported that it was not disgust but boredom that made them stop playing. What became the most problematic to these players was not the portrayal of aimless killing but the fact that the game was so boring, such an un-emotional act of repetitive actions ("Brian" (19), individual interview, October 13, 2016). For these respondents, a strong emotion, such as excitement, fear, or even disgust, would have been preferable to the feeling of meaningless repetition. If there was a sense of outrage, it was directed toward the designers of the game because they had created a less-than-mediocre and boring game, and then manipulated the players' curiosity by promises of ultra-violent, transgressive content ("Mary" (24), focus group interview, October 16, 2015). Other participants described how their expectations toward *Hatred* rarely were met. One player expected to be provoked and to be forced to reflect; he wanted to feel bad about his actions as that feeling would have been congruent with the norms about killing in his regular life ("Danny" (22), individual interview, October 7, 2016). In a way, the transgression of *Hatred* was *a lack of* discomfort and offense, which created a transgression of the player's personal ethics and morals, where the player registered his own lack of provocation as uncomfortable.

One of the main problems with norms is that they are invisible from the inside of a particular culture, and they cannot be discerned from the outside. This is a dilemma in the study of culture, and media scholar John Fiske discusses this dilemma through his exploration of Madonna fandom in a text on British Cultural Studies (1992). In this article, Fiske demonstrates how ethnography, with observations and interviews, connects with a semiotic, interpretative approach, to offer an understanding of this fandom both as the fans are seen by others and as they speak about themselves (Fiske 1992). One of our options for our work to achieve a kind of cultural shift in point of view that may make the norms of both mainstream and game culture visible is to use material that we know both game fans, players, and critics have access to and to see what happens in the cross sections. The different public controversies surrounding games and gaming display such cross sections.

We can see one expression of culturally grounded controversies by looking at the "List of controversial video games" on *Wikipedia* (Wikipedia 2019) – flagged as "incomplete" despite its more than 100 references. The list shows a user-curated list of games that have been the subject of a public controversy, have been banned or regionally censored, and the reasons for the public outrage. A Wikipedia list obviously is not always an authoritative source of information, but it has some interesting implications. When we choose to point to it here, it is because, to frequent Internet users such as the game audience, Wikipedia is a well-known and often used resource. The audience – as well as the authors – of this particular list is likely to be comprised of people particularly interested in games in general; in game controversies; or in outrageous, offensive, or transgressive games in particular. They are likely to be players themselves, and they need to have a minimum of computer literacy.

If we look beyond the nine legal controversies relating to copyright infringement and similar disputes in this Wikipedia article, we see that the controversies concern the topics and contents of the games. While the list indeed includes cases relating to stereotypical representation and sexual content, and some relating to the inclusion of drugs or alcohol, the main reason for outrage and controversy is violence. Mostly the problem is excessive and graphic violence, although "graphic" is a definition that has changed over the years. If we look at *Doom* (id Software 1993), which has been linked to splatter, gore, and graphic violence since it was first published, the early, pixelated images are almost nostalgic and quaint in their abstract distribution of red to indicate blood. We do however see one additional trend in the outrage over violence. The early games tend to be flagged for combining violence with other controversial topics. One such example is *Custer's Revenge* (Mystique 1982) for the Atari platform, where the player in the role of the historical US Army General Custer dodged arrows to reach a Native American woman tied to a pole. The reward for surviving was to have sex with her in a context that was easily interpreted as rape. The transgressions pile up in this game, as it takes what was a pyrrhic victory for the Native Americans over Custer and the US troops, makes fun of it, and allows General Custer to survive only to violate the natives in the shape of a trapped woman. The Wiki page of controversial games cites several sources from 1982 claiming the controversy at the time was concerned with whether or not the woman consented.[1] However, the topic and affordances of the game comprise a long list of potential cultural outrage. We can speculate that the pixilation, which makes the game look clumsy and naive, may be one reason why it did not cause more outrage, while another might be that at its release, home console gaming was, after all, a niche practice. The game is however almost 40 years old, and our speculations are based on interpretation of surviving texts – and also most likely biased by our knowledge of game controversies in Western culture today.

Although the more recent titles on the list of controversial games illustrate that video game controversies today are more diverse, games still cause debates over similar topics – or the combination of topics – as *Custer's Revenge*: Racist language, the use of Nazi symbols, references to explicit violence, and sexual violations. The controversies and the changes the discussions around them lead to in the games are often limited to certain countries, such as the removal of Nazi imagery before *South Park: The Stick of Truth* (Obsidian Entertainment 2014) was released in Germany. While the combination of violence with ideology and sex in certain contexts is still provocative, the increased detail in games has caused a widening vocabulary of controversy, and today's debates also look beyond fiction-level content to sophisticated game mechanics such as loot boxes, which include potential gambling elements in games available to children and youths (Macey and Hamari 2019; Nielsen and Grabarczyk 2018; Zendle and Cairns 2018).

It is also interesting to see what is absent from this list. With a few exceptions, we find very few references to so-called "hentai" or "eroge" games, pornographic games of manga-inspired, often Japanese, animation (Lewdgamer n.d.). A recurring topic in these games is rape and nonconsensual sex, and with its basis in anime style, they are visually sophisticated and very graphic. We would expect such games to be prominent on a list of controversial games, and when they are not, this is most likely caused by the language barriers. Wikipedia lists games that have caught the eye of the English-speaking society, and games exclusively in Japanese rarely make headlines in English. There are still two eroge games on the controversy list, the most recent being *RapeLay* (Illusion Soft 2006), in which the protagonist stalks and rapes a mother and her two teenage daughters. *RapeLay* caught the attention of the European and American public several years after publication (Lah 2010). As eroge games operate within the legal limits in Japan, the transgression of this game comes from the context in which it was discussed. The international human rights organization

Equality Now launched a campaign against Japanese "rape-simulation games" for normalization of sexual violence against women and children, and put pressure on Japanese companies and policy makers. Law professor Hiroshi Nakasatomi points out that this international pressure was important for the public attention that the game was given in Japan and the following self-regulation of Japanese game producers (Nakasatomi 2012), including banning the production and sales of "rape games" and rebranding of such games under production (Ashcraft 2010). In this sense, *Rape-Lay* demonstrates the importance of culture and context for the perception of transgression, even criminal transgression.

A more recent controversy on sexual violence in games concerns the unreleased game *Rape Day*, an apocalypse-themed visual novel by developer Desk Plant where harassing and raping women is central to gameplay. The announcement of its release inspired an online petition to have it banned from Valve's online game platform Steam (Evans 2019) and reflects the *RapeLay* controversy in its concern for whether sexual violence is acceptable for games. In light of the fact that Valve's publishing policy is to allow any game content unless it is an obvious case of trolling or explicitly breaks the law (Johnson 2018), it is clear that this game tests the boundaries of Valve, whether intentional or not. Either way, this is an example of controversy and transgression being used to determine boundaries.

This attempt of listing controversial games generally underlines the importance of context in the definition of anything as controversial or transgressive. Despite attempts at finding descriptive criteria, "transgressive" is a normative label, and carries social and political meaning. So how can we research something which is disputed and provocative in a meaningful manner? Our approach considers that to understand transgression in games, we need to not only look for the subjective experience but also take into consideration the norms of a given culture and society. This is also why this research has potential to reach beyond game studies. The controversies that are sparked by transgressive games are as revealing about the society surrounding game cultures and the norms dominating the context games operate in as they are about form, content, and play styles.

Context

The problem with speaking about transgressions that relate to game culture is that there is no unified game culture (Downing 2011; Muriel and Crawford 2018). Figures show that approximately half the population in the US and Western Europe plays video games daily either on console, PC, smartphones, or tablets. Close to 50% of Western European players are female, and US figures show that the average video game player is 34 years old (Entertainment Software Association and Ipsos Connect 2018; Interactive Software Federation of Europe and Ipsos Connect 2018). In other words, there are too many players and too many people engaged with play and games in different manners for the culture related to games to be unified. There is also severe cultural bias toward identification with the different aspects of game culture. According to the Pew Research Centre, for instance, *gamer* is a term that men will be three times more likely to use to describe themselves than women (Duggan 2015). To break it further down, Hispanic Americans are more likely to talk about themselves as gamers than African Americans and Americans of Northern European descent. This may have something to do with the prevalent, but misleading, stereotype about gamers, as described by game researchers Rachel Kowert, Ruth Festl, and Thorsten Quandt (2014). In a large study of people playing games, with a control group of people who did not play, they tested the stereotype of gamers as young, socially inept males and found that the average online player does not fit the stereotypical category (Kowert, Festl, and Quandt 2014). Before this, games and gender scholar Adrienne Shaw questioned the term *gamer* used as a targeting phrase and an identity, and pointed out that it was weak and problematic because gamer identity is not isolated from other identities or from a diversity of social contexts, and

> that targeted marketing's overemphasis of discrete identity categories like gender, sexualities, and races might actually have a negative impact on players' relationship to the medium. It also argues that researchers must be more attentive to the fact that playing games does not define one as a gamer.
>
> (Shaw 2012)

The term *gamer* has also become problematic over the last few years through appropriation by groups attempting to make points related to cultural politics. In 2014, an online campaign, supposedly about ethics in game journalism but better known for the anonymous participants harassing women in game design and criticism, attacked game studies researchers based on the belief that they were part of a "cultural Marxist" conspiracy to make games "politically correct" (Chess and Shaw 2015; Massanari 2015; Mortensen 2018). Using the term #gamergate as their calling card, this group of more or less anonymous activists took hold of the term *gamer* and gave it a specific meaning. Through their connection to the men's rights activists (MRA) and the so-called "alt-right" (Hawley 2017, 45–49), they underlined the importance of Shaw's argument that "gamer" was not a neutral term for all who play games, but an identity that intersects with other identities.

As we attempt to understand the context for transgressive games, we can also take note of how certain players have reacted to games that in other contexts might not have been controversial. For instance, the game *Dishonored 2* (Arkane Studios 2016) was marketed with a female protagonist and two playable main characters, one male and one female. If we are to believe some of the discussions relating to the Steam game platform (Souldomain

TM 2017), the option to play as a woman was deeply controversial, with the discussing players characterizing this design choice as an example of social justice run wild, and in forums such as GameFAQs it was claimed that the game had been "infected" (Tearast 2018).

Another example of debates among players concerning topics that would not have been controversial in other contexts is the debate on whether or not *The Witcher 3* (CD Projekt RED 2015) should feature more people of color (Kain 2015). On the one hand, the game is based on a Polish book series and designed by Polish designers, so it may come as no surprise that there are mainly white characters in it. On the other hand, why struggle to defend the realism of a game that features magic and dragons? It is not as if adding characters of different skin colors would in any way compromise the actual realism of the series. It would however challenge our preconceptions and biases toward the so-called high fantasy genre, and in particular the fantasy world of this particular book series, which closely resembles a mythic Medieval Eastern Europe. The discussions around *The Witcher* and other fantasy productions outline these preconceptions neatly while also revealing the concerns, values, and comfort zones of the active fans of these games. By studying which content and which game forms transgress against the norm of different segments of culture, we understand the values, ethics, and politics of the most expressive and verbal representatives of game subcultures as well as the values of the society at large.

Transgressive aesthetic in games

In this book, we focus not only on player experiences of transgression in games but also on the aesthetic of transgression in games or what we can see as the principles that can be revealed by studying transgressive texts. Beyond the texts themselves, games are, in many ways, ideal media for the study of transgression also because of how players engage with them: Through play. In his discussion of what he called "Scriptor Ludens" or the playing writer, literary scholar Robert R. Wilson observed that transgressive practices are a lot more acceptable when they relate to play (Wilson 1986, 74). According to Wilson, in literary criticism "transgression" tends to morph into a positive description when approaching "play", and he speculates that this is due to the transformative power of play. In our further discussion, this is one of our main points: That the process of playing mitigates transgressions. While games have transgressive potential, and people who play can experience games and gameplay as transgressive, play changes the content of terms used to describe it, seen most clearly on how "wipe out" and "destroy," for instance, become expressions of skill (Wilson 1986).

It is this movement of meaning, this shift in perspective, that becomes visible as we study how games play with difficult and provocative topics, and it is what we chase as we track the paradox of transgression in games.

Note

1 Among the 1982 sources, all available online, are an article in *InfoWorld* November 8, an article from *Milwaukee Journal* December 26, and a notice in *Billboard* December11 mentioning two lawsuits against the game.

References

Aldama, Frederick Luis, and Herbert Lindenberger. 2016. *Aesthetics of Discomfort: Conversations on Disquieting Art*. Ann Arbor: University of Michigan Press. https://muse.jhu.edu/book/44685.

Arkane Studios. 2016. *Dishonored 2*. Bethesda Softworks LLC. Xbox One.

Ashcraft, Brian. 2010. "Why Is CNN Talking About Rapelay?" *Kotaku*, March 31, 2010.

Bicchieri, Cristina. 2005. *The Grammar of Society: The Nature and Dynamics of Social Norms*. Cambridge: Cambridge University Press. doi:10.1017/CBO97 80511616037.

Bicchieri, Cristina, Ryan Muldoon, and Alessandro Sontuoso. 2018. "Social Norms." *The Stanford Encyclopedia of Philosophy*. Metaphysics Research Lab, Stanford University. https://plato.stanford.edu/archives/win2018/entries/social-norms/.

Brookhaven National Library. n.d. "History:The First Video Game?" Stony Brook University. Accessed May 26, 2017. www.bnl.gov/about/history/firstvideo.php.

Budick, Sanford, and Wolfgang. Iser. 1996. *Languages of the Unsayable: The Play of Negativity in Literature and Literary Theory*. Stanford, CA: Stanford University Press.

Caillois, Roger. 2001. *Man, Play and Games*. Urbana: University of Illinois Press ; Wantage: University Presses Marketing.

Cashell, Kieran. 2009. *Aftershock: The Ethics of Contemporary Transgressive Art*. London: I.B. Tauris.

CD Projekt RED. 2015. *The Witcher 3: Wild Hunt*. CD Projekt.

Chess, Shira, and Adrienne Shaw. 2015. "A Conspiracy of Fishes, or, How We Learned to Stop Worrying About #GamerGate and Embrace Hegemonic Masculinity." *Journal of Broadcasting & Electronic Media* 59 (1): 208–20. doi:10.1080/08838151.2014.999917.

Consalvo, Mia. 2007. *Cheating: Gaining Advantage in Videogames*. Cambridge, London: MIT.

Coughlan, Sean. 2014. "Violent Video Games Leave Teens 'Morally Immature.'" *BBC News Education*, 2014. www.bbc.com/news/education-26049333.

Destructive Creations. 2015. *Hatred*. Destructive Creations. www.hatredgame.com/.

Downing, Steven. 2011. "Retro Gaming Subculture and the Social Construction of a Piracy Ethic." *International Journal of Cyber Criminology* 5 (1). www.cybercrimejournal.com/downing2011ijcc.pdf.

Duchamp, Marcel, and R. Mutt. 1917. "Fountain." New York: The Blind Man.

Duggan, Maeve. 2015. "Gaming and Gamers." www.pewinternet.org/2015/12/15/gaming-and-gamers/.

Entertainment Software Association, and Ipsos Connect. 2018. "2018 Sales, Demographic, and Usage Data. Essential Facts About the Computer and Video Game Industry." www.theesa.com/wp-content/uploads/2018/05/EF2018_FINAL.pdf.

Evans, Patrick. 2019. "Rape Day Game Pulled by Steam Platform after Outcry." *BBC News – Trending*, March 7, 2019. www.bbc.com/news/blogs-trending-47484397.

Fassone, Riccardo, and William Huber. 2016. "Game Studies in the Cinquecento. Prolegomena to a Historical Analysis of the Rhetorics of Play." *Ludica* 2015–2016 (21–22): 10–13.

Fiske, John. 1992. "British Cultural Studies and Television." In *Channels of Discourse, Reassembled; Television and Contemporary Criticism*, edited by Robert C. Allen, 2nd ed., 284–326. London: Routledge.

Foucault, Michel. 1977. *Language/Counter-Memory/Practice*. Ithaca, NY: Cornell University Press.

Hawley, George. 2017. *Making Sense of the Alt-Right*. New York: Columbia University Press.

Huizinga, Johan. 1955. *Homo Ludens; a Study of the Play-Element in Culture. Humanitas, Beacon Reprints in Humanities*. Boston, MA: Beacon Press.

id Software. 1993. *Doom*. GT Interactive.

Illusion Soft. 2006. *RapeLay*. Illusion Soft.

Interactive Software Federation of Europe and Ipsos Connect. 2018. "Gametrack Digest: Quarter 1 2018." www.isfe.eu/sites/isfe.eu/files/gametrack_european_summary_data_2018_q1.pdf.

Jenkins, David. 2015. "Hatred Review – The Most Violent Game on Earth." *Metro Gaming*, 2015. http://metro.co.uk/2015/06/02/hatred-review-the-most-violent-game-on-earth-5225932/.

Jenks, Chris. 2003. *Transgressions*. London: Routledge.

———. 2013. "Transgression: The Concept." *Architectural Design* 83 (6): 20–23. doi:10.1002/ad.1669.

Johnson, Erik. 2018. "Who Gets to Be on the Steam Store?" *Steam Community*. June 6, 2018. https://steamcommunity.com/games/593110/announcements/detail/1666776116200553082.

Julius, Anthony. 2002. *Transgressions: The Offences of Art*. Chicago, IL: University of Chicago Press.

Kain, Erik. 2015. "Should 'The Witcher 3' Feature More People of Color?" *Forbes*, 2015. www.forbes.com/sites/erikkain/2015/06/04/should-the-witcher-3-feature-people-of-color/#15275d787e28.

Klepek, Patrick. 2016. "That Dragon, Cancer's Developers Are OK with Asshole Steam Discussions." *Kotaku*, 2016. www.google.com/url?q=http%3A%2F%2Fkotaku.com%2Fthat-dragon-cancer-s-developers-are-ok-with-asshole-st-1753044712.

Köhne, Eckart., Cornelia. Ewigleben, Ralph. Jackson, and British Museum. 2000. *Gladiators and Caesars: The Power of Spectacle in Ancient Rome*. Berkeley: University of California Press.

Kowert, Rachel, Ruth Festl, and Thorsten Quandt. 2014. "Unpopular, Overweight, and Socially Inept: Reconsidering the Stereotype of Online Gamers." *Cyberpsychology, Behavior, and Social Networking* 17 (3): 141–46. doi:10.1089/cyber.2013.0118.

Lah, Kyung. 2010. "'RapeLay' Video Game Goes Viral amid Outrage – CNN.Com." *CNN*, March 31, 2010. http://edition.cnn.com/2010/WORLD/asiapcf/03/30/japan.video.game.rape/.

Lessig, Lawrence. 2006. *Code: Version 2.0 ; Lawrence Lessig*. Electronic. New York: BasicBooks ; London: Perseus Running, distributor.

Lewdgamer. n.d. "Lewdgamer." Accessed March 10, 2017. www.lewdgamer.com.

Lynch, Teresa, Jessica E. Tompkins, Irene I. van Driel, and Niki Fritz. 2016. "Sexy, Strong, and Secondary: A Content Analysis of Female Characters in Video Games across 31 Years." *Journal of Communication* 66 (4): 564–84. doi:10.1111/jcom.12237.

Macey, Joseph, and Juho Hamari. 2019. "ESports, Skins and Loot Boxes: Participants, Practices and Problematic Behaviour Associated with Emergent Forms of Gambling." *New Media & Society* 21 (1): 20–41. doi:10.1177/1461444818786216.

Macfarlan, Tim. 2015. "Fury over 'Slave Tetris' Game Cramming Africans into a Ship's Hold." *Daily Mail Online*, September 1, 2015. www.dailymail.co.uk/news/article-3218677/Fury-Slave-Tetris-game-players-squeeze-Africans-ship-s-hold.html.

Massanari, A. 2015. "#Gamergate and The Fappening: How Reddit's Algorithm, Governance, and Culture Support Toxic Technocultures." New Media & Society. doi:10.1177/1461444815608807.

Mortensen, Torill Elvira. 2018. "Anger, Fear, and Games: The Long Event of #GamerGate." *Games and Culture* 13 (8). doi:10.1177/1555412016640408.

Muriel, Daniel, and Garry Crawford. 2018. *Video Games as Culture. Considering the Role and Im-Portance of Video Games in Contemporary Society.* London and New York: Routledge.

Mystique. 1982. *Custer's Revenge.* Mystique.

Nakasatomi, Hiroshi. 2012. "'Rapelay' and the Problem of Legal Reform in Japan. Government Regulation of Graphically Animated Pornography." *Electronic Journal of Contemporary Japanese Studies* 12 (3). http://www.japanesestudies.org.uk/ejcjs/vol12/iss3/nakasatomi.html.

Nielsen, Rune Kristian Lundedal, and Paweł Grabarczyk. 2018. "Are Loot Boxes Gambling? Random Reward Mechanisms in Video Games." In *Proceedings of DiGRA 2018.* Digital Games Research Association (DIGRA).

Numinous Games. 2016. *That Dragon, Cancer.* Numinous Games.

O'Neill, Maggie., and Lizzie Seal. 2012. *Transgressive Imaginations: Crime, Deviance and Culture.* Basingstoke: Palgrave Macmillan.

Obsidian Entertainment. 2014. *South Park; the Stick of Truth.* Ubisoft.

Ringhieri, Innocenzo. 1551. *Cento Giuochi Liberali et d'ingegno.* Bologna: Anselmo Giaccarelli.

Salen, Katie, and Eric Zimmerman. 2004. *Rules of Play: Game Design Fundamentals.* Cambridge: MIT Press.

Serious Games Interactive. 2015. *Playing History: Slave Trade.*

Serrano, Andres. 1987. "Piss Christ." Southeastern Center for Contemporary Art.

Shaw, Adrienne. 2012. "Do You Identify as a Gamer? Gender, Race, Sexuality, and Gamer Identity." *New Media & Society* 14 (1): 28–44. doi:10.1177/1461444811410394.

Souldomain T.M. 2017. "Seems Obvious Now That SJWism Back Fired." Steam Community. 2017. http://steamcommunity.com/app/614570/discussions/0/2333276539591292689/.

Suits, Bernard (Bernard Herbert). 1990. *The Grasshopper: Games, Life, and Utopia.* Boston, MA: David R. Godine.

Sutton-Smith, Brian. 1997. *The Ambiguity of Play.* Cambridge, MA, London: Harvard University Press.

Tearast. 2018. "The New Dishonored: Another Case of a Game Becoming Infected by the SJWs?" GameFAQs. 2018. https://gamefaqs.gamespot.com/boards/916373-pc/75632145.

Waters, John. 1972. *Pink Flamingos*. United States: New Line Cinema.

Wikipedia. 2019. "List of Controversial Video Games." Wikipedia. 2019. https://en.wikipedia.org/wiki/List_of_controversial_video_games.

Wilson, Robert R. 1986. "Play, Transgression and Carnival: Bakhtin and Derrida on 'Scriptor Ludens.'" *Mosaic: An Interdisciplinary Critical Journal* 19: 73–89. doi:10.2307/24777518.

Zendle, David, and Paul Cairns. 2018. "Video Game Loot Boxes Are Linked to Problem Gambling: Results of a Large-Scale Survey." Edited by George Joseph Youssef. *PLOS ONE* 13 (11): e0206767. doi:10.1371/journal.pone.0206767.

2 Form and content of transgressive games

Whether a game is transgressive or not depends on the responses it creates in players. In other words, if a game provokes discomfort, provocation, or disgust or strong criticism, then this is an indication that the game may include elements that will be deemed transgressive by audiences. When a game is considered transgressive, this may be due to the topics it portrays and the way these topics are displayed, or it may be due to the activities that the player is invited to join in or perform. These aspects may indeed be combined, so that a sense of transgression may emerge from how the game models these activities as well as from the status of such mechanisms inside the narrative. Hence an important part of our project is to understand how form and content interact with the player to produce an experience of transgressive aesthetics.

This chapter presents some of the central terms we will use in the discussion of the games we have chosen for our player study. These terms will then be revisited as we discuss the games in Chapter 3.

Form and content in games

Like other media, games consist of two layers – form and content. From a general text theoretical perspective, *form* is how the mediated text is structured and organized, while *content* is the subject matter of the work (Baldick 2015, 74–75, 144). *Form* often refers to aspects relating to the medium and the medium-specific properties of a text, while *content* is associated with the message of the texts. Following this reasoning, in games, *form* can be considered the structural features relating to the game system, rules, and mechanics, while *content* is the representational aspects relating to fiction and narrative. Like with preceding media, a game's form concerns the materiality of the medium or the medium-specific aspects of the text. The content, then, is the theme of the game or the gameworld environment that works as a metaphor for the game system beyond (Jørgensen 2013; Klastrup 2009; Klastrup and Tosca 2004). Some games appear to be more driven by form, such as *Tetris* (Pazhitnov 1985) or *Pac-Man* (Namco et al. 1980), where the graphical interfaces are fairly minimal representations of the game mechanics. Other games appear to be more driven by the content, and there are large, long-running game franchises that follow and develop complex storylines such as *The Legend of Zelda* (Miyamoto and Tezuka 1986) or the *Warcraft* series (Blizzard Entertainment 1994). In both of these games, the storyline is represented in moving and still images, music, voice, and written text, creating a developing, unfolding fiction, set in a vast explorable world where it is easy to consider the mechanics as a tool to represent the story rather than a goal in and of itself.

Form and content are often closely related and tend to affect each other. In games, the meaning of game mechanics is colored by how they are represented in the gameworld, and the representational aspects are often not considered meaningful without being explicitly linked to the game system. However, whether game mechanics should actually be considered *form* or *content* in a game context is disputable. Let us consider the status of game mechanics in respect to the game system. While the game mechanics are indeed a part of the game system that defines games as a medium, the player also engages with this game system through specific game mechanics in the process of play. The game system is here understood as the overall infrastructure of the game, including rules, objects, their attributes, an environment, and the internal relationships between all features (Salen and Zimmerman 2004), while the game mechanics are "methods invoked by agents for interacting with the game world" (Sicart 2011) in the sense that it concerns relatively formulaic or fixed combination of rules that together create a framework for how players interact with game rules. The relationship between the two can then be understood in this manner: The game system involves a range of systemic features relating to the form of the game. These systemic features include hidden processes that the player does not engage with, features that govern how the gameworld works relating to the graphic and physics engines, and tangible and manipulable interactive elements involving game mechanics. As a part of the larger game system, game mechanics become the specific "game elements that offer certain interactions with the game state" (Jørgensen 2013). All these processes have a certain expressive power. In a game where all the objects are designed to be threats, obstacles, or tools for defense in progressing through the game, the player will experience everything as dangerous, even silly adversaries like candy, vegetables, toys, or flowers in *Cuphead* (StudioMDHR 2017), and plants can become defensive weapons as in *Plants vs Zombies* (PopCap Games 2009). The meaning of an object depends not only on its reference in the real world but just as much or even more on its function in the gameworld.

Because games demand hands-on interactivity and engagement, and include processes that the player engages with in a meaningful manner in the process of play, the game system and mechanics are not *form* in the traditional sense of the term, but they also have attributes that make them part of the *content*. To illustrate: Game physics engines simulate the laws of physics in the gameworld, thereby becoming vital for the player's inter-action with the game environment. In *Prince of Persia* (Ubisoft Montreal 2008), for example, central to gameplay is navigating through a treacher-ous environment of climbable ledges and pillars as well as bottomless pits. It is the physics engine – an obvious part of the game's form – that creates the affordances of the environment, but at the same time, this is what struc-tures the content and the fiction central to the player's interaction with the game. Not least, it is central for creating fictional involvement and a nar-rative experience: The system forms the functional base of the gameworld that the player interacts with and is a part of. Within this system, the game mechanics guide the player's direct interaction with the game, and the ex-perience of engaging with the mechanics is an indelible part of engaging with the content. For comparison, it is only rarely that the mechanic of turning a page becomes a major part of the way we experience the content of a book, but in games reaching new content is a challenge in itself.

We may further explore the complexity of the relationship between form and content in games through the concept of *interface*. Interface is tra-ditionally understood as the boundary between different regions (Collins English Dictionary 2017) or the point where independent systems interact (American Heritage Dictionary 2017). New media scholar Lev Manovich argues that in new media, the interface is what frames or mediates the content and what allows the user to access the content. It is "the work's interface that creates its unique materiality and a unique user experience" (2001, 66–67). Thus, instead of a division between content and form or content and medium, he finds a dichotomy between content and interface. At the same time, he argues that the interface is so closely intertwined with the content that it is difficult to separate it from the content that it mediates:

> [T]he choice of a particular interface is motivated by a work's content to such a degree that it can no longer be thought of as a separate level. Content and interface merge into one entity, and no longer can be taken apart.
>
> (Manovich 2001, 67)

In *Gameworld Interfaces*, Jørgensen (2013) argues that the gameworld en-vironment must be seen as an aspect of the interface, because it is the chan-nel that allows for communication between the player and the game system. In this sense, the interface is a structural feature of the game and may for this reason be considered part of the game medium's form. However, supported by Lisbeth Klastrup (2009), she argues that there is little doubt that the gameworld, as an interactive environment for play and as fictional world, also is a central part of the game content – perhaps even the ultimate and defining part of the content of a game.

In the further discussion, we will address game mechanics and rules as a part of the game's form, and the representational elements consisting of theme, narrative, and gameworld as content, but with the philosophy in mind that the relationship is as complex and intertwined as the previous discussion suggests. We may for this reason with confidence, and without sloganism, state that the medium *is* indeed the message: Perhaps not in the sense of media theorist Marshal McLuhan, but in a more literal sense. In McLuhan's understanding, the dramatic changes brought by new media technology are a more important message than what we communicated while using it (1964). In games, form *is* content.

Meaningful play in transgressive games

The debate of fiction expressed through mechanics is reflected in game scholar Jesper Juul's discussion about the relationship between rules and fiction in *Half-Real*. Juul's argument that modern games consist of *rules* that form a material reality and *fiction* that provides a representational environment can be seen as just another way to describe *form* and *content* in games. In *Half-Real*, Juul states that fiction "plays an important role in making the player understand the rules of the game" (2005, 163). Thus, the representational aspects work as a concretization of the more abstract game rules, a phenomenon that interaction research calls *reification* (Beaudouin-Lafon and Mackay 2000; Jørgensen 2013). Reification, as defined by HCI researchers Michel Beaudouin-Lafon and Wendy Mackay, "is a process for turning concepts into objects. In user interfaces, the resulting object can be represented explicitly in the screen and operated upon" (2000). Reification and the close relationship between form and content in games have particular impact on how transgression in games is experienced, as any transgression may be caused, enhanced, mitigated, or suppressed by the mechanics as much as by the content.

This fluid boundary between mechanics and fiction leads to an important discussion in game studies as to whether the meaning of a game springs out of the representation or out of the rules of the game. This debate also reflects public controversies on games. Often when a game is deemed transgressive in public discourse, it is due to their *content*. When games are accused of including sexual topics, excessive violence, or problematic gender representations, it is a reaction to the content of games. The idea that meaning springs out of the representational aspects of games are also fundamental to the European and American game rating systems, such as Pan-European Game Information (PEGI) and Entertainment Software Rating Board (ESRB), in which age regulation is based on the content and themes of games (Van Vught and Schott 2012). At other times, however, the controversy has concerned the *form* of games; in other words, the activities that the game system allows players to perform – the affordances and procedures of the game. The skepticism toward including serious topics into games, based on the idea that games – frequently thought of as toys – are supposed to be fun, safe, and playful, is an example of this. The idea that interactivity makes certain activities more "real" than watching mere visual representations and that games for this reason should be heavily regulated is another.

We believe that we cannot reduce the meaning-making potential of video games to only one of these aspects. As modern video games feature an amalgamation of both representational aspects as well as game mechanics, we argue that the meaning-making process that takes place in the mind of the player emerges from the combination of the two, and that they work together in communicating a meaning that is more than the two parts alone.

Meaning through content

Society pays a large amount of attention to the fact that different people may respond differently to specific kinds of media content, and age regulation is an example of this. Systems such as the PEGI and the ESRB have been built around this idea. Both are systems for evaluating game content according to age-appropriateness and provide guidance for consumers of whether a certain game includes violence, bad language, gambling, sex, drugs, and other topics of potential concern. In terms of game content, these ratings show a degree of sensitivity toward the fact that the decoding of game content is subjective and often also contextual. As guidance for parents, PEGI stresses that "every child is different. Ultimately parents should decide what their children are capable of viewing or experiencing", inviting parents to play together with their child and helping contextualize and explain why certain games may be unsuitable (Pan European Game Information PEGI 2019). Despite the fact that PEGI indeed categorizes certain topics as being of potential concern, this quote demonstrates the important fact that we cannot decide whether game content is transgressive or not simply by identifying certain topics. On the contrary, the quote shows that it is not always easy to identify what content is transgressive for whom and in what situations, and that subjective factors, such as maturity and preference, count. Further, the focus on playing together and talking about the content indicates that context matters.

Like with other media, to understand whether the inclusion of certain content is problematic or not, it is important to also take the fictional or in-game context into consideration. This means that whether something is deemed transgressive by the player often depends on how a narrative is told, how characters are depicted, and the audiovisual style of the game in question. Also, the empathic bond that players have established with characters will contribute to the player's response (Lankoski 2011) and their sense of whether game content is transgressive or not. This also means that topics such as violence, abuse, sexism, and racism may be justified by players when they are integrated into the narrative in a way that is experienced as meaningful and which gives depth to the story. Further, rhetorical devices such as humor, fantasy, or particular kinds of visual styles will also contribute to framing the content as different from the actual world. In other words, it is often not the inclusion of the topic in itself that creates a sense of discomfort, disgust, or provocation, but the way it is treated. Hence identifying a controversial topic is not enough to identify transgression. To understand whether a game has transgressive content or not involves a degree of involvement or time spent with the game in question. As is central to our player-centric perspective, we cannot simply look at the game, but we also need to play it or at least observe play.

Meaning through form

As we have argued, content alone does not help us understand whether a game can be experienced as transgressive for people playing it. This also explains why the game ratings sometimes may appear randomly assigned. As content descriptors, PEGI and ESRB ratings are not evaluations of gameplay. With the exception of indicating whether a game is played online or not, PEGI and ESBR do not say anything about the difficulty level or the relationship between game mechanics and representation. However, games can also transgress the sensibilities of players on the level of game rules and mechanics; in other words, through its *procedures* (Bogost 2007). As such, a game may be transgressive through the actions that it invites the player to take, either because the actions represent transgressions in the real world (such as violence and crime) or because of the way actions are modeled in the game.

The idea that meaning comes out of the interaction with rules in games is reflected in what scholars and game designers Katie Salen Tekinbaş and Eric Zimmerman call *meaningful play*. In their view, meaning in games "emerges from the relationship between player action and system outcome" (Salen and Zimmerman 2004, 34). Meaningful play happens when the relationship between player actions and system outcomes is discernible and integrated into the larger context of the game. To be discernible in this context means that the "result of game action are communicated to the player in a perceivable way", and to be integrated means that the player action has immediate significance, but also that it has an effect on the player experience at a later point in the game (Salen and Zimmerman 2004, 34–35). Thus, Salen and Zimmerman's idea of meaningful play indicates that playing a game is in itself a meaningful experience, even in games with abstract representations such as *Tetris*. In such games, the meaning springs out of the mechanics, not out of the representation.

An example from a video game where the sense of transgression is found on the level of game mechanics is found in the infamous torture scene in *Grand Theft Auto V (GTAV)* (Rockstar North 2013), where the player inflicts torture on an innocent. While the fact that the player is invited to inflict torture in itself may create a sense of discomfort, this is also further stressed by how the torture is modeled: The player must themselves select what tools to use, and it is not enough to simply press a button to, for instance, pull a tooth. Instead the player must wiggle the analogue stick to simulate loosening the tooth and then forcefully jerk at the stick to pull the tooth out. While simply pressing a button would trivialize the act of torture, here the torture sequence is given extra impact through an interaction that simulates the act of pulling the victim's tooth to a relatively detailed level. Now the relevance of this example may be questioned as the *GTA* franchise is well known for its humor and satire, and wiggling a controller stick in order to pull a virtual tooth has large comedy potential. Satire is an important aspect of gameplay, and we will discuss that further in Chapter 7. For this argument, however, we will treat this as a straight-forward example.

Following Bogost's argument that as games carry and create meaning and arguments through rules and game mechanics (Bogost 2007), when *GTAV* asks the player to interact with the game in a particular way and it is the modeling of this interaction that makes the game situation feel uncomfortable, the *procedurality* of the game is at work in the meaning-making process. Here the in-game act of torture does not simply refer to overcoming a gameplay challenge of being able to press buttons in the specific sequence; instead, it refers to an act of torture, and this is given emphasis by the discomfort that players feel when pulling the tooth.

Meaningful play: a marriage of form and content

This situation where the *form* plays a defining role in the meaning-making process puts game form into a position where it is not possible to separate clearly between form and the content. Instead we see that game form and game content are entangled in an intricate interplay with each other in the meaning-making process. If we move to the specific case of transgression in video games, we see that it is rarely the game mechanism alone that creates a sense of transgression; rather, the sense of transgression is created because the game mechanism is combined with a particular kind of representation. Keeping the torture scene of *GTAV* in mind, wiggling the analogue stick is in itself not a transgressive act; as a matter of fact, many games use this mechanic as a metaphor for any kind of wiggling act. For instance, *The Last Guardian* (genDESIGN and SIE Japan Studio 2016) uses the same wiggling action as *GTAV*'s torture scene for a completely different purpose. *The Last Guardian* is an adventure and puzzle game where the player goes on a journey to free himself and his giant animal companion from captivation. In this emotional-laden game, wiggling the analogue stick lets the player free treats buried in the ground to feed their big animal companion Trico, an act which is not likely to feel transgressive and is more likely to be experienced as a bonding event between the character and their companion, where the player struggles to dig a treat out of the ground for their friend. It is when the wiggling is combined with the representation of social taboos, such as pulling a tooth in the torture scene, that it becomes potentially disturbing for the player. In this sense, it is difficult to claim that the sense of transgression is created by the procedural power of the game mechanics alone.

Comparatively, transgressive representations alone may not have the same impact as representations and game mechanics together. This can be demonstrated with an example from the isometric shooter *Hatred* (Destructive Creations 2015). The game opens with a cinematic cutscene that introduces the player character as he prepares for a killing spree with no other motivation than simply hating the world. While the game appears to have an intentionally provocative theme, this is not reflected in the game mechanics. The game uses game mechanics that are standard for the shooter genre, with little modification that might have stressed the transgressions of the player character. Shooting is just a press of a button; even the finishing move that allows the player to kill already downed enemies – although admittedly visually disturbing – utilizes trivial game mechanics. The only exception to standard shooter mechanics is that the player can heal his character by killing downed people. The consequence is that while initially visually disturbing, the game soon feels like any other mediocre shooter, something that was observed by the participants in our studies.

In conclusion, we see that while meaningfulness, and hence transgression, can indeed spring out of either game mechanics or representation, the combination of the two has a different potential for meaning-making than each alone. In combination, the two contextualize each other, sometimes with the effect of being able to show the games' true potential for expressing the transgressive while in other situations helping to sanitize or mitigate the sense of transgression.

Beyond form and content: ludic transgressions

As we have seen, it can be difficult to make clear distinctions between form and content in games, particularly due to the meaning attached to processes of play. The play activity, in which players appear to be *doing* the actions the game invites, can make play look very different when *observed* from different positions, from within or without the play experience. So it becomes vital to distinguish not only between form and content, but also between transgression within the specific context of play or outside of it. As we discussed in Chapter 1, games tend to be more controversial when they refer to something in the real world, something outside the game.

Ever since *Death Race* (Exidy 1976) allowed the player to run over "gremlins" with their racecars, games have regularly been targeted for controversy. As we saw in the discussion in Chapter 1 of game controversies, historically, most controversies relate to the game's content in the shape of themes or narratives (NCAC 2019; Wikipedia 2019), spanning stereotypical representation and sexual content, and the inclusion of drugs or alcohol, but the main reason for outrage and controversy is violence. Public controversies have largely focused on the representational content explicitly, but sometimes criticism is also directed at the gameplay – what the player is allowed to do in the game. In the *Death Race* controversy, the game's close relationship to the film *Death Race 2000* (Bartel 1976), in which road race competitors were awarded for running over pedestrians (Kocurek 2012), created a discussion over whether the game encouraged violent behavior in the actual world, but there was apparently little attention toward the in-game playful context of the actions. Up until today, we still see that controversies concern the visuals of the game and the presumed relationship between the visuals and the gameplay rather than the actual game experience itself. The *GTA* series has, for instance, repeatedly been criticized for excessive violence, featuring huge explosions and massive police chases, but whether causing simulated havoc feels like a crime or a transgression for the player is rarely asked. On the contrary, horror games, which players frequently describe as disturbing, are rarely considered controversial by society. The same is true for particularly tactile scenes in certain games, such as a scene in *The Walking Dead Season 1* (Telltale Games 2012), where the player must cut off the avatar's arm to avoid a zombie infection: While the idea of cutting off one's arm certainly may be stressful, watching it being done in a game from an observer's perspective is not nearly as disturbing as it is for the player. When there is a discrepancy between the gameplay and the public reception of the game like this, we are dealing with an example of a *superficial transgression*, because it is based on a superficial understanding of the game by observers about how the topic is treated from a gameplay perspective.

These examples show that when a game is understood as transgressive by someone, the sense of transgression can either be evoked because the game breaks with the norms of society, what we will call *extraludic* or game-external transgressions, or because the game breaks with norms inside the game context, what we will call *intraludic* or game-internal transgressions. This reflects philosopher John Richard Sageng's discussions of intraludic and extraludic norms in games (2018, 65). *Extraludic* and *intraludic transgressions* are sometimes combined, but it is not given that what breaks with norms outside the game will be the same as what breaks with norms inside the game. While extraludic transgressions concern the relationship between the game and society, and are often associated with ideas of what content or representation may or may not be appropriate for games and play, play behavior, or play time use, intraludic transgressions are closely associated with the fictional and ludic context of the game. While extraludic transgressions are about public outrage and controversy, intraludic transgressions concern discomfort created by situations encountered as part of the gameplay context.

As this book concerns the transgressive aesthetics of games and the subjective interpretation of it by players in a gameplay context, our focus is on intraludic transgressions. However, as a certain game may cause both intraludic and extraludic transgressions at the same time, and because it is important to understand the difference and relationship between the two, our discussion here will start with extraludic transgressions. We need to consider how and why certain games become the target of public controversies, while other games with uncomfortable and mature content do not. In the following, we will employ media and games scholar Holger Pötzsch's term *transgressivity* to investigate how video games can be transgressive on both the extraludic and intraludic level.

While we have attempted to define transgression as a concept, understanding exactly when something becomes transgressive for whom and in what context is a contextually and culturally dependent question. With his term *transgressivity*, Pötzsch wants to grasp the move from formal definitions to contextual perceptions and experiences of transgressive games. From this perspective, he presents a typology of forms of transgressivity in video games, stressing how game content and mechanics may evoke a sense of transgression. The categories in Pötzsch's typology are described through three parameters; first, the frames or discourses that are transgressed; second, the practices of play encountered or performed in the transgression; and third, the game mechanics and design features of the game in question (Pötzsch 2018). The typology is concerned with the games' content and mechanics, and does not concern overarching conceptual debates about what is and is not appropriate content in games. As it does not distinguish with respect to where the transgressions originate and offers a descriptive and non-normative perspective on transgressive content in games, Pötzsch's categories are useful when we attempt to understand the relationship between *intraludic* and *extraludic* transgressions. This will allow us to discuss whether the sense of transgression stems from the game itself and emerges as a result of gameplay or whether the sense that a game is transgressive stems from how the game is discussed in public discourse. To include a higher sensitivity to the player perspective, we will also discuss whether the game offers options for the player to transgress or whether it is the game that transgresses against the player.

Extraludic transgressions

Extraludic transgressions stem from situations in which the sense of transgression has little to do with the actual form or content of the game, but emerges from the idea that certain societal norms are broken. Often extraludic transgressions are related to the fallacy of play and the idea that there are certain topics that in themselves are inappropriate for play, regardless of how these topics are treated. As we have pointed out in Chapter 1, there is obviously a cultural factor involved in the idea of what topics are inappropriate for play and what stirs controversy in, say, Europe or North America may be quite different from what stirs controversy in Asia.

When different controversies, such as the *RapeLay* outrage, where a game legal in Japan created problems in the US (Ashcraft 2010), lead to discussions of censorship, we see an example of what Pötzsch calls *juridical transgressivity*, which indicates that the game includes "[m]echanics and content deemed illegal for particular groups at particular times and places" (Pötzsch 2018, 57).

These are extraludic transgressions, which often concern situations that are not solely associated with the form or content of a particular game. Instead, they are often the subject of cultural debates about games as medium rather than detailed discussions about the gameplay of specific games themselves. For instance, the so-called #gamergate controversy can be seen as an extraludic transgression so far as it concerned the gamer identity and conservation of the medium, where there was a perceived transgression against the expectations of one audience by the wishes of another game audience (and vice versa). We will discuss aspects of this in closer detail in the context of *hegemonic transgressivity* below. Another kind of extraludic transgression that many players encounter, associated with specific game titles, is the so-called toxic culture associated with certain online gamer cultures (Boudreau 2018; Consalvo 2012). While toxic gamer culture can be experienced as transgressive for many players, some would also argue that the perceived toxicity is part of the vernacular of gaming culture and not to be taken seriously, suggesting that this is experienced as a transgression only by certain groups of players.

The fine line between extraludic and intraludic transgressions

One of the strengths of Pötzsch's typology is that it highlights the fact that when games are considered transgressive, they are considered such due to multiple, often complex, reasons, which leaves no obvious boundary between extraludic and intraludic transgressions. Many game transgressions do not spring out of either the game or public discourse alone, but out of an amalgamation of associations relating both to the game and to real world situations. *Critical* and *hegemonic transgressivity* are two of Pötzsch's forms of transgressivity that are potentially transgressive both because of their game-internal characteristics – the content and mechanics – and because of their relationship to society at large. Critical and hegemonic transgressivity are both examples of games that appear to explicitly aim at stirring controversy and debate, reaching for a dialogical relationship with society. For this reason, we can call critical and hegemonic games *transgressive by intent.*

Critical transgressivity is intentionally provocative for the purpose of social criticism and "aims at questioning and possibly subverting prevailing discourses and power relations" (Pötzsch 2018, 53). Critical transgressivity has for this reason an oppositional character with respect to dominating trends in society, presenting a particular worldview or ideological perspective that there are strong opinions about. Such games may be best known through activism-related games in the serious game genre and popularized through sites such as Newsgaming.com, the publication platform for a team of independent game developers seeking to combine games and simulations with political cartoons, but critical transgressivity is also found in an increasing number of commercially available games. Pötzsch's example is *Spec Ops: The Line* (Yager Development 2012), a game that we also used for discussion material in our focus group study. Illustrating the darker side of military operations such as war crimes, civilian causalities, and post-traumatic stress syndrome, *Spec Ops: The Line* subverts the traditional hero story and simultaneously presents an anti-war message.

Contrary to critical transgressivity, *hegemonic transgressivity* uses transgressions in a speculative or suppressed way for the purpose of reinforcing or capitalizing dominating power structures (Pötzsch 2018). Instead of questioning established hegemonic frameworks, games that exploit hegemonic transgressivity may instead aim for provocation for provocation's sake, such as using excessive violence for its shock value rather than for delivering a deeper critical message. Pötzsch's example here is the "No Russian" mission of *Call of Duty: Modern Warfare 2* (Infinity Ward 2009), in which the player must go undercover as a terrorist during a massacre of civilians at an airport security check. The game does not invite the player to problematize the act; rather, it is framed as justified because it can hinder a greater atrocity. This is why Pötzsch finds that the scene is a speculative inclusion that "reiterates received mantras of war as a necessity in the face of incomprehensible evil" (Pötzsch 2018, 56). Arguably, we see the same in *Hatred*, which was included in both the focus group and journal studies, where the acts of the mass murderer avatar are never contextualized or problematized. In the example from *Modern Warfare 2* above, the player may choose to opt out of the mission, and during the mission they may also choose not to fire their weapon; however, if they follow along with the mission as directed, the player can be said to actively engage in transgression. In *Hatred*, however, we can ask whether the player is a *transgressor*, through portrayals of violence the player participates in, or a *transgressee* being transgressed against since there is no opting out apart from quitting the game. This is an experience related to the hegemony, which can be both empowering and oppressive, depending on your relative position at any given time.

Hegemonic transgressivity and the case of Anita Sarkeesian

To illustrate the complexities of in particular hegemonic transgressivity, we will briefly touch on the curious controversy surrounding media critic Anita Sarkeesian's project *Tropes vs Women in Videogames* (Sarkeesian 2012b). This rather innocuous analysis of gendered tropes in games met surprising and hateful resistance from a very active group of mainly male gamers (Sarkeesian 2012a), protesting what they expected to be the end of overt female sexiness and male sex-laced power fantasies in games. Their protests turned to personalized attacks on Sarkeesian (Wingfield 2014), and random individuals online were uncovering and constantly repeating both justified problems – continuing their criticism after these were corrected – and hypothetical or plain erroneous grievances (Daemonpro 2014), while stating that Sarkeesian's criticism of games would hurt women in games (KindRAness 2016). The attackers, criticizing Sarkeesian, were a minority among people who play games, and the support she received as her crowdsourced project was funded way beyond expectations, indicates that she had a strong group of followers willing to put their money behind her message. And the support Sarkeesian subsequently received, all the way up to presenting her view on the expressed misogyny in games and gamer culture in the United Nations (Alter 2015), indicates that her expressed views on gender representation in games were not transgressive, at least not to the establishment. However, the hateful and active resistance she met, to the point of death threats, indicates that her point of view made Sarkeesian a transgressor against an active subset of game culture.

Although we can hardly claim that sexist gender representation in games is a form of critical transgressivity, Sarkeesian did point out a feature of certain games that can elicit criticism by the establishment – or the hegemony – of Western society. This made her a hegemonic transgressor; her transgressions strengthened what the establishment at least pay lip service to. However, the outrage that she caused signals that she was indeed stirring up and transgressing against a different, perceived hegemony – that of a group of gamers who saw themselves as the most important segment of game culture. Sarkeesian was thus a critical transgressor against dominant power structures in game culture because she was asking for a *change* from the establishment of game culture.

The case of Sarkeesian is also tied to what Pötzsch calls *situational transgressivity*, which refers to "[m]echanics and content breaching requirements of particular settings" (Pötzsch 2018, 51). Following sociologist Erving Goffman's (1967) frame analysis, situational transgressivity concerns the breaking of rules relating to particular social frames. What Sarkeesian did by adapting the scholarly discourse of feminist criticism on games to YouTube videos, a medium that is frequently used for game streams, Let's Plays, and walkthroughs, was an obvious break of frame. Since situational transgressivity concerns transgressions that depend on particular situations or settings, it is difficult to identify certain games as being situationally transgressive. Instead, this concerns the setting of play rather than the game itself, and any game played in an inappropriate setting would be considered a situational transgression. Pötzsch's example is the politician who plays mobile games during parliamentary hearings (Pötzsch 2018). However, it could also be argued that games that have options for in-game situational transgressivity are examples of this form. For instance, MMOs that allow player versus player offenses like griefing and ganking, such as *World of Warcraft* (Blizzard 2004), can be considered games with the potential for situational transgressivity against the player. Moreover, as we will see in the discussion below, situational transgressivity can also be connected to the fictional situations of a game.

Deviant play practices (Mortensen 2008) can also be considered a break with the hegemony. Deviant play practices can be both intraludic and extraludic at the same time because they can include player activities that break the rules of the game as well as the norms and social expectations. An example of a situation concerning playing within the rules, but against the hegemony of the straight white male, can be found in what gender studies scholar Jenny Sundén with reference to Espen Aarseth's idea of transgression discusses in her examination of gameplay in an LGBT (lesbian, gay, bisexual, transgender) *World of Warcraft* guild. She demonstrates how simply by acknowledging each other's queer sexuality, players could transgress within the often very narrow and conform community of gamer culture. In this context, she described how it was common to use "rape" as a metaphor for victory and "gay" as a metaphor for silly or stupid, but it was unacceptable to announce that a guild actually was friendly to people who identified as queer, making queerness at least as transgressive in a fantasy land of elves and shape-shifters as it is in our physical reality (Sundén 2009).

Last, another form of transgression that further complicates the relationship between extraludic and intraludic transgressions is what Pötzsch calls *idiosyncratic transgressivity*, which "[f]eatures subjectively experienced as transgressive by specific individuals" (2018, 51). This form is difficult to design around and is focused on individual, subjective sensibilities. As this form concerns reactions that stem from individual interpretations, opinions, and experiences, it is difficult to identify certain games as being idiosyncratically transgressive per se. Sometimes subtle and even innocent game content can create intense responses in players with particular traumas, for instance. Certain games with a particular social realist approach, such as games that deal with traumas, can be expected to have a triggering effect on some, such as *Spec Ops: The Line*, which deals with post-traumatic stress; *This War of Mine*, featuring being a civilian in war; or *Life is Strange* (Dontnod Entertainment 2015), which is concerned with suicide and bullying, among other things. However, although players may find these games transgressive due to previous traumatic experiences, they may also experience being uncomfortable because of the particular situations in which they put the player and the protagonist. In such cases, we are dealing with a form of diegetic transgressivity rather than an idiosyncratic one. In our journal studies, players found that *GTAV* and *Beyond: Two Souls* (Quantic Dream 2013) were games that created a sense of idiosyncratic transgressivity in certain players. Idiosyncratic transgressivity on the part of the player happens when the player must actively do something that breaks with their basic sensibilities (such as inflicting torture in *GTAV*), and it is against the player when the player is a victim of it (such as almost becoming a victim of rape in *Beyond: Two Souls*).

These transgressive experiences that spring out of neither the game nor the public discourse, but from both, simultaneously, can be called *metaludic* transgressions. We will return to this shortly, after having elaborated on intraludic transgressive experiences.

Intraludic transgressions

Intraludic transgressive experiences emerge from interaction with the game itself, are connected to in-game features, and stem from the in-game context itself rather than from public discourse. It concerns the breaking of game rules, but can also concern the treatment of specific topics inside the game, be it through representational or game mechanical means. Intraludic transgressivity is of particular interest in the discussion of transgressive aesthetics in games.

Intraludic transgressions cover what Pötzsch identifies as *ludic* and *diegetic transgressivity* (2018). *Ludic transgressivity* includes features that "enable a break with the rules and mechanics as well as to the practices of creating and exploiting such formal potentials" (2018, 50). He mentions features that allow bug exploitation and other design weaknesses, a type of transgression in so far that it threatens to break the coherence and appreciation of the gameplay experience. Here, Pötzsch refers to deviant play practices that are concerned with rule breaking and cheating rather than subverting the social frame the way Sundén was discussing. While there is a body of research into this kind of transgression (Aarseth 2007; Consalvo 2007; Juul 2002; Meades 2018; Salen and Zimmerman 2004; Smith 2001), it did not come up as a concrete example of transgression in any of our studies. The reason for the absence of such data may be connected to the idea that the participants did not experience this as a meaningful transgression against them, nor did they engage in activities where they felt they transgressed against others in this manner. While some players may feel that breaking the rules of a game is cheating and for this reason wrong – typically because it gives them an undeserved advantage in single-player games, which were the focus of this study – breaking the game rules may not feel transgressive since the only person to feel the consequences is the player herself. Based on our data, we would however like to expand this category to include games that transgress *against* the player: Dark game design (Zagal, Björk, and Lewis 2013); that is, games that make players act against their own interest, such as games based on gambling mechanisms like freemium or pay-to-play games, are examples of this (Karlsen 2018). This can also include games that are imbalanced in favor of the system rather than the player or where the challenges are so high that players are likely not to be able to succeed. Examples of this are the *Souls* games (From Software 2011) and by extension *Bloodborne* (From Software 2015), which was used in our gameplay journal study.

While ludic transgressivity concerns breaking the rules of the game, *diegetic transgressivity* is connected to the fictional aspect of the game. *Diegetic transgressivity* refers to the "breaking of the rules, laws, and conventions that are intrinsic to fictional gameworlds" (Pötzsch 2018, 52). Examples are game mechanics that allow for the breaking of fictional laws in the game, and Pötzsch refers to the fact that in *The Elder Scrolls V: Skyrim* (Bethesda Game Studios 2011) stealing is possible, but guards will attack the avatar if they catch her in the act. Another example, which we will address in closer detail later, was provided by one of our respondents who stressed that she felt bad for running over pedestrians in *GTAV*. However, when we discuss diegetic or fictive transgressivity, it is important to stress that breaking the in-game laws of a game may not always be experienced as a profound transgression. As indicated above, ludic transgressivity may not actually feel transgressive unless the combined ludo-narrative explicitly frames the event as something the player should feel bad about. For instance, when the *Skyrim* guards confront the avatar for breaking the law, the player gets three choices: Pay a fine, go to jail, or resist arrest. Paying the fine can be tough enough for players early in the game, and if jailed, the player loses their skill progression toward the next level and has their equipment confiscated. Once the sentence is served, the equipment is returned and everything goes back to normal. If the player resists arrest, the guard will attack, and if the player kills that guard, a new guard will arrive, and the player will eventually be attacked on sight. At a certain point, the villages under a particular chieftain's rule can no longer be visited unless the player sneaks in at the dead of night. While the criminal act has consequences that may impact gameplay heavily, it does not change or make important storylines unavailable and does not reduce the player's ability to progress. For this reason, the player may not experience this as transgressive.

Another example that shows the complexity of intraludic transgressions is *Assassin's Creed II* (Ubisoft Montreal 2009), in which the player takes on the role of an assassin. This means that in order to play, the player must accept that representations of killing are central to their activities in the game, regardless of the fact that killing is a highly transgressive act in the actual world. In the game, it is the goal to kill given individuals, and for this reason, stalking and killing chosen individuals is not transgressive in context of the game. Assassinating specific individuals and also killing their bodyguards are acceptable acts within the norms of the game. While this is a form of violence that is not permitted in real life, it is important to remember in this discussion that there are certain contexts in which we are permitted to kill. As British intellectual Raymond Williams points out (Williams 1974), the police and the military are permitted, and sometimes even required, to use lethal force. Whether or not violence is a transgression is, as this demonstrates, very much a matter of context or framing, and in the world of *Assassin's Creed*, the player accepts the frame in which it is not just allowed, but also expected that they fictionally assassinate their targets. As a matter of fact, the player *must* choose this framing; if they were cringing from the act, they would not be able to play the game at all. Indeed, taking on the fictional role of an assassin is one of the attractions of the game: The player is allowed to perform transgressive actions inside a fictional realm where actions do not mean what they mean in the real world and have no actual consequences. Further, the game is not designed to make the player cringe in discomfort of the actions they are carrying out; rather, the violence is sanitized (Pötzsch 2017) to function in the context of interesting gameplay. When we address the actions that are considered transgressive by the game, this is signaled by indications in the graphical user interface and in the way characters in the environment act, and while the player may recognize the transgression against in-game norms and act accordingly (for instance, by hiding from guards), this may be experienced as a break of a game rule, but not as a break of a social norm, because it happens as part of a game.

At the same time, however, killing is depicted as transgressive in this fictive game universe. This means that if a civilian game character is witness to a killing or any kind of violence, they will run screaming. Moreover, guards will also chase the assassin on sight if they are trespassing. The game does not allow the player to kill civilians; in such cases, the game will flash a message to the player informing them that "Ezio did not kill civilians". The fictive rules thus state that even though assassins are supposed to kill, this is still viewed as a criminal and ethical transgression.

A metaludic form of transgression?

In the previous discussion on extraludic and intraludic transgression, we have seen that it is not always clear cut whether the sense of transgression emerges from the game itself or from how the game interacts with issues in the actual world. To further complicate matters, we have seen that transgressivity may emerge from both form and content – and in many cases it is how these operate together that matters.

These complications show that transgression sometimes can be understood as *metaludic*. Metaludic transgression is neither intra- or extraludic, but can simultaneously stem from both the game and the outside world. For instance, diegetic transgressivity, perhaps expressed through the killing of an in-game child, may be experienced as harrowing because of the empathic bond that the player has formed with the child in-game. But the player's response can simultaneously be related to real-world norms.

While it is very much a subjective interpretation whether something is experienced as transgressive or not, metaludic transgression highlights how a game can be transgressive on a number of levels. This means that it is often not possible to categorize games strictly according to the discussions above. Instead it may be more useful to think of transgressive experiences as happening in a triangle with intraludic, extraludic, and metaludic at the tips. Any experience of outrage and transgression may be plotted into this triangle, but it is rare that two players will position the experience at exactly the same point.

Breaking fictive norms and ludic rules

By stating that killing is part of the fictive role and also part of the ludic goal of the game, but at the same time stressing that killing is indeed transgressive in the fictive game universe, the fictive norms and the ludic rules partly contradict each other – creating a partly incoherent fictive world (Juul 2005, 123). When rules and fiction contradict each other in communicating transgressive acts, the player can choose to ignore the transgressivity. Since the ludic goal of *Assassin's Creed II* concerns taking out certain targets, the player can choose to ignore the in-game norm that killing is transgressive. We have seen that this happens for some of our respondents and will later discuss this in terms of game scholar Anders Frank's theory of *gamer mode*, a mind-set that allows players to ignore fiction while focusing on game mechanics (Frank 2012). Thus, the players maintain interest in the game and the intraludic perspectives, but redirect their attention from immediate content to played content and form. This also highlights a function that we keep observing in the studies in this project: Players change their focus in the process of playing. This points toward our discussion in Chapter 4, concerning player-response theory, addressing how games train the player, and the player learns how to approach the game on the game's own premise, adopting what we can call an intraludic logic. Chapters 4 and 5 will go deeper into the discussion of how we understand the connection between game and player, and an important aspect of these discussions is exactly how players mitigate the sense of transgression when they encounter it in gameplay.

However, when players decide to focus on game mechanics rather than representation, this does not mean that they avoid all sense of transgression. On the contrary; since a prerequisite for playing games is that one takes the ludic context and the game rules seriously (Jørgensen 2014), discomfort, anger, and sense of transgression may easily spawn from the game's inherent qualities. A player must get into the right mind-set of playing, a *lusory attitude* (Suits 1990), and must allow themselves to be attached to the outcomes of the game (Juul 2003). When this mode is activated, the player takes the game seriously as an autotelic frame of reference that allows them to give value to in-game results such as failure and success. The player may then find that otherwise not particularly provoking features, such as premature game-character death, unclear game design, a high difficulty level, or other players' game actions, create an experience of transgression. Although it is the in-game processes that matter in such situations, the influence of the in-game experience goes beyond the game itself by affecting the player's emotions. And this is one of the hallmarks of transgressive experiences: Our emotions get involved.

This chapter does not answer where exactly the transgressions happen in games; instead, it opens the field further and shows that transgressions can happen not only in form, in content, and in the way form affords content and content affords form but also in the context of play and the players' experience of the game. If there is a key to transgressive aesthetics, it is in the *experience* of transgression, and in the next chapter, we will look at how the games used in our study can be experienced as transgressive.

References

Aarseth, Espen. 2007. "I Fought the Law: Transgressive Play and the Implied Player." In *3rd Digital Games Research Association International Conference: "Situated Play", DiGRA 2007*, 130–33. Digital Games Research Association (DIGRA). doi:10.1057/9781137429704.

Alter, Charlotte. 2015. "U.N. Says Cyber Violence Is Equivalent to Physical Violence Against Women." *Time*, September 2015.

American Heritage Dictionary. 2017. "American Heritage Dictionary Entry: Interface." *American Heritage Dictionary*. Houghton Mifflin Harcourt. https://ahdictionary.com/word/search.html?q=interface.

Ashcraft, Brian. 2010. "Why Is CNN Talking About Rapelay?" *Kotaku*, March 31, 2010.

Baldick, Chris. 2015. *The Oxford Dictionary of Literary Terms*. 4th Ed. Oxford: Oxford University Press.

Bartel, Paul. 1976. *Death Race 2000*. New World Pictures.

Beaudouin-Lafon, Michel, and Wendy E. Mackay. 2000. "Reification, Polymorphism and Reuse." In *Proceedings of the Working Conference on Advanced Visual Interfaces – AVI '00*, 102–9. Palermo, It. New York, NY: ACM Press. doi:10.1145/345513.345267.

Bethesda Game Studios. 2011. *The Elder Scrolls V: Skyrim*. Bethesda Softworks LLC.

Blizzard. 2004. *World of Warcraft*. Blizzard Entertainment Inc.

Blizzard Entertainment. 1994. *Warcraft*. Blizzard Entertainment Inc.

Bogost, Ian. 2007. *Persuasive Games: The Expressive Power of Videogames*. Cambridge: MIT Press.

Boudreau, Kelly. 2018. "Beyond Fun: Transgressive Gameplay, Toxic and Problematic Player Behavior as Boundary Keeping." In *Transgression in Games and Play*, edited by Kristine Jørgensen and Faltin Karlsen. Cambridge: MIT Press.

Collins English Dictionary. 2017. "Interface Definition and Meaning." *Collins English Dictionary*. Harper Collins Publishers. www.collinsdictionary.com/dictionary/english/interface.

Consalvo, Mia. 2007. *Cheating: Gaining Advantage in Videogames*. Cambridge, London: MIT.

———. 2012. "Confronting Toxic Gamer Culture: A Challenge for Feminist Game Studies Scholars." *Ada: A Journal of Gender, New Media, and Technology*, no. 1 (November). doi:10.7264/N33X84KH.

Daemonpro. 2014. "My Many Problems with Tropes vs Women and Anita Sarkeesian." *Tumblr*, 2014.

Destructive Creations. 2015. *Hatred*. Destructive Creations. www.hatredgame. com/.

Dontnod Entertainment. 2015. *Life Is Strange*. Square Enix Co., Ltd.

Exidy. 1976. *Death Race*. Exidy.

Frank, Anders. 2012. "Gaming the Game." *Simulation & Gaming* 43 (1): 118–32. doi:10.1177/1046878111408796.

From Software. 2011. *Dark Souls*. Namco Bandai Games.

———. 2015. *Bloodborne*. Sony Interactive Entertainment.

Goffman, Erving. 1967. *The Presentation of Self in Everyday Life*. 1990th ed. London: Penguin.

Infinity Ward. 2009. *Call of Duty: Modern Warfare 2*. Activision.

Jørgensen, Kristine. 2013. *Gameworld Interfaces*. Cambridge: The MIT Press. doi:10.7551/mitpress/9780262026864.001.0001.

———. 2014. "Devil's Plaything. On the Coundary Between Playful and Serious." DiGRA Nordic '14. Proceedings of the 2014 International DiGRA Nordic Conference. 2014. www.digra.org/digital-library/publications/devils-plaything-on-the-boundary-between-playful-and-serious/.

Juul, Jesper. 2002. "The Open and the Closed: Games of Emergence and Games of Progression." In *Computer Games and Digital Cultures Conference Proceedings*, edited by Frans Mäyrä, 323–29. Tampere: Tampere University Press.

———. 2003. "The Game, the Player, the World. Looking for the Heart of Gameness." Proceedings of the 2003 DiGRA International Conference: Level Up. 2003. www.digra.org/digital-library/publications/the-game-the-player-the-world-looking-for-a-heart-of-gameness/.

———. 2005. *Half-Real: Video Games between Real Rules and Fictional Worlds*. Cambridge: MIT Press.

Karlsen, Faltin. 2018. "Exploited or Engaged? Dark Game Design Patterns in Clicker Heroes, FarmVille, and World of Warcraft." In *Transgression in Games and Play*, edited by Kristine Jørgensen and Faltin Karlsen, 219–233. Cambridge: MIT Press.

KindRAness. 2016. "Anita Sarkeesian and the Bad Feminism – KindRAness – Medium." Medium. 2016.

Klastrup, Lisbeth. 2009. "The Worldness of EverQuest: Exploring a 21st Century Fiction." *Game Studies: The International Journal of Computer Game Research* 9 (1). http://gamestudies.org/0901/articles/klastrup.

Klastrup, Lisbeth, and Susana Tosca. 2004. "Transmedial Worlds – Rethinking Cyberworld Design." In *2004 International Conference on Cyberworlds*, 409–16. Tokyo: IEEE. doi:10.1109/CW.2004.67.

Kocurek, Carly A. 2012. "The Agony and the Exidy: A History of Video Game Violence and the Legacy of Death Race." *Game Studies: The International Journal of Computer Game Research* 12 (1). http://gamestudies.org/1201/articles/carly_kocurek.

Lankoski, Petri. 2011. "Player Character Engagement in Computer Games." *Games and Culture* 6 (4): 291–311. doi:10.1177/1555412010391088.

Manovich, Lev. 2001. *The Language of New Media. Leonardo*. Cambridge: MIT Press.

McLuhan, Marshall. 1964. *Understanding Media: The Extensions of Man*. 2013 Kindl. Ginko Press.

Meades, Alan. 2018. "The American Arcade Crusade and the Amusement Arcade Action Group." In *Transgression in Games and Play*, edited by Kristine Jørgensen and Faltin Karlsen, 237–255. Cambridge: MIT Press.

Miyamoto, Shigeru, and Takahashi Tezuka. 1986. *The Legend of Zelda*. Nintendo.

Mortensen, Torill Elvira. 2008. "Humans Playing World of Warcraft: Or Deviant Strategies?" In *Digital Culture, Play, and Identity: A World of Warcraft Reader*, edited by Hilde G. Corneliussen and Jill Walker Rettberg, 203–224. Cambridge: The MIT Press.

Namco, Toru Iwatani, Shigeo Funaki, and Toshio Kai. 1980. "Pac-Man." Namco & Atari.

NCAC. 2019. "A Timeline of Video Game Controversies." National Coalition Against Censorship. 2019. https://ncac.org/resource/a-timeline-of-video-game-controversies.

Pan European Game Information PEGI. 2019. "Online Safety Tips | Pegi Public Site." PEGI. 2019. https://pegi.info/page/online-safety-tips.

Pazhitnov, Alexey. 1985. "Tetris." Microsoft Windows.

PopCap Games. 2009. *Plants vs Zombies*. PopCap Games & Electronic Arts.

Pötzsch, Holger. 2017. "Selective Realism: Filtering Experiences of War and Violence in First- and Third-Person Shooters." *Games and Culture* 12 (2): 156–78.

———. 2018. "Forms and Practices of Transgressivity in Videogames: Aesthetics, Play, and Politics." In *Transgression in Games and Play*, edited by Kristine Jørgensen and Faltin Karlsen, 45–61. Cambridge: MIT Press.

Quantic Dream. 2013. *Beyond: Two Souls*. Sony Interactive Entertainment.

Rockstar North. 2013. *Grand Theft Auto V*. New York: Rockstar Games.

Sageng, John Richard. 2018. "The Bracketing of Moral Norms in Videogames." In *Transgression in Games and Play*, edited by Kristine Jørgensen and Faltin Karlsen, 63–80. Cambridge: MIT Press.

Salen, Katie, and Eric Zimmerman. 2004. *Rules of Play: Game Design Fundamentals*. Cambridge: MIT Press.

Sarkeesian, Anita. 2012a. "Image Based Harassment and Visual Misogyny." Edited by Anita Sarkeesian. *Feminist Frequency*.

———. 2012b. "Tropes vs Women in Videogames." *Kickstarter*.

Sicart, Miguel. 2011. "Against Procedurality." *Game Studies: The International Journal of Computer Game Research* 11 (3). http://gamestudies.org/1103/articles/sicart_ap.

Smith, Harvey. 2001. "The Future of Game Design: Moving Beyond Deus Ex and Other Dated Paradigms." *Multimedia International Market*. Montreal: IGDA. www.witchboy.net/articles/the-future-of-game-design-moving-beyond-deus-ex-and-other-dated-paradigms/.

StudioMDHR. 2017. *Cuphead*. StudioMDHR.

Suits, Bernard (Bernard Herbert). 1990. *The Grasshopper: Games, Life, and Utopia*. Boston, MA: David R. Godine.

Sundén, Jenny. 2009. "Play as Transgression: An Ethnographic Approach to Queer Game Cultures." In *Proceedings of DiGRA 2009: Breaking New Ground: Innovation in Games, Play, Practice and Theory*. www.digra.org/digital-library/publications/play-as-transgression-an-ethnographic-approach-to-queer-game-cultures/.

Telltale Games. 2012. *The Walking Dead: Season One*. San Rafael, CA: Telltale Games.

Ubisoft Montreal. 2008. *Prince of Persia*. Ubisoft.

———. 2009. *Assassin's Creed II*. Montreal: Ubisoft.

Vught, Jasper Van, and Gareth Schott. 2012. "Player Experience: Articulating Suspense as a Configurative Encounter." *Westminster Papers in Communication and Culture* 9 (1): 91. doi:10.16997/wpcc.152.

Wikipedia. 2019. "List of Controversial Video Games." Wikipedia. 2019. https:// en.wikipedia.org/wiki/List_of_controversial_video_games.

Williams, Raymond. 1974. *Television Technology and Cultural Form*. *Technosphere*. London: Fontana/Collins.

Wingfield, Nick. 2014. "Feminist Critics of Video Games Facing Threats in 'Gamer-Gate' Campaign." *New York Times*, 2014. www.nytimes.com/2014/10/16/ technology/gamergate-women-video-game-threats-anita-sarkeesian.html.

Yager Development. 2012. *Spec Ops: The Line*. 2K Games.

Zagal, José, Staffan Björk, and Chris Lewis. 2013. "Dark Patterns in Game Design." In *Proceedings of Foundations of Digital Games 2013*. www.fdg2013. org/program/papers/paper06_zagal_etal.pdf.

3   Transgressive games
An overview

Attempting to pin down exactly what a transgressive game is, reducing it to a precise definition, would either be a work of overwhelming hubris or an ongoing documentation of how culture changes. Transgressive aesthetics, being contextual depending on the norms of society, will never be precisely definable or quantifiable. Instead, we want to offer a better understanding of how complex the transgressive aesthetic of games can be, and how easy it is to let provocation or offense overshadow a diverse and sensitive analysis. To demonstrate the need to make a distinction between different transgressive experiences, we offer a discussion of games we suggest to be, in different manners, transgressive, with a focus on the game we use in this study.

When we present the selected games here, we use terminology introduced in the previous chapter, particularly concerning the typology of transgressivity and the distinction of intraludic and extraludic transgressive experiences. And as we can see from Chapter 2, transgressivity always concerns how a particular individual interprets something in a given context. This means that it is not possible to make a definitive and complete overview of transgressive games. As will be documented in Chapter 5, we have seen in our studies that what one player finds transgressive may not correspond to the opinions of a second player. Even if two players find the same content or mechanics to be transgressive, *why* it is transgressive and how they respond to that given content may differ. In our selection of examples, both for our discussions in general throughout the book and for the players who have participated in the research project, we have looked for games that are transgressive on different parameters. We have asked when a game is considered transgressive on its own terms. This means looking at the form and content of games as well as the player experiences – at mechanics and fiction, and how these are interacted with and interpreted rather than what players may do toward other players within the rules of the game. However, as controversies in the game community have shown, sometimes there can be a gap between the *encoding* and the *decoding* of the game (Hall 2006) – between the intended message of a game and how this message is received by the players. Looking at examples of game readings, we have also identified certain categories of content that seem to invite an oppositional reading by groups of players in the sense that the response to the game is in opposition to what appears to be the intended message.

This chapter discusses the games we have used for player studies and highlights our reasons for choosing these particular games in a study of transgressive aesthetics. When selecting case games for our research, we have chosen games that have been targets of debate and criticism, but for different reasons. Since we are not aiming at exploring the full range of transgressive potential in games, there are certainly categories of games that we have not covered in our data collection. Examples of such games are games as art projects, like the experimental horror game *The Static Speaks My Name* (thewhalehusband 2015). We avoided art project games because we wanted to look at the more common games and styles. But by expanding our discussion here to additional examples and research conducted by others, for instance, the work by Brian Schrank on games and the avant-garde (Schrank 2014) or the work represented in the *Transgression in Games and Play* anthology (Jørgensen and Karlsen 2018), we are able to illustrate a wide range of transgressive games and how they are received by the playing audience. By demonstrating situations that are offensive and uncomfortable as well as situations where discomfort is wanted and even experienced as something valuable, these examples also question the idea of transgression in games. But the main goal of this work is to explore the limits in the more mainstream field of games, considering what role transgressions play in well-known games. When do regular players meet their limits? What are the most common experienced transgressions? The selected games are presented in the following, and an overview of the games, on what grounds they are deemed transgressive, and how they were generally received by our player participants are found in Table 3.1.

Table 3.1 Overview of games used in the empirical studies

Game	Genre	Intraludic transgressivity	Extraludic transgressivity	Gameplay journal responses	Focus group responses
Alien: Isolation	Horror	Diegetic/ludic		**Mixed:** High suspense until figured out alien behavior pattern. For two, the suspense was enjoyable.	
Beyond: Two Souls	Action-adventure/ interactive drama	Diegetic	Situational, idiosyncratic	**Largely positive:** High character empathy. One player experienced idiosyncratic transgressivity that made him stop playing.	

(*Continued*)

Game	Genre	Intraludic transgressivity	Extraludic transgressivity	Gameplay journal responses	Focus group responses
Bloodborne	Action-RPG	Ludic		**Mixed:** All found the difficulty to be high. Players with little progression were negative and players with progression were positive.	
GTAV	Sandbox third-person shooter	Diegetic	Critical, hegemonic	**Mixed:** All recognized attempt at satire, but disagreed whether it was successful or not.	**Mixed:** All recognized attempt at satire, but disagreed whether it was successful or not.
Hatred	Isometric shooter	Diegetic	Juridical, hegemonic	**Negative:** Uncomfortable game, but sensation wore off over time.	**Negative:** Appears provocative for the sake of being provocative.
Life is Strange	Episodic adventure game	Diegetic	Situational, idiosyncratic		**Positive:** Emotional impactful.
Spec Ops: The Line	Third-person shooter	Diegetic	Critical		**Positive:** Successful in war criticism and making the player feel complicit.
This War of Mine	Survival/ management	Diegetic	Critical, hegemonic	**Mixed:** Disagreement whether it was able to create discomfort and reflection.	

Hatred

In the isometric shooter *Hatred* (Destructive Creations 2015), the player plays the role of a mass murderer who hates the world and who wants to take as many lives as possible before getting neutralized. As breaking the rules of the fictional gameworld is central to gameplay, the game is an example of diegetic transgressivity (Pötzsch 2018). Featuring largely black-and-white graphics, the game is played from the third-person perspective from the top down, providing distance from events and an overview of the environment around the avatar. Most game mechanisms are action-based, with focus on the selection and use of up to three weapons, including grenades, as well as the driving of vehicles. In the beginning of the game, the player largely fires at running civilians, but difficulty soon changes and rapidly increases as the police and later the military show up to stop the player. In the later parts of the game, the player breaks into heavily guarded locales such as a military camp and a nuclear power plant. An important game mechanism is the "execution" of downed enemies, which is the only way to regain health and involves a cinematic switch of the camera to a close-up view of an animation of the execution.

As mentioned, the game was for a period banned from Steam, making it an example of juridical transgressivity. The game was chosen not only due to its reputation as "the most violent game on earth" (Jenkins 2015) but also because it features traditional shooter game mechanics, making it relevant as a case for studying the relationship between the fictional representation and the game mechanics. The game is an example of hegemonic transgressivity, in that it at first appears to threaten established norms for what is acceptable in games, but in the end only reinforces dominant attitudes about shooter games as being shallow, violent, and not very innovative in terms of game mechanics. Our hypothesis was that the underdeveloped narrative context would limit fictional involvement, and traditional game mechanics would make it easy for the player to take on an instrumental or strategic mind-set, in other words, a *gamer mode* (Frank 2012, 120). Following this hypothesis, we believed that these issues would mitigate the sense of transgression when playing the game. *Gamer mode* has come to stand out as a central term to our further discussion, particularly in relation to mitigation, and we will return to this later in this chapter and in Chapters 4 and 5.

Hatred was used both in the focus group study and the game journal study. Three players in focus groups 1 and 4 had played the game, and with the exception of two players in groups 3 and 4, the rest was familiar with it. Across the focus groups, the general attitude was that the game appeared speculative in its attempt to create controversy, but also that its exaggerated style makes it difficult to take the game seriously. While some of the participants who had not played the game believed they would find playing the game uncomfortable, those with experience with the game stressed that there is a discrepancy between the speculative appearance and how it feels to play. The gameplay was described as mediocre and over time dull, and the respondents interpreted the exaggerated and excessive violence as a way to draw attention toward an otherwise uninteresting game.

Three men completed the *Hatred* journal, while two women abandoned the study without offering any explanation why, one after having filled in one journal entry. Among the respondents, the general emotions toward the game were negative. "Brian" and "Keith" explicitly stated that they were "repulsed" by the concept of the game, but all three stressed that over time, the excessive violence became monotonous and lost its impact. Comparing

Hatred to other violent mainstream action games, "Keith" concludes that the discomfort is all about the context. "Danny" believes that creating a controversy was a "marketing trick" on the part of the developers in that it speculates in explicit violence for public attention without any attempt of problematizing the representation.

We expected this game to be experienced as transgressive in the sense that it violates the general sensibilities of society through its representation of exaggerated violence without much context and because it makes entertainment out of it. It may also be seen as transgressive by violating the idea that games are growing out of its sub-cultural status as a rebellious medium and maturing into a serious medium of communication.

Grand Theft Auto V

Grand Theft Auto V (GTAV) (Rockstar North 2013) is an open world action-adventure shooter, in which the player switches between the roles of ex-con Michael, who is living a middle-class life under witness protection with his family; fellow bank robber and sociopath Trevor, who is living an under-par life in a trailer park; and young Franklin, who is involved in small-time crime. Focusing on how the characters become entangled with the crimes of their pasts, the game is an example of diegetic transgressivity. Following the storyline mission of the game, the player completes one mission at a time as one of these characters, with the opportunity to do side missions in between. The gameworld is an open environment, with a focus on action-oriented gameplay. Missions typically include travelling to a certain location where the player carries out a task, often through violent means, before returning to a previous location to finalize the mission. With the exception of static structures such as buildings, most objects as well as characters in the gameworld can be acted upon or interacted with. Within these limitations, the gameworld can be explored at will. Since weapons and cars are central to gameplay, and the game importantly includes a sanction system where the police will chase the avatar with increased force based on the level of violence that is being inflicted, gameplay often includes action-packed and spectacular events, including car chases and violence.

GTAV was used both in the focus group study and in the gameplay journal study. The game was chosen as a representative of a kind of a game that has been the subject of much public outrage, but where defenders have claimed that the game must be understood as parody and satire, and that this mitigates the seriousness of the actions represented. The game was also chosen due to its open world and exploratory design, which was believed to encourage a different level of playfulness than the other games of the study. As a parody of certain aspects of Californian life and culture, *GTAV* may be seen as an example of critical transgressivity, but we want to point out that the game is an example of a particular kind of critical transgressivity: Namely, satire. As a particular sub-genre of humor and parody, satire is a rhetorical art designed to attack vice and folly through the use of wit and ridicule (Griffin 1994). However, a problem with humor and satire is that it is a difficult art form that may evoke very different responses in the audience, from acceptance of the dominant-hegemonic message of the game to opposition (Hall 2006). *GTAV* was also the game in our studies that created most diverse responses from the participants, as there was disagreement concerning whether the game actually succeeds in the attempts of humor and satire, and the respondents also disagreed with regards to whether the game was experienced as transgressive or not.

Among the 13 focus groups participants, only two had no experience from the *GTA* series. The groups discussed a much-debated mission in *GTAV*, in which the player inflicts torture upon a non-player character. While some participants embraced the game as satire with focus on the exaggerated and parodic characters, and the absurdity of the situations that both fiction and gameplay put them in, some also had problems identifying with the characters and the situations. The scene itself, which we introduced in Chapter 2, was described by most with a certain kind of discomfort; some found it tasteless and said that the attempt to make it humorous was not successful.

Three women and one man completed the gameplay journal study, while two women abandoned the study before starting to fill in their journals. All four participants appreciated parts of the gameplay, but even though they could recognize the satire, they did not agree on whether it was successful or not. Three of them identified content as problematic due to racism, sexism, or classism, indicating that for them the game was largely an example of hegemonic transgressivity because of its inability to sufficiently problematize the stereotypes it represents. However, for "Sally", the game represented critical transgressivity because in her opinion, the satire is able to target a broad range of groups in American society on equal terms. This variation in responses also demonstrates how the idea of transgression depends on the individual player's viewpoint.

Spec Ops: The Line

Spec Ops: The Line (Yager Development 2012) is a third-person perspective, military-themed shooter game strongly influenced by Joseph Conrad's literary classic *Heart of Darkness* (Conrad 1899). The player takes the role of Captain Walker leading a Delta Force team on a special operations reconnaissance mission in Dubai, which soon turns into a search for Walker's former colleague, Colonel Conrad, who has gone rogue with the 33rd Battalion. *Spec Ops: The Line* follows the gameplay conventions of the military shooter, where combat and the use of firearms are central for the ability to progress in the game. The most central game mechanisms are combat-oriented, relating to the use of different weapons, dodging gunfire, and giving simple tactical commands to the player's two squad mates. One important mechanism is the "execution" mechanism, a finishing move that allows the player to execute a downed enemy for extra ammo. Also, during moments of particular narrative importance, the player is given a choice between two actions. While the gameplay is traditional, the meaning of gameplay actions is subverted through a powerful narrative. When the player follows the missions of the game and adapts to the behavior that the game design invites, they are soon lured into becoming part of a dark narrative that features post-traumatic stress syndrome and the consequences of a military operation gone wrong. The game features a photo-realistic style, which are made more sinister and dramatic as Captain Walker's mental state deteriorates. The game's challenges relate to the traversal of an enemy-packed environment, and game objectives are presented as commands given by military leaders in a hierarchy that is not to be questioned. For this reason, there is initially little in the game that suggests diegetic transgressivity. However, this changes during gameplay, as the mentally unstable Captain Walker's becomes the decisive agent in the absence of higher-ranking military leaders. Here, the hesitant questions from the two squad mates indicate that diegetic boundaries are being crossed.

Spec Ops: The Line was chosen as a case in the focus group study not only due to its reputation as a classic relating to its ability to inspire reflection through discomfort (Dyer 2012; Garland 2012; Klepek 2012; Sicart 2013) but also because there is disagreement with regards to its ability to successfully do so. Some reviewers argued that the use of conventional mechanisms of the shooter genre created a situation where any deeper narrative message would necessarily fall through (Keogh 2013, 8; Lindsey 2012), while others recognized the horrors that were displayed, but did not find the integration between gameplay and narrative to be particularly uncomfortable (Björk 2015, 182).

In the focus group study, groups 1 and 4 made unsolicited mention of *Spec Ops: The Line*, and players in groups 1, 3, and 4 had previous experience with the title. In the three groups, the game was discussed as an example of critical transgressivity, in that it created a sense of "positive discomfort" by making the participants feel *complicit* to the game events (Jørgensen 2016; Sicart 2013; Smethurst and Craps 2015). By combining traditional gameplay and game mechanics with an uncomfortable narrative, the game ensures that players who play as intended are punished by the narrative consequences and thereby are invited to reflect about the consequences of war. The game can be understood as an example of critical transgressivity in two ways. In addition to subverting the conventions of the military shooter through a narrative that communicates the terrors of war rather than a hero story, the game also provides an unexpected and potentially uncomfortable experience laden with ideology in a genre that normally is sanitized (Pötzsch 2017). Also, following from this, *Spec Ops: The Line* is diegetically transgressive because the narrative puts the player into an uncomfortable position of complicity that forces them to reflect (Sicart 2009, 2013).

We decided not to use *Spec Ops: The Line* in the gameplay journal study due to the fact that the game had been heavily discussed both in games media and on forums after its release. To find participants who had not heard of the game would be a challenge, and a simple Internet search would also disclose too much of the game's plot, turning point, and other players' reactions to the game to secure a lack of bias among participants, and more importantly for this study, to avoid having their pre-knowledge spoil the sense of shock or outrage.

This War of Mine

This War of Mine (11 bit studios and War Child 2014), is a management simulator set among civilians in a war-ridden fictional situation inspired by the Siege of Sarajevo during the Bosnian War. The game received critical acclaim for representing civilians rather than soldiers in the time of war (Grayson 2014). It features a somber black and white sketch-inspired style and a third-person side-scrolling perspective, and in it, the player controls a group of civilians who have taken up shelter in a derelict building; the goal is to survive until ceasefire. Central game mechanics include nighttime scavenging of resources such as food, medicine, repair equipment, and fuel, and to reinforce the shelter both against the upcoming winter and raiding parties. Based on the characters' individual abilities, the player will assign them to different missions – the fastest runner may be allocated to scavenging, while the best cook creates the meals. Over time, the player will have to take greater risks when scavenging in order to find the needed resources, and ethical issues arise as this means breaking into other civilians' homes to steal their belongings and sometimes getting into combat. Hostile encounters with other survivors also take their toll on the player characters, which may become injured or suffer from psychological trauma – which hinder them from contributing to reinforcement and scavenging while still requiring upkeep. The game dynamic can be compared to a downward spiral, as the situation becomes hard to change once things start going bad: When the expert scavenger is injured, another less proficient character must take over. The less proficient scavenger brings home fewer resources, which affects the psychological state of all characters. Depressed characters have reduced capacity for working, and in the situation where one of the characters dies, either from injury, sickness, or suicide, the mood of the remaining characters becomes even lower. The game features diegetic transgressivity in many ways: By forcing the player to break the laws of ordinary situations, it actualizes the lawless situation of wartime. Further, the player must do an ethical evaluation of the situations and see the consequences of their actions.

This War of Mine was used in the gameplay journal study and was chosen due to its critical reception. Another issue was its use of game mechanics in order to present ethical dilemmas. The game was used in the game journal study, where it was played by three men and one woman. Participants' response to the game was mixed and ranged from acceptance to rejection. Two of the respondents found the game to be emotionally powerful, but while "Stan" said that he loved the game because it made him uncomfortable and thus made him think, "Fred" prefers games that are fun and entertaining rather than reflective and stated for this reason that he hated the game. For these participants, the game was a case of critical transgressivity. However, the two remaining respondents found the procedural rhetoric unconvincing. "Leon" found the simulation to be too simple to convincingly make a good argument, while "Jane" was disappointed by how the simplistic simulation reduced a profound problem to something fun. From this variation in reception, the game appears to be potentially transgressive on two levels: First, there is a potential emotional disturbance that may either break the interest in the game or strengthen it. Also, for others, the attempt of simulating a complex and profound situation through the use of simple game mechanics may in itself be problematic and an example of hegemonic transgressivity because of its inability to accurately or interestingly model the situations in question.

Life is Strange

Life is Strange (Dontnod Entertainment 2015) is an episodic narrative-based adventure game that situates the player in a high school drama where they take on the role of the teenage girl, Max, who must tackle traumatizing situations related to bullying, online harassment, and teenage suicide, as well as the estrangement and death of a dear friend, and discovers that she has the supernatural ability to turn back time. Gameplay allows the player to move Max around in the virtual environment consisting of a set of limited locations relating to the particular narrative chapter and interact with selected objects. Central to the game mechanics are dialogue options that offer a branching narrative, although they do not provide a sense of agency for the player because what Max says is often misunderstood by the non-playing characters she interacts with. Another central mechanism is the ability to turn back time a few seconds, allowing the player to reset events and test out different options. This is integrated into the narrative, and much puzzle-solving is executed through this mechanism. Also, from a later point in the game, the rewind mechanism can also be used to put Max back in time to when a photograph was taken, thus allowing for the exploration of alternative timelines and possible worlds.

Life is Strange caught our interest due to the public attention that it got for its inclusion of teenage suicide. Its social-realist perspective on traumatic teenage experiences that are recognizable for many was the reason we wanted the focus group participants' input on the game. The game's potential for transgression lies in its ability to recreate uncomfortable social situations that are familiar to most, but also in its attempt of addressing difficult and sensitive issues through ludic means. *Life is Strange* was discussed during the focus groups. While three of the respondents did not know the game beforehand, three had played it. The remaining seven knew about the game through reviews or videos. The game appeared dramatic and emotionally laden for most of the participants, and the respondents who had played the game before the study supported this impression by describing playing the game as emotionally impactful. Having played the game, "Luke" describes it as an example of an uncomfortable game experience due to the difficult choices the player has to make and the fact that whatever one decides to do, the results are always uncomfortable due to escalating social situations or the agendas of other characters. While many of the other diegetically transgressive games feature the breaking of laws or ethics in the fictional world, in *Life is Strange* diegetic transgressivity is *situational* because it often relates to making the right choice in a particular complex fictional situation. These are choices of an ethical nature or simply of an instrumental nature, such as avoiding the attention of an uncomfortable classmate. *Life is Strange* is also a game that may spawn idiosyncratic transgressivity, as it may trigger a sense of transgression due to the personal experiences of the players. In focus group 1, "Tony" mentioned that the game's treatment of suicide was particularly impactful due to personal experiences.

As with *Spec Ops: The Line*, we did not choose *Life is Strange* in the journal study because of the public attention that was on it while we were planning the study.

Beyond: Two Souls

Like *Life is Strange*, *Beyond: Two Souls* (Quantic Dreams 2013) stresses diegetic and situational transgressivity by its strong focus on narrative and puts the player into emotionally laden situations based on building empathy with the main character and situating them in emotionally or socially uncomfortable situations. *Beyond: Two Souls* is a cinematic-style, narrative-based adventure game where the player takes the role of Jodie, a young girl who is growing up as a lab rat at a special military facility due to her psychic powers. The girl experiences situations of loss and betrayal as she is abandoned by her foster parents and exploited for her powers by her father figure inside the lab. Not unlike *Life is Strange*, the player can move around a selected number of locations based on the objectives relating to the particular mission and interact with certain objects in the environment. For special actions and conversation options, interface prompts will turn up on the screen. Important to the game is Jodie's spiritual companion Aiden, who is the source of her psychic powers. Jodie can call on Aiden for assistance and, through him, knock persons or objects around, but Aiden can also provide protective shields, help Jodie see things in the past, and heal injured people. The player has relative freedom with respect to Aiden's more violent actions, but as many of the game's scenes are situations where Jodie is frustrated or in distress, for instance, being bullied by peers, the victim of attempted rape, or pressed to her physical edge by researchers, there is incentive to let Aiden act out by throwing objects around or even being violent to people. Here the fact that transgressions are carried out *against* the player-protagonist, emphasizes the idea that such scenes are intended to create discomfort in the player. This discomfort is unrelated to the consequences of the situation.

The game was used in the game journal study, and was chosen due to its narrative focus on the suffering of a young person, and as an example of a game where potential experiences of transgression appear to be mainly connected to the narrative rather than the game mechanics. While we originally were considering using the game's predecessor *Heavy Rain* (Quantic Dream 2013), we chose *Beyond: Two Souls* because it is a lesser-known title than *Heavy Rain*, which was bundled with the PlayStation 3 at release. The game was also mentioned as particularly captivating by one respondent in one of the focus groups.

Two women and two men completed the study, while one man abandoned the study before starting to log their gameplay. Three of the participants reported being moved by the game and also that this made the game a positive experience for them. The potential transgressions of the game seem thus to be connected to an experience of discomfort related to witnessing a person suffer, and is an example of situational transgressivity as the fictional situations in which the character finds itself is detrimental to this experience. Similar to *Spec Ops: The Line, This War of Mine*, and *Life is Strange*, the recognizability of this discomfort is rewarding for some, while for others, the discomfort crosses the line of what they want to endure when playing a game. However, the game can also be a source of idiosyncratic transgressivity. As we will discuss more closely in Chapter 6, "Theo" decided to quit after only logging one entry, and in the subsequent interview, he explained that this was connected to his personal sensibilities relating to the discomfort of seeing children suffer. Thus, while it is the in-game fictional situation that evokes the sense of discomfort, this would not be possible were it not for the fact that we recognize the situations from real life.

Alien: Isolation

The first-person survival horror game *Alien: Isolation* (Creative Assembly 2014) was used in the gameplay journal study as a representative of the horror game genre. Intraludic transgression is central to the horror game genre, which purpose is to create a sense of unease and high levels of adrenaline in the player. In horror games, such responses are connected to diegetic transgressivity in that it is created by a scary fictional setting, but is often combined with ludic transgressivity against the player by the use of difficult or subversive game mechanics that decrease a sense of control. Horror games are interesting from the perspective of transgressive aesthetics, because for players attracted to the genre, such games may indeed create a high level of discomfort even though they are not experienced as transgressive in a profound sense. In Bernard Perron's words, the appreciator of the genre "is playing at frightening himself" (Perron 2009, 3). Horror games are an acquired taste, and there are many players who do not play them because they create discomfort and remove them of the sense of power and control that many other genres offer. At the same time, we would claim that players are rarely *offended* by horror games; even though the genre may include violent deaths, monstrous representations, and unspeakable terrors, these issues are conventions that are expected of the genre. Also, the situations of horror games also tend to be so far removed from our social reality that they can rarely be considered extraludic transgressivity.

Attempting to replicate the atmosphere of the original *Alien* film (Scott 1979), *Alien: Isolation* stresses suspense through empty, claustrophobic spaces and combines this with what Henry Jenkins has called *embedded narratives* – signs in the surroundings that point toward events that have occurred (Jenkins 2004, 126). The player takes the role of Amanda Ripley, who is stuck in a space station in search of information about what happened to her mother on the spacecraft Nostromo 15 years ago. While the first-person perspective tends to be associated with action-packed shooters, there are few weapons in *Alien: Isolation*, and those that are present only have limited effect. While they can be used against hostile humans and androids, they have no use against the alien monster itself. Instead gunshots may attract the monster to your location, and only the flamethrower has the potential of fending the monster off for a few seconds. The game received attention for its use of artificial intelligence that rendered the alien unpredictable. Due to the alien's use of ventilation shafts in order to move around, an important game mechanics is the radar that allows the player to detect its relative location to avoid it. The game focuses on stealth, and when noticed by the alien, the player must hide under tables or in closets and even hold their breath as the monster searches for them. The game includes puzzle elements that force the player to access computers, talk to survivors, or find key cards that give access to new areas of the space station. Focusing on creating a suspenseful experience for the player through conventions from both horror films and games, the game aims for a particular kind of discomfort, but whether this is a wanted discomfort or a discomfort that causes a player to stop playing the game depends on player preferences.

Four men and one woman participated in the *Alien: Isolation* journal study. Common for all was that they found themselves frightened by the game, with heart thumping and hands shaking, at least in the initial hours of playing the game. All also described using techniques for mitigating their fear, such as taking breaks or, in "David's" case, first looking at the phone and later challenging himself by actively seeking out the danger. The five participants all found that the game became less scary, and for some, even boring over time. "David" and "Mel" both stressed that the game changed once they had figured out the game mechanics, in particular when they learned that the alien's movement patterns could be studied and exploited. While "David" does not generally play horror games because he becomes scared, "Paul", however, does not describe the adrenaline rush as uncomfortable but stresses that he likes horror games and finds *Alien: Isolation* to be both fun, thrilling, scary, and challenging, and he describes this adrenaline rush as a pleasant feeling.

Bloodborne

A game that focuses on ludic transgressivity over diegetic transgressivity is *Bloodborne* (From Software 2015). This form of transgressivity does not so much concern the fictional realities of the game as it concerns the gameplay itself, and for this reason the sense that this game transgresses one's boundaries and makes one wants to stop playing can be isolated to the game itself. Described as a frustrating game with high difficulty level, *Bloodborne* is an example of a game where failure (Juul 2013) and frustration are central to the game experience. By including this game in our selection, we wanted to also explore whether games also can be experienced as transgressive through testing the player's patience. Also, in an otherwise Western-focused selection, this Japanese game adds a degree of diversity.

Bloodborne is a third-person perspective action, role-playing game focusing on a high difficulty level that gave its predecessors, the so-called *Souls* series (*Demon's Souls* and *Dark Souls I–III)* (From Software 2009, 2011), their reputation as relentless and unforgiving. In *Bloodborne*, the player is a Hunter traversing the streets of Yharnam, where the city's inhabitants have been stricken by a disease and turned into monstrous, zombie-like creatures. The player may roam the streets freely, but is restricted by infected inhabitants, locked gates, and the city's maze-like organization. "Learning by dying" is here a design feature rather than a flaw (Grammenos 2008, 1445), and as saving points are rare, the player must try and fail a number of times. To progress in the game, the player must fight their way through groups of infected in order to access levers that open locked gates that grant access to new areas. The infected are many, strong, and often hidden or located at places where they are difficult to reach. The player's avatar will fall prey to the enemies one or several times before being able to complete an area, and identifying the behavior pattern of the monsters is crucial for success. A key feature is to unlock shortcuts that allow the player to skip areas once it has been successfully completed. *Bloodborne* also provides less information than the typical AAA game. The narrative and the role of the protagonist are murky, and the controllers and interface are clumsy to use. For instance, when a monster hits the player, the health bar animation has a short delay, making it difficult to fall back or dodge in time. The dark, Gothic visual style favors dark colors and a lot of shadows, which makes it difficult to discern gameworld elements clearly, thus contributing to less than clear communication between the game and the player.

Bloodborne was used in the gameplay journal study and was played by four men and one woman. While all experienced the game as a frustrating game experience, the degree of frustration varied. For "Sarah" and "Josh", the lack of progression made the game monotonous and in the end boring, while "Henry" found lack of progression so frustrating that the game became unplayable. "Nathan" and "James", on the other hand, were more successful at gameplay and experienced the game in more positive terms, appreciating the high difficulty level, even though in the end that was what also made them quit. *Bloodborne* is interesting from the perspective of transgressive aesthetics because it shows us that it is not only games that provoke or offend on the level of content that can be described as transgressive and that game mechanics must be coupled with content in order to be experienced as transgressive. On the contrary, formal elements such as game mechanics can indeed in themselves create emotional responses of outrage that are similar and sometimes also stronger than the emotions evoked by offensive game content.

Other forms of transgressive games

With the focus on transgressive aesthetics in games, it may not be surprising that most of the games above are examples of diegetic transgressivity. Although we have covered many categories of transgressive games in our data, it is certainly possible to identify additional categories of transgressive games. Examples of extraludic transgressive games that have not been covered here are *taboo games*, that is, games that concern topics that are taboo in most cultures, such as, for instance, pedophilia, cannibalism, or genocide. More importantly, to be considered a taboo game, the game must treat these topics not in a sanitized or cushioned way, but in a way that is experienced as taboo, repulsive, or offensive when playing the game. The first-person shooter *Ethnic Cleansing* (National Alliance 2002) created by an American white nationalist organization may be an example of such a game. Another is the beforementioned *RapeLay* (Illusion Soft 2006), a Japanese eroge video game in which the player takes the role of a stalker who kidnaps and rapes a mother and her two daughters. However, both of these games are symptomatic for taboo games in that they are not aimed at a mainstream audience but rather toward a small subculture that will not take offense from the game and instead find the breaking of taboos in itself to be attractive.

However, it is possible to identify games that are transgressive in other ways. If we consider play scholar Jaakko Stenros's overview of transgressive play forms, we see that many of the games in our selection can be characterized as *parapathic*: They are meaningful and worthwhile although they are neither fun nor makes the player feel good. This appears to be the case for *This War of Mine, Beyond: Two Souls, Spec Ops: The Line, Life is Strange,* and to a certain extent *Alien: Isolation* and also *Bloodborne*. *Hatred* does not fall in this category because it feels neither meaningful nor good, and *GTAV* does not feel uncomfortable and meaningful at the same time. However, these games may indeed be seen as examples of *brink play*, where playing the game becomes an alibi for doing things that would not be acceptable in our social reality. *Bloodborne* and *Hatred* could also be seen as transgressive because they are examples of *repetitive play* (Stenros 2018, 19–22). Based on Stenros's categories, it is also possible to identify additional kinds of transgressive games: Free-to-play games and games that use dark design patterns to convince players to spend more time or money on the game than is in their interest would be an example of games with *instrumentalized* play. In this category, we can include so-called *gamification* or the use of game elements in non-game systems (Deterding et al. 2011). Gamification has been used mainly in service-oriented communication to increase the motivation to use systems due to their game-like affordances (Huotari and Hamari n.d., 25). Following Stenros further, *The Artwork Formerly Known as Painstation* (Morawe and Reiff 2001), which we will discuss in more detail in Chapter 8, could be seen as an example of a *violent* game, because it asks players to subject themselves to physical harm. Not least, games in which bodily stimulation such as masturbation is a central mechanic would be an example of *sensation-centric locomotor* games (Stenros 2018, 18–23).

The games we have chosen demonstrate the delicacy of transgression. It is an ephemeral sensation that changes the moment one or more elements framing the experience changes. This may seem counterintuitive, considering the large controversies games occasionally cause, but we are not focusing at the controversies, but at the sense of being part of something transgressive, a sense of taking a step over your own boundaries. This makes it particularly difficult to choose games for the study of transgression, because knowing you are playing a game that is supposed to be transgressive may change everything.

Tackling transgression in games

In Chapter 2, we discussed different typologies of transgressive game experiences and how games, through their representational or game mechanical content, transgress players' interest. Transgressive games create a sense of discomfort, opposition, or offense that breaks with the willingness to play the games. As the data above shows, what kind of game content that breaks with a player's sensibilities depends on socio-cultural background, attitudes, and personal experiences. However, the data also points to certain situations or kinds of content that to a greater degree risks transgressing against player sensibilities and thus disrupting the players' interest in continued play.

To sum up the explanations given by respondents concerning transgressive games, game content can be opposed because it is excessive, such as the excessive violence of *Hatred*. Also, when in-game actions and fictional situations goes against their ideological or ethical sensibilities, for instance, through stereotypes and prejudice in *GTAV*, this may in many cases be experienced as unacceptable for certain players. Expanding this, game content can also be experienced as transgressive because it hits "too close to home", that is, it becomes uncomfortably close to actual, real situations, as in *Spec Ops: The Line* or *This War of Mine*, or it addresses issues that are difficult for the player due to personal experience, as in *Beyond: Two Souls* or *Life is Strange*. Game content can also be experienced as inappropriate or as not tackling a particular topic in a meaningful or respectful manner, as is the case of "Jane's" experience with *This War of Mine*. Not least, players may decide to quit a game because it is too scary, as is the case for some players' experience with horror games such as *Alien: Isolation*.

References

11 bit studios, and War Child. 2014. *This War of Mine*. 11 bit studios.

Björk, Staffan. 2015. "Fabricated Innocence: How Players Can Be Lured into Feel-Bad Games." In *The Dark Side of Game Play: Controversial Issues in Playful Environments*, edited by Torill Elvira Mortensen, Jonas Linderoth, and Ashley M. L. Brown, Routledge, 171–87. New York, London: Routledge.

Conrad, Joseph. 1899. *Heart of Darkness*. London, Edinburgh: William Blackwood and Sons.

Creative Assembly. 2014. *Alien: Isolation*. Sega.

Destructive Creations. 2015. *Hatred*. Destructive Creations. www.hatredgame.com/.

Deterding, Sebastian, Dan Dixon, Rilla Khaled, and Lennart Nacke. 2011. "From Game Design Elements to Gamefulness." In *Proceedings of the 15th International Academic MindTrek Conference on Envisioning Future Media Environments – MindTrek '11*, 9. New York: ACM Press. doi:10.1145/2181037.2181040.

Dontnod Entertainment. 2015. "Life Is Strange." Square Enix Co., Ltd.

Dyer, Mitch. 2012. "The Story Secrets of Spec Ops: The Line." *IGN*, 2012. www.ign.com/articles/2012/07/20/the-story-secrets-of-spec-ops-the-line.

Frank, Anders. 2012. "Gaming the Game." *Simulation & Gaming* 43 (1): 118–32. doi:10.1177/1046878111408796.

From Software. 2009. *Demon's Souls*. Namco Bandai Games.

———. 2011. "Dark Souls." Namco Bandai Games.

———. 2015. *Bloodborne*. Sony Interactive Entertainment.

Garland, Jordan. 2012. "Aftermath: Crossing The Line with Walt Williams." *GamingBolt.Com: Video Game News, Reviews, Previews and Blog*, 2012. https://gamingbolt.com/aftermath-crossing-the-line-with-walt-williams.

Grammenos, Dimitris. 2008. "Game Over." In *Proceedings of the Twenty-Sixth Annual CHI Conference on Human Factors in Computing Systems – CHI '08*, 1443. New York: ACM Press. doi:10.1145/1357054.1357281.

Grayson, Nathan. 2014. "Heavy: This War of Mine Is a War Game about Civilians." *Rock, Paper, Shotgun*, 2014. www.rockpapershotgun.com/2014/03/13/heavy-this-war-of-mine-is-a-war-game-about-civilians/.

Griffin, Dustin H. 1994. *Satire. A Critical Reintroduction*. Lexington: The University Press of Kentucky.

Hall, Stuart. 2006. "Encoding/Decoding." In *Media and Cultural Studies: Keyworks*, edited by Meenakshi Gigi Durham and Douglas M. Kellner, 163–172. Malden, Oxford, and Carlton: Blackwell Publishing.

Huotari, Kai, and Juho Hamari. n.d. "A Definition for Gamification: Anchoring Gamification in the Service Marketing Literature." *Electronic Markets*. Accessed June 26, 2019. doi:10.1007/s12525-015-0212-z.

Jenkins, David. 2015. "Hatred Review – The Most Violent Game on Earth." *Metro Gaming*, 2015. http://metro.co.uk/2015/06/02/hatred-review-the-most-violent-game-on-earth-5225932/.

Jenkins, Henry. 2004. "Game Design as Narrative Architecture." In *First Person: New Media as Story, Performance, and Game*, edited by Noah Wardrip-Fruin and Pat Harrigan, 118–30. Cambridge: MIT Press.

Jørgensen, Kristine. 2016. "The Positive Discomfort of Spec Ops: The Line." *Game Studies: The International Journal of Computer Game Research*. 16 (2). http://gamestudies.org/1602/articles/jorgensenkristine.

Jørgensen, Kristine, and Faltin Karlsen. 2018. *Transgression in Games and Play*. Cambridge: MIT Press.

Juul, Jesper. 2013. *The Art of Failure: An Essay on the Pain of Playing Video Games*. Cambridge: MIT Press.

Keogh, Brendan. 2013. "SpecOps: The Line and the Subversion of the Military Shooter." DiGRA 2013: Defragging Game Studies. 2013. www.digra.org/digital-library/publications/spec-ops-the-lines-conventional-subversion-of-the-military-shooter.

Klepek, Patrick. 2012. "This Is All Your Fault." *Giant Bomb News*, 2012. www.giantbomb.com/articles/this-is-all-your-fault/1100-4291/.

Lindsey, Patrick. 2012. "Spec.Ops.: The Line Isn't Profound, It's a Shooter." *Pixels or Death*, August 29, 2012. http://pixelsordeath.com/features/spec-ops-the-line-isnt-profound-its-a-shooter.

Morawe, Volker, and Tilman Reiff. 2001. "The Artwork Formerly Known as Pain-Station." Cologne. www.painstation.de/history.html.

National Alliance. 2002. *Ethnic Cleansing*. Resistance Records.

Perron, Bernard. 2009. "Introduction: Gaming After Dark." In *Horror Video Games: Essays on the Fusion of Fear and Play*, edited by Bernard Perron, 3–13. Jefferson: McFarland & Company, Inc., Publishers.

Pötzsch, Holger. 2017. "Selective Realism: Filtering Experiences of War and Violence in First- and Third-Person Shooters." *Games and Culture* 12 (2): 156–78.

———. 2018. "Forms and Practices of Transgressivity in Videogames: Aesthetics, Play, and Politics." In *Transgression in Games and Play*, edited by Kristine Jørgensen and Faltin Karlsen, 45–61. Cambridge: MIT Press.

Quantic Dream. 2013. *Beyond: Two Souls*. Sony Interactive Entertainment.

Rockstar North. 2013. *Grand Theft Auto V*. New York: Rockstar Games.

Schrank, Brian. 2014. *Avant-Garde Videogames: Playing with Technoculture*. Cambridge: MIT Press.

Scott, Ridley. 1979. *Alien*. United Kingdom, United States.

Sicart, Miguel. 2009. *The Ethics of Computer Games*. Cambridge: MIT Press.

———. 2013. *Beyond Choices*. Cambridge: MIT Press.

Smethurst, Toby, and Stef Craps. 2015. "Playing with Trauma." *Games and Culture* 10 (3): 269–90. doi:10.1177/1555412014559306.

Stenros, Jaakko. 2018. "Guided by Transgression: Defying Norms as an Integral Part of Play." In *Transgression in Games and Play*, edited by Kristine Jørgensen and Faltin Karlsen, 13–25. Cambridge: MIT Press.

thewhalehusband. 2015. *The Static Speaks My Name*. https://thewhalehusband.itch.io/thestatic.

Yager Development. 2012. *Spec Ops: The Line*. 2K Games.

Part 2

Experiences with transgressive games

4   Transgressive games and the player-response perspective

Games are interactive media that can be traversed in different ways. While the user experience with non-interactive media also varies greatly depending on personal sensibilities, political leniency, social background, taste, and media literacy, the interaction with non-interactive texts remains an interpretative engagement. Games, on the other hand, require input from the player beyond interpretation in order to be engaged with at all. In games, this input cannot be reduced to the input provided when browsing a website or using productivity software. With its stress on game mechanics that must be mastered, tactics that must be employed, and processes that must be manipulated, games also require a different form of interaction than other interactive media. This understanding is an acknowledgment not only of the medium-specific aspects of games but also of the fact that a particular game can be engaged with in a number of different ways based on the player's in-game choices, playstyle, and game literacy.

When discussing transgressive games, it is vital to understand this complexity of games and how players interact with them in order to understand why game content may be experienced as provocative for certain players and profound and meaningful for others, or trivial for some players and disturbing for others. Understanding transgressive games means understanding that people may have different preferences or sensibilities with regards to particular kinds of content or that they may interpret it in different ways; it also means acknowledging that players interact with games in different ways, with different motivations and intentions, and with different skills and abilities. These abilities change during play and the change in ability is part of the process of playing, which reflects back to the preferences and sensibilities regarding both content and playstyle. Games are in this manner moving targets for analysis, as the object of analysis itself will change with the abilities of the user. This is why we are highlighting what we call a player-response approach to understanding transgressive games, that is, a perspective in which we do not simply analyze the games we are researching, but take into account the interpretations of other empirical players as well.

The legacy from reader-response theory

The player-response approach follows reader-response theory in highlighting the important fact that media texts are not realized without the presence and interpretation of the reader (Iser 1978). Reader-response theory downplays the role of the author in the hermeneutic process while stressing the reader's role in focusing on the idea that the meaning of a text comes into being through the interpretative process. However, as reader-response theory is developed for literature, it cannot be applied to games without revision (Mortensen 2003, 25). The flexible nature of games, their adaptability, and procedurality make it questionable to reduce them to "texts", and the ludic and playful interactions required by games necessitate a modification of reader-response theory that takes into consideration the active, non-trivial process of traversing games. This is why we talk about the player-response approach. It aims to empower the player in the meaning-making process in a similar way as the reader-response theory empowers the reader. The player-response approach implies that we cannot understand games as a medium or the meaning-making process associated with it without taking into account players and the fact that there is a plethora of responses to a single game.

Of particular importance to our discussion here is understanding reader-response theory's idea of the *reader* – the individual receiver of the text and in certain ways comparable to the player. Reader-response theory postulates that there can be different readers, such as an *empirical reader*, understood as a historical reader who actually engages with a text, but also an *implied reader*, who is a conceptual reader as presupposed by the structure of the text itself (Iser 1978, 34). Author and literary scholar Umberto Eco also differentiates these readers from the *model reader*, which is the possible reader that the author has in mind when composing the text (Eco 1979, 7). The empirical reader, or, as literary scholar Wolfgang Iser says, the real reader, "is invoked mainly in study of the history of responses, i.e., when attention is focused on the way in which a literary work has been received by a specific reading public" (Iser 1978, 28). Studying the empirical reader can give us new, surprising insights, as can be seen from cultural studies scholar Janice Radway's groundbreaking work from 1984 on how women read romance novels. She discovered that the assumptions about women's use of a particular genre of literature were flawed, and the readers she studied gained a wide range of gratifications from the reading which had as much to do with the context to the reading process as it had to do with the words in the text (Radway 1984).

The implied reader, however, is understood from the text and is the reader figure as defined by the structure of the text – a construct implied by the writing style, address, and organization of the text. According to Iser, in order to understand how literary works affect us, we must not assume anything about the nature or context of the reader. The implied reader is a construct of the text and only exists in the structure of the text, but he embodies all the qualifications for the literary work to have an effect (Iser 1978, 34).

Iser's implied reader is not the target reader or the reader imagined by the author (Booth 1961). Iser's implied reader is a dynamic construction that steps out of the text through close scrutiny. To understand the implied reader, we need to understand how the real reader interacts with the text. Here Iser uses the term *interaction*, which in literary theory does not indicate the kind of interaction that changes the structure of the work or which is discernable to an outside observer; it is an interaction of comprehension. What it changes is the reader's relationship to the text and the desire to "create the conditions necessary for the effectiveness of that text" (Iser 1978, 9). This can cause some confusion in the study of games, since game studies uses interaction to mean an action that leads to some discernible change, a change that can be observed from the outside. Games are built on a wide range of such interactions, where the player's input and the technology's response creates the game in itself. To use the game *Candy Crush* (King 2012) as an example: The ability to move a piece of candy may not change the comprehension of the game, but the understanding that moving them in certain manners leads to new benefits that change the chances of winning, and the behavior of more than the one candy you move can trigger a cascade of realizations about how the game works, changing the player's approach, strategy, and behavior. It is thus clear that the *interaction of player and game*, while related, is different from the *interaction of reader and text*. This makes interaction a very imprecise term to use in this discussion, and when we talk about the player's internal process of engagement, we will attempt to describe it in other terms, such as comprehension or interpretation. Interaction will be used only to describe the actual process of input and response expressed in game play.

For our below discussion of the implied player, it is also important to distinguish Iser's implied reader from Eco's model reader (Eco 1979, 7). The model reader is an anticipated reader, a tool by the author in the writing process. This assumed reader is able to interpret the codes the author generates in the writing. Different texts have different model readers. For Eco, open texts are those that allow multiple readings, while closed texts strictly guide the reader toward one intended meaning. The model reader of a closed text can be any random audience that happens to approach it. Due to the unpredictable nature of this model reader, the text needs to lead the reader by hand, signaling each twist and turn in advance, because it cannot assume that the model reader knows the genre, the topic, and direction of the story. In an open text, on the other hand, the model reader is assumed to know the topic, and the model reader is predictable – a skilled, engaged, able reader, who can decode the complexity of the text (Eco 1979, 8–9). Eco's model reader for an open text is however approaching the implied reader since this reader can be extrapolated from the text itself. This reader is not random, but closely integrated into the structure and the writing.

When we choose to dwell on Iser and partly Eco in this context, it is due to their emphasis on the reader as a vital participant in the realization of the text. Where Radway focuses on the reader and her use of the text rather than the text itself, Iser and Eco both look to the reader to find the mechanisms that bring the text alive. In other words: While Radway studies the reader in order to understand readers, a parallel to player-oriented studies in game studies, Iser and Eco study the reader in order to understand the text. They demonstrate the importance of the activity of the reader in the face of the text. Together with literary critic Roland Barthes and his understanding of the importance of the reader in relationship to the author (Barthes 1977), they all introduced an understanding of the text as something that depended on a reader to be fully realized. In player-response theory, we are stressing the same approach: Games cannot be actualized without the player's interaction, and for this reason we argue that we must study players in order to understand games.

Toward an implied player

Analyzing media texts from the perspective of the implied reader has been a central strategy to reader-response theory, and the term *implied player* has been adapted into game studies (Aarseth 2007; Mortensen 2003) to reflect the idea that game design provides clues as to how the model player is supposed to play a certain game. However, although we agree that game design indeed says a lot about the role that the designers have intended the model player to take, we also believe that this only tells part of the story. To clarify how the player-response perspective significantly breaks with the reader-response theory of Iser, and in what ways the implied player indicates a different position than the implied reader, it is crucial to understand the nuances of what it means to interact with a game. For a nuanced understanding of games, it is also necessary to take into consideration the accounts of empirical players and to understand how they actually interact with a game. In the following, we will argue that this is related to the fact that games are *designed as systems* and because interacting with such systems needs a *certain kind of effort* on the part of the player.

Games are designed as systems

If we argue that the implied player is the player intended by the game design, we must also ask whether there is an authorial voice in the game that steers the player in a certain direction. In order to explore this argument, we must take a closer look at game design and how it compares to authorship. Game design is often referred to as *second-order design* because game designers cannot design a particular behavior – they are limited to design tools and systems with which the players can interact (Salen and Zimmerman 2004). This means that designers can only create an activity space that offers opportunities for interaction, not the interaction itself. What designers create is a system consisting of an *environment* and *rules of behavior*. As systems, games consist of parts that work together as a whole (Salen and Zimmerman 2004, 152). There is little doubt that how the environment and its rules are designed have a strong impact on gameplay by facilitating and guiding how players interact with the game, but to understand the extent of this impact, we need to understand how players come to learn the properties and behavior.

In order to play the game, the player must learn the interaction possibilities that the game offers, also known as its *affordances* (Gibson 1979, 127). In his seminal work on the ecology of visual perception, psychologist James J. Gibson argues that we perceive the environment around us in terms of potentials for interaction. According to this theory, affordances are properties of an object or environment that allow a human or animal to interact with that object or environment. Affordances help us identify the possibilities and constraints in the environment: They guide our interaction. In the physical world, we may see a ladder and perceive it as offering the possibility for climbing; or we may encounter a door and understand that it offers the option for opening and closing. Although they are designed environments that offer stricter interaction possibilities than the physical world, video games are also perceived in a similar manner: The game controllers have properties that allow us to interact with the gameworld, and inside, we learn that certain objects, such as walls and rivers, may restrict our actions, and others, such as weapons and tools, offer potential for action. Understanding the affordances of the gameworld allows us to learn the range of options that are available for us. The gameworld and everything it contains is of course designed with the intention of gameplay, but would it then be reasonable to call a player who interacts accordingly an *implied player*? The implied player would obviously use in-game explosives for destruction that leads to progress in the game – but what if they use the explosive for throwing their avatars into the air to reach areas that they were not meant to reach? Are these players unpredictable empirical players that it is impossible to design for? Or are they model players of an open game text? Depending on the answer, such actions should be taken into consideration in the design of the game.

In order to complicate matters more, let us consider a particular set of affordances that concerns the rules and behavior of the game system – the procedural aspect of games. According to digital media scholar Janet Murray, procedurality is one of the essential properties of digital artifacts, and she refers to procedurality as the computer's "defining ability to execute a series of rules" (Murray 1997, 71). Procedurality is an affordance that concerns the ability to carry out processes, which makes games into an engine "[d]esigned not to carry static information but to embody complex contingent behaviors" (Murray 1997, 72). Through interacting with the game, the video game player learns the procedural behavior of the game environment and uses their understanding of the system to play the game in the manner they find most interesting. Through manipulating affordances, procedures included, players are invited to creatively engage with the rules laid out by designers, and due to procedural nature of the game, this creativity may go far beyond what the designers had in mind. While one may argue that this level of freedom is what the designers had in mind for the typical player, this is far from how an implied reader is positioned in a literary text. Individual empirical players will approach the game in just as many ways as people will use a building: The organization of rooms of a hospital definitely has an impact upon the use as there will be surgery rooms, patient rooms, examination rooms, offices, and so on, and there will be intended users of that hospital such as patients, nurses, doctors, janitors, and others. However, calling them "implied users" in the same vein as the implied reader would be to miss the fact that studies of empirical users and their needs are the point of departure for the design of such buildings. If we move into the field of User Experience and interaction design, we also see a similar approach: Designers do not look at their product to find out who the users are; on the contrary, like Radway does when she studies how real women actually use Romances, designers ideally look at actual, empirical users of comparable tools and spaces to get insight into how their product should be designed. As systems designed for interaction and use, and with a high degree of focus on usability and a meaningful user experience, games should then also be understood through the lens of empirical players.

At the same time, we do not ignore the fact that games are also expressive media and that the designers often may have an authorial ambition in which they have an implied player in mind. Building on Murray, Bogost stresses that procedurality should be understood as "the core practice of software authorship" due to its basis in algorithms that model the behavior of things. In making a system behave procedurally, its authors create code that "enforces rules to generate some kind of representation, rather than authoring the representation itself" (Bogost 2007, 4). Meaning, then, is created through the interaction with algorithms, which takes us to the idea that procedures also can be rhetorical. Bogost argues that even though rules are often considered to limit behavior, such constraints may also create a space for expression or a logic that guides our activities. When talking about rhetoric, Bogost refers to "effective and persuasive expression" (Bogost 2007, 3), and draws a historical line of the development of different forms of rhetoric, spanning the oratory of Antiquity via written expressions and visual rhetoric before moving on to digital rhetoric and, last, procedural rhetoric. Procedural rhetoric, as defined by Bogost, is "the practice of using processes persuasively" (Bogost 2007, 28–29). This presupposes an intention on the part of the designer in that procedural rhetoric entails the authoring of persuasive arguments through the construction of rules of behavior and of dynamic models.

While the concept of procedural rhetoric stresses the important idea that there is an authorial voice behind design and that a game's mechanics and procedures may very well be designed with the *intention* of promoting a particular argument, *how* the argument is received by the individual empirical player is entirely subjective. If we follow Stuart Hall's theory of encoding and decoding, which we briefly discussed in the introduction, it is vital to understand that the communicative process includes both an authorial intention – an *encoding* – and an interpretation by the audience – a *decoding* (Hall 2006, 165). In other words, regardless of how explicitly an author stresses their goal of their communication in their message, there is no guarantee that the individuals on the receiving end will accept the intention of the message. Hall's theory stresses that decoding can be separated into three categories: The *dominant-hegemonic* reading, where the message is decoded in the way the author intended stands opposing the *oppositional* reading, where the message is decoded in a resistant way, and the decoder questions the message and looks for alternative interpretations. The *negotiated* decoding lies somewhere between the two, in that the message is partly accepted by the decoder (Hall 2006, 173). Hall's theory stresses the fact that interpretation is a complicated process where both cultural codes and the socio-historical context of both author and audience matter. The model is relevant to most kinds of media communication – from the reception of news as made visible in the recent debates about "fake news" to the reception of games. This has been demonstrated in gamer culture debates about the content of video games, where, for instance, Anita Sarkeesian's feminist criticism has been treated as an attack not only on games but also on gamers (Mortensen 2016). While Hall's theory helps us understand the discrepancy that may happen in the communicative process generally, complex affordances and variable procedurality are two aspects that put the reception and use of games in a particular context that differentiates them from other media. In combining the encoding/decoding model with the theory of affordances, game scholar Adrienne Shaw has expanded the model to account for the configurative processes that are central to interactive media such as video games. She shows that practices such as modding and cheating may not necessarily be inherently oppositional because such activities are often encouraged or at least made possible by the developer (Shaw 2017, 598–99), but it is important to stress that it also means that a game developer, to an even lesser extent than an author, can be in control of their own message.

Games require effort

While the procedurality and affordances of games create a situation where the author loses control over the communicative process, it is important to stress that how the player engages with the game is also critical in the player-response theory. It is not only the game structure that creates a particular situation different from the situation that reader-response theory discussed; how the player *interacts* with the game text is central in the player-response theory.

Within game studies, gameplay is understood as characterized by a very high degree of player autonomy, described by, for instance, Murray as *agency* (1997, 126), and by stressing the exploratory and creative freedom of the playful or paratelic mind-set, relating to intrinsic motivation, exploration, and experimentation (Stenros 2015, 66–67). Examples of this are found in the variety of descriptions of subversive game practices such as the exploration of the limitations of the game system (Aarseth 2007) or the use of games for other purposes not intended by the game design such as *queering* (Sihvonen and Stenros 2018). Compared to the reader, the player is often perceived as much more in control of the experience as the game comes into being through play.

In stressing the important point that the activity is a central part of the player's response in relation to games, we would also like to bring to the attention how games relate to Espen Aarseth's idea of ergodic texts. As a form of literature that needs "nontrivial effort" on part of the reader to traverse the text, ergodic literature is contrasted with literature "where the effort to traverse the text is trivial, with no extranoematic responsibilities placed on the reader except (for example) eye movement and the periodic or arbitrary turning of pages" (Aarseth 1997, 1–2). In ergodic texts, the dependence on the reader is not only a way to describe the process of comprehension and realization that depends on the intellectual and emotional abilities of the reader but a direct dependence on the actions of the reader in order to make the text progress and to determine the progression of the text. One of Aarseth's examples of ergodic texts is the ancient Chinese divination system *I Ching* (Wilhelm 1923). In order to make sense of the collection of sentences and sentence fragments *I Ching* is comprised of, the person approaching the text needs to follow certain rules, which include throwing coins and then referencing the places in the book which the coin throws indicate. Together with the question asked, this creates an answer. There are other "texts" that do much the same, for instance the *Tarot* divination cards, where the shuffling of the cards serves to randomize the response (Waite 2005) like the toss of the coins in *I Ching*. Both systems lean on the numbers of random combinations in order to appear driven by divine chance when the diviner delivers the interpretation. The unpredictability created by the shuffling, throwing, and sheer number of possible combinations these lead to is what connects the manually realized *I Ching* with the electronically or digitally realized *cybertext*, defined by of Aarseth as "texts that involve calculation" (1997, 75) in the production of "strings of signs as they appear to the reader" (1997, 62). The idea of the cybertext distinguishes texts that are put together by choosing different paths from section to section, from texts where the production depends on numbers, such as rolling dice or letting the computer roll the dice to come up with somewhat random pieces of text.

It is possible to argue that since we find numbers at the bottom of any code, all digital texts – including video games – are cybertexts, but that does not mean cybertexts and video games are the same thing. First, while the cybertext presupposes the existence of an interactor, this interaction is not necessarily anything similar to gameplay, which includes playful exploration and creativity, tactical overcoming of certain challenges, and the experience of trying to master the system. Sometimes, the interaction of a cybertext may be limited to entering a question (*Eliza* (Weizenbaum 1964)) or – unlike the interaction of many games – it may not be connected to planning or skills (*I Ching*). Further, what Aarseth calls cybertext is distinguished from the wider term hypertext: While a hypertext refers to a particular kind of structure and is an alternative to other formats for organizing texts, a cybertext is based on calculations (Aarseth 1997, 75, 76). This indicates that having an underlying code dependent on numbers is not enough to create a cybertext. Rather, the events in the text need to depend on calculation rather than choice, most commonly activated through a randomizer similar to the coin toss in *I Ching* but determined by the processing power of a digital device. This is where cybertexts and video games come close and at some points may overlap. This randomizing function, through the use of dice or other mechanisms, is at the heart of a majority of games and is an important element of many games of skill as it functions to create unpredictability that in analogue games can be introduced by factors such as weather or other physical conditions. At the same time, however, there are abstract games, games that are fully devoid of outside randomizers, and here the unpredictable element is introduced through human ability. While there are a few abstract, analogue games, like chess, this is not a common feature in video games. Unpredictability is a vital part of the definition of games, and in video games this is an integral part of what creates a sense of risk, the potential for failure, without which the pleasurable, non-productive activities we may be engaged in cease to be gaming and become play.

This detour into cybertext is aiming at the broader understanding of the relationship of games to interaction that we pointed out earlier. While traditional texts put the reader at the receiving end of the communication process, cybertexts, including games, situate the user in a more ambiguous position where interaction is not simply user input, and effort may point to more or less goal-driven exploration and concern figuring out how the system works and what is the most interesting way of manipulating it. Cybertexts presuppose that efforts of the player or user contribute to the creation or configuration of the text itself (Aarseth 1997). Addressing literary theorist Roland Barthes's argument for the death of the author and the subsequent empowerment of the reader, Aarseth questions the sender position:

> When I fire a virtual laser gun in a computer game such as *Space Invader*, where, and what, am 'I'? Am I the sender or the receiver? I am certainly part of the medium, so perhaps I am the message. (...) just as

the game becomes a text for the user at the time of playing, so, it can be argued, does the user become a text for the game, since they exchange and read to each other's messages according to a set of codes. The game plays the user just as the user plays the game, and there is no message apart from the play.

(1997, 162)

Aarseth questions the familiar relationship between the reader and the text by indicating that the text that demands interactivity may not be passively submitting to the manipulations of the user, but rather steers the steps of the player through the text. This is, in Aarseth's reading, a political question as it challenges not only the relationship between author, text, and reader, as did reader-response theory, but also the relationships between consumer and creator. This is an expression of the discussions around the role of the active media user that the digital media permits, and it blooms into terms such as *prosumer*, coined in 1970 by the futurist Alvin Toffler but raised to more common understanding and use with the recent and current analysis of digital media production and consumption structures (Bruns 2006).

Further, Aarseth's discussion highlights the positions of power of the reader and questions whether the reader of a cybertext actually can change anything at all. If we assume that the cybertext in this case is a game, the reader becomes the player, and what Aarseth discusses is whether the player can change anything or is being played – being led through the labyrinth of the game, never seeing the wizard behind the curtain. When talking about the response to transgressive games, then, this points toward the ambiguous relationship between players and transgressive games: While the player may have a certain power over the actions and events, the game will also guide the player's actions in a certain way. In certain cases, this means that the player, regardless of their choices of action, may end up with a situation – for instance, a cutscene – where their actions are limited. Being cornered in this way may – intentionally or unintentionally by the designer – lead players into having transgressive experiences.

Who is the implied player?

Above, we have argued that the player-response perspective and the idea of an implied player must take into consideration the fact that games are designed systems, and traversing them needs a particular kind of effort on the part of the player. This means that while there is a high level of authorial guidance in a game, it is not absolute. The player still has agency within the systemic properties that the gameworld offers. While reading needs to be mastered, once we know it, we rarely struggle to master every single book after that. But a game is something we learn, train at, and then, at the end, master – supposedly. If we follow the logic relating to Aarseth's idea of cybertext and Bogost's idea of procedurality, what we have done is to become extremely good at taking direction. The *model player* would be a player able to follow every lead of the game, and hence overcome every obstacle, as the game, the rules, and the affordances leads her through the procedures making it up. But is this the *implied player*?

We have earlier described how Iser understands the implied reader not as the intended target audience of the text but as a concept or idea created by the structure of the text itself (Iser 1978, 34). While this can be reminiscent of how game design guides players, on the basis of the above discussion, it is important to stress that a game design, and thus also a game structure, will always need to be played, and realized, by real, empirical players. These players may, during the production of the game, be hypothetical or potential players for the developers, but since the game cannot move forward without actual players, the player constructed by the game is more closely aligned with the *personas* of goal-directed design (Cooper 1999) than with the implied reader. While based on empirical users encountered in user studies, personas are hypothetical archetypes of actual users (Cooper 1999, 124), descriptions of model individuals created to represent actual users of a particular system. Designers use personas as a tool in the design process in order to keep their mind focused on the behavior, motivations, and preferences that actual users of their system would have. Personas allow designers to redirect their attention from an unspecified, generic "user" to focus on defined individuals; the creation of personas should be based on actual user studies and representations of actual end users (Baxter, Courage, and Caine 2015, 41). So, while the implied reader is a product of the structure of the text, personas are – like the implied player – the product of actual empirical users.

With this comparison in mind, we must understand the implied player thus: First of all, not as an implied player, but as *implied players*. Although hypothetical, implied players are representations of actual empirical players; but instead of being one or more empirical individuals, they are an amalgamation of some of the typical traits found among certain actual groups of players. Thus, the implied player is not one, but can be a collection of typical players. Implied players are players to whom the game has been tailored, a tailoring that centers on the design of affordances and rule systems that create an activity space inside which the player can execute playful agency through interacting with game mechanics. In our player-response theory, this delimitation of implied players is important because it demonstrates the importance of taking into account empirical players. And as we have pointed out, in order to understand implied players, we cannot keep the focus on the text only; we also need to understand the position of play. Despite this tailoring, they are neither empirical nor model players since the game may afford actions which were not planned in the design and which no players have actually performed.

What this means is that the implied players can never be perfectly shaped by the game, because if that happens, then the game ceases to be a game. The implied players, as such, are both the players revealed by understanding the game rules, affordances, and structures, but also the players who do not always utilize them all in the strictly planned manner. The implied players must, in order for the game to remain a game, be flawed, dependent on human impulses, and occasionally irrational and emotional. So a player-response theory is a theory of understanding game structures, which includes an understanding of the empirical player as much as the model player. We can learn all the rules of the game, but it is not a game until it is realized by a human being – that is, until it is played.

The player-response approach in practice

Where the reader-response theory looked at the implied reader almost exclusively through looking at a text's form and structure, player-response theory stresses the idea that the structure includes the empirical player. Any digital game structure makes so many assumptions about the context of the implied players that context becomes hard to ignore. First of all, there is the technological part, as digital games assume access and the ability to use a particular kind of technology. Where a book is a self-contained delivery system, in which the combination of human skill and object is all that is needed, even the simplest digital game demands an electrical power source and a particular type of machine on which to play. Then, there are also the controllers, which tend to favor people with full control of both hands, and the image, which demands decent vision, all before we have started to look at the structure and content of the particular game. However, while contextual factors are indeed central to understanding all media consumption, for games a focus on the empirical player is paramount due to the ergodicity and procedurality of games. The fact that games respond differently to different player choices as well as their game literacy stresses the fact that two instances of the same game are unlikely to ever be the same, even for the same empirical player. As the process of approaching the game as text is not mundane, we cannot ignore the material, economic, and political context within which games are consumed. The player certainly cannot ignore this aspect as she approaches the game as the investment in gaming technology is significant and will influence the availability of games, the genres, and the potential social use of any given game.

This does not mean that every single instance of analyzing a game, its form and its content, needs to start with a full analysis of the technology it is consumed on or the range of possible playstyles and how it affects the gameplay experience or the game outcome, but it means that we cannot assume that any digital game is consumed in a vacuum, where these aspects have no meaning. If nothing else, then lag, interface distortion, or the need to use emulators to make a game run on alternative technology will change how a game's structure work. If a process is meant to be quick and fluid, but ends up slow and erratic, be it due to playstyle or technical shortcomings, this changes the very structure of the game significantly. And where a hypothetical one-armed reader has few problems reading a printed book, she will need a special input device to play, which may end up either removing several features of a digital game or making them irrelevant, if it is necessary to introduce shortcuts to move beyond a point in the process. This makes it vital to look also at empirical players' responses to any given game in order to fully understand how a system creates its implied players and in order to understand how the realization of form and content takes place. We need to understand how games are played and how people feel about playing them. With the human being as an integrated part of the game, we have added a third aspect to the model of analysis: A game contains form, content, and player. All this is obviously also crucial for studying transgressive aesthetics in games, and our study looks at all the three in unison.

However, to do a game analysis using close reading from the perspective of the idea of an implied player has certain weaknesses, weaknesses that are more prominent in games compared to linear media, due to games' adaptability with regards to playstyles and the individual player's gameplay competence. First, as we take on the roles of both players and researchers, we can hardly claim that our gameplay is anywhere near the implied players' perspective. Researchers are a distinct group of players who even when they play according to the game's design are not close to neither the average nor the model player, because they often play with a particular goal in mind. Even when playing for leisure, a researcher's professional, often analytical, relationship to the medium will affect the way they experience the game. A researcher may also play for the purpose of exploring a theory, for material for a questionnaire, or for the revision or checking of certain facts to offer some non-casual reasons for research play. Further, while it is possible to examine the game's design, and on that basis identify what activities that particular design invites, we cannot know whether the design actually makes the player participate in the actions they are invited to. Aarseth's examples of transgressive gameplay that seeks to exploit the game simulation demonstrate this. This issue is also well illustrated with a reference to gamification: While proponents of gamification stress that certain kinds of game design are effective because they tap into psychological mechanisms (Linehan, Kirman, and Roche 2014), this claim is speculative as long as we know that human response is more flexible than behaviorism states. This is also why user testing for a long time has been a standard component in different areas such as advertising, market research, software development, and media research. To understand at least a minimum of the variation in how games are understood, interpreted, and interacted with, we cannot be limited to looking at what the design invites the hypothetical player to do.

For this reason, the player-response approach we are advocating implies taking into account the experiences and interpretations of other empirical players apart from ourselves for the purpose of understanding the particular games better, indicating that the *implied player* is not only a factor of the game structure, but also of the game in its many instances of play. The primary aim of the player-response perspective is not to understand players better, but to understand the games better, and since play is what realizes the games, we need to include the play experiences. In our understanding of this, games are realized as a dialogue between the text and the user. This leads to a side effect of the player-response perspective – that the approach leads to a better understanding of player practices.

References

Aarseth, Espen J. 1997. *Cybertext: Perspectives on Ergodic Literature.* Baltimore, MD: Johns Hopkins University Press.

———. 2007. "I Fought the Law: Transgressive Play and the Implied Player." In *3rd Digital Games Research Association International Conference: "Situated Play", DiGRA 2007*, 130–33. Digital Games Research Association (DIGRA). doi:10.1057/9781137429704.

Barthes, Roland. 1977. *Image—Music—Text.* New York: Hill and Wang.

Baxter, Katie, Catherine Courage, and Kelly Caine. 2015. *Understanding Your Users: A Practical Guide to User Requirements Methods, Tools, and Techniques. Second Edition.* Burlington, MA: Morgan Kaufmann.

Bogost, Ian. 2007. *Persuasive Games: The Expressive Power of Videogames.* Cambridge: MIT Press.

Booth, Wayne C. 1961. *The Rhetoric of Fiction.* Chicago, IL.: University of Chicago Press.

Bruns, Axel. 2006. "Towards Produsage: Futures for User-Led Content Production." In *Cultural Attitudes towards Communication and Technology 2006*, edited by Fay Sudweeks, Herbert Hrachovec, and Charles Ess. Tartu, Estonia. https://eprints.qut.edu.au/4863/.

Cooper, Alan. 1999. *The Inmates Are Running the Asylum.* Indianapolis, IN: Sams Publishing.

Eco, Umberto. 1979. *The Role of the Reader. Explorations in the Semiotics of Texts.* Bloomington: Indiana University Press.

Gibson, James J. 1979. *The Ecological Approach to Visual Perception.* Boston, MA: Houghton Mifflin.

Hall, Stuart. 2006. "Encoding/Decoding." In *Media and Cultural Studies: Keyworks*, edited by Meenakshi Gigi Durham and Douglas M. Kellner, 163–172. Malden, Oxford, and Carlton: Blackwell Publishing.

Iser, Wolfgang. 1978. *The Act of Reading: A Theory of Aesthetic Response.* London: Routledge and Kegan Paul.

King. 2012. *Candy Crush Saga.* King.

Linehan, Conor, Ben Kirman, and Bryan Roche. 2014. "Gamification as Behavioral Psychology." In *The Gameful Worlds: Approaches, Issues, Applications*, edited by Steffen P. Walz and Sebastian Deterding, 81–105. Cambridge, London: The MIT Press.

Mortensen, Torill Elvira. 2003. "Pleasures of the Player: Flow and Control in Online Games." *Thesis for Dr. Art, University of Bergen.*

———. 2016. "Anger, Fear, and Games: The Long Event of #GamerGate." *Games and Culture*, April, 1555412016640408-. doi:10.1177/1555412016640408.

Murray, Janet. 1997. *Hamlet on the Holodeck. The Future of Narrative in Cyberspace.* Cambridge: MIT Press.

Radway, Janice. 1984. *Reading the Romance.* Chapel Hill: The University of North Carolina Press.

Salen, Katie, and Eric Zimmerman. 2004. *Rules of Play: Game Design Fundamentals.* Cambridge: MIT Press.

Shaw, Adrienne. 2017. "Encoding and Decoding Affordances: Stuart Hall and Interactive Media Technologies." *Media, Culture & Society* 39 (4): 592–602. doi:10.1177/0163443717692741.

Sihvonen, Tanja, and Jaakko Stenros. 2018. "Queering Games, Play, and Culture through Transgressive Role-Playing Games." In *Transgression in Games and Play*, edited by Kristine Jørgensen and Faltin Karlsen, 115–129. Cambridge: MIT Press.

Stenros, Jaakko. 2015. "Playfulness, Play, and Games. A Constructionist Ludology Approach." Tampere: University of Tampere.

Waite, Arthur Edward. 2005. *The Pictorial Key to the Tarot.* Mineola, NY: Dover.

Weizenbaum, Joseph. 1964. "Eliza." Cambridge: MIT Artificial Intelligence Laboratory.

Wilhelm, Richard. 1923. *I Ching or Book of Changes.* 1989th ed. London: Arkan/Penguin.

5   Transgressive gameplay experiences

While few video games are experienced as transgressive all the time, there are many modern video games that have moments that can be experienced as transgressive. As we showed in Chapter 3, while *Hatred* (Destructive Creations 2015) is a game that all our respondents experienced as speculative and tasteless in the introductory cutscene, they found that, when playing over time, the sensation of offense diminished. The sensation of transgression was not a constant – for some it quickly disappeared, while for others it returned during certain in-game events. Also, one of the players of *Grand Theft Auto V (GTAV)* reported that at first the game was okay, but over time the racial slurs became unbearable.

Here we need to ask whether every experience of discomfort is transgressive. Distinguishing between different experiences of discomfort is difficult, and we have, due to the exploratory nature of the study, been generous in defining transgressive experiences. At the same time, our attention has been either on the moments when the players have reported a high level of discomfort, enough that it has been at the edge of making them abandon gameplay, or the moments when they, in retrospect, have pointed out that an experience has been pushing at their boundaries. This is in line with our distinction between profound transgression and transgressive aesthetics. Our focus is not on the *offense* that makes the players stop playing, but on the *aesthetics* that is pushing at their boundaries, forcing them to deal with a sense of dissonance between the desire to traverse the game and the discomfort of the experience.

An important question in our study has been to ask how players deal with transgressive game experiences. What happens to the players' sense of engagement in the game, and is the playful mindset affected in any way? What is it that makes players continue to play, even when the game content rubs them against the grain, and when do the transgressions become so profound that the players quit the game? In order to understand the potential power of transgressions in video games, we have to take a look at how players engage with games, not only by interpreting them or by issuing commands, but through *play* as activity and through a *playful* mindset. In this chapter, we will take a deeper look at player engagement and the mindset that people employ when they play, and what impact transgressions have on this mindset. We will argue that in a game context, transgressions can be moderated and become bearable for a number of reasons that all connect to the fact that the transgressive experiences happen within a ludic and also a fictional frame. This frame is an aesthetic frame, but it is also characterized by a playful mindset.

Approaching the study of how play *happens* from more than one angle gives us no definite answer about how people play their games. Instead it reveals the extreme variety of play, including the multitude of factors that can influence it. More importantly, it also reveals that how we perceive play practice will depend on the parameters we apply to the study of it. We could have looked at game genres and discussed how these can be determined by play practice as much as by content and theme, or at age groups and discussed how play practice is determined by free time, responsibilities, and social circle at different stages of life. The practice of play is endlessly flexible and will serve the individual player. Media scholar Faltin Karlsen interviewed players who invested a lot of time in their play and found that, for many of them, excessive play was something they did for a period in their life (Karlsen 2013). This indicates that the play practices of the empirical player are not firm and stagnant but alive and flexible. A player who is very serious about a game can be serious about enjoying it casually; a casual game can be played in a hardcore manner. This means that many common play practices must be described on a case-by-case basis, where each game will have player communities developing their own styles, while certain communities may change the games they play to suit their own practice.

For the study of games, it underlines the necessity of a player-based understanding of the structure, because the intentions and engagement one brings to the game significantly changes the meaning of the game even if it does not change anything else. This is why the game *Gnav* is a traditional children's game in the Nordic countries today, despite its history as a forbidden hazard game. The players, their intention, and the context in which it is played can move a game from one category to another, from one genre to another, from one legal definition to another.

The fallacy of play

Play is not a single thing that is easy to isolate. Rather, it is everything from free-form creative behavior to a choreographed ritualistic expression of movement. This makes it extraordinarily difficult to define and, oddly enough, easy to ignore. Play is ubiquitous, and often counter-productive and rebellious, which tend to lead to its being waved aside as non-serious or, at best, a distraction to break the monotony of a routine work. *Play* refers to a range of different activities, including the playing of music, participation in theatrical play, and the playing of games and with toys. Also, the word is used to denote joking, deception, and make-believe (Salen and Zimmerman 2004, 303; Schechner 2013, 91). While we *play* structured and rule-bound games, *play* alone is a free-form and more permeable activity. Roger Caillois uses the terms *ludus* and *paidia* for the play of games and free-form play, respectively (Caillois 2001, 27). In many languages, *play* denotes the activity itself, while *game* refers to the rule system or even the game object when it comes in a box. Katie Salen and Eric Zimmerman define play as "free movement within a more rigid structure" (Salen and Zimmerman 2004, 304), and argue that play is something that occurs both in opposition to and through exploring and experimenting with the rigid structures. Further, in Salen and Zimmerman's view, play can be understood as an overarching category of activities that includes games, but also as one of several essential components of games. In the following discussion, we are focusing on play as a specific activity; it is what players do when they engage with games.

Play is a word that tends to be associated with something that is harmless because it happens within the boundaries of not being "real". However, as we stated in the introductory chapter, it is a fallacy to see play as non-serious, fun, safe, and not having any consequences to life (Csikszentmihaly 1981, 14; Geertz 1973, 432–33; Jørgensen 2014; Linderoth and Mortensen 2015; Malaby 2007, 107; Montola 2010; Schechner 2013, 118–19; Stenros 2015, 72–76). Play has never been isolated from reality; on the contrary, play has always had a grain of seriousness to it. Already in 1901, philosopher Karl Groos argued that children's play involves skills necessary for survival and is therefore not separate from reality (Csikszentmihaly 1981, 14). In this sense, at the core, play reflects the sinister issue of a potential threat. Play theory pioneers Johan Huizinga and Roger Caillois showed how games and play spring out of culture and also affect culture at large (Caillois 2001; Huizinga 1955). More recently, cultural anthropologist Thomas Malaby has argued that while games and play are socially constructed to be separable from life "to some degree", he questions whether there is a strong boundary between play and ordinary life (Malaby 2007, 109). Also, in their research on hard-core gamers, game scholars Daniel Pargman and Peter Jakobsson (Pargman and Jakobsson 2008) found that it is difficult to conceive of a clear absolute border between play and everyday life.

Psychologist Mihaly Csikszentmihalyi argues that play is paradoxical: Play performs socializing functions and is the origin from which cultural and social institutions are built; but at the same time, play is also supposed to be disengaged from reality. As a subset of life that is both inside and outside of everyday life, play allows us to "rehearse for the serious business of adaptation" (Csikszentmihaly 1981, 14). Performance theorist Richard Schechner takes a similar but different approach in claiming that "playing is double-edged, ambiguous, moving in several directions simultaneously" (Schechner 2013, 89). To play is at once very real and highly exploratory, and a playful situation may have sudden shifts between serious and fun. Schechner points out that the mood in a play situation may change completely and swiftly, illustrated by children's play where a child may laugh at one moment, then cry, then be angry, before abruptly shifting into laughter again. This happens not only in free-form play, but also in well-structured game situations such as sport events, where an injury to a player in the field risks collapsing the playful mood (Schechner 2013, 96). For Schechner, however, this ambiguity is not paradoxical, but an inherent characteristic of play: To engage in play means to put oneself at a certain risk, either emotionally or physically, and it is a central feature of play that ties in with its creative and exploratory aspects. Play is not interesting unless it can explore its own boundaries, or as Jonas Linderoth and Torill Elvira Mortensen state, play is "something precarious, a balance that needs to be maintained unbroken but at the same time needs to be challenged and put at risk in order to remain interesting" (2015, 6).

This also points to the idea that there is not a long distance between play and transgression. Closely related to Clifford Geertz' description of *deep play*, which is play that involves so high stakes that it may seem unreasonable to engage in it in the first place (Geertz 1973, 454), Schechner introduces *dark play*: Play that stresses "risk, deception, and sheer thrill", and that "subverts order, dissolves frames, and breaks its own rules – so much that the playing itself is in danger of being destroyed" (Schechner 2013, 119). These are examples of what Jaakko Stenros labels *bad play*, which he defines as norm-defying play that goes against the idealized understanding of play as inherently positive (Stenros 2015, 75). He borrows the term from David Myers who describes bad play as "play that is threatening, risky, or otherwise harmful to the self and others; and play that is against the rules" (Myers 2010, 17). Bad play thus includes play practices that subvert the game rules; that disrupts other player's sense of play; and play that is potentially harmful. Bad play can be dangerous, irresponsible, taboo-breaking, or unsportsmanlike, and Stenros later describes such forms of play as transgressive, referring to play activities which are not always identified as play, but which may be carried out *as* play, that is, from within a playful mindset (Stenros 2018). Calling such play transgressive, Stenros also expands it to play that challenges power structures, illegal play, and taboo play (Stenros 2015, 74).

If we move on to the digital evolution of games, bad play is further exemplified through practices such as *ganking* and *griefing*, which is play in multi-player games that aim for other players' distress. When such play practices are combined with the dramatic aspects of modern game worlds that support narrative content and fictive universes, this merger opens up for complex situations where the playful exploration of the boundaries of the game mechanics interacts with character empathy and drama. This leads to play events such as the classic situation in *The Sims* (Maxis 2000) where the player kills a character by removing the swimming pool ladder to watch them drown, or the player rejects the love interest in *Dragon Age: Origins* (Bioware 2009) just for the curiosity of exploring how they react.

Having argued against the idea of play as fun, safe, and apart from life, and having established that a central characteristic of play is a form of exploration and creativity which challenges norms and the idea of what is and is not appropriate or good, we may now conclude that play does not have to be of the norm-abiding kind, and that players may often be attracted to games due to the ambiguous nature of play and the fact that it invites the exploration of the boundary between what is and what is not play. Although few players enjoy being the transgressee, the target of transgressive play; by joining play, they have agreed to a social contract that states that there is a risk of discomfort and disappointment.

Throughout this chapter, we will see how the player respondents in our study engage with transgressive game content and how their engagement challenges the idea of idealized play. The first half of the chapter discusses how player motivation, engagement, and playfulness are affected by transgressive game content. The latter part of the chapter discusses the different mitigation techniques that the player respondents employ in order to continue playing when they encounter game content that they experience as transgressive. As we will see, in many situations there is a reciprocal relationship between the transgressive content and the specific ludic mindset, and this relationship contributes to the players' interpretation of the transgressive game content and thus of the gameplay situation.

Engaging in play

A long-standing question in game studies concerns how players engage with video games. Although play is a central form of engagement, there are also a number of other motivations, player styles, and attitudes that provide a context for why people play in the first place. In game studies, researchers have developed different concepts and overviews that describe and characterize player engagement in games, spanning from game designer and scholar Richard Bartle's famous categorization of players of MUDs into the four types – *killers, achievers, socializers,* and *explorers* (Bartle 1996) – to the descriptions of experiential phenomena, such as *immersion* (Brown and Cairns 2004; Calleja 2014; Ermi and Mäyrä 2005; McMahan 2003; Murray 1997), *engrossment* (Brown and Cairns 2004; Ermi and Mäyrä 2005), *incorporation* (Calleja 2014), and *flow* (Isbister 2016; Salen and Zimmerman 2004). While Bartle's categories describe four cardinal player types that are often observed in online game environments based on whether their interests are primarily based on interacting with the game environment itself or with other players, the other concepts are attempts at grasping the deep focus and concentration that often characterize descriptions of the experience of involvement that players have with games. Another focus has been on motivations and mindsets. Psychologist and game scholar Nick Yee used Bartle as a starting point for a survey of the motivations of more than 30,000 MMORPG players (Yee 2006). For understanding the psychological foundations for play and the playful mindset, Jaakko Stenros has demonstrated the relevance of reversal theory by discussing how different playful mindsets correspond with *telic* and *paratelic metamotivational states* (Stenros 2015). Below, we will discuss engagement with games with this terminology as our point of departure, showing how it integrates with other understandings of playful involvement; at the same time, it helps illuminate player engagement with transgressive games.

The seriousness of play

Whatever we call the engagement that players experience when playing games, it is clear that it is fueled with intrinsic motivation and a high level of attention and commitment. As Jørgensen has argued elsewhere, there is always a core of seriousness in gameplay, in the sense that players need to take the social contract of play seriously (Jørgensen 2014). Engaging in gameplay thus implies that players take a sincere attitude toward the gameplay situation and indicates a willingness to submit to the frames set up by the game, regardless of whether these are open-ended, such as in free-form play, or more restrictive, such as in rule-bound games. During gameplay, players take on what Bernard Suits calls the *lusory attitude*, in which players accept restricted freedom of action for the sake of engaging in gameplay (Suits 1990, 38–39). When this mode is activated, the player takes the game seriously as a frame of reference that allows them to give value to in-game results such as failure and success. To take on this attitude is a requirement for playing and demands a certain degree of commitment, since the player cannot simply quit in the middle of the game without disrupting the game for the other players (Salen and Zimmerman 2004, 97). Although this seriousness is grounded in the gameplay situation, it often goes beyond the game itself, illustrated by the fact that gameplay often may affect the players' moods. Examples include players' becoming frustrated when they fail a challenge over and over again or when they experience other players sabotaging their strategy. When players let their frustration affect their mood outside the game, they are often accused of taking the game too seriously, but in certain contexts, players are expected to take the game situation seriously. So-called hardcore gamers are known, for instance, for their dedication to a game in that they often enjoy difficult games and invest much time and resources into playing them (Bosser and Nakatsu 2006; Juul 2010, 29). In some cases, hard core is associated with playing according to specific rules that make the game more complicated than it might otherwise be: For instance, increasing in strength through leveling but according to very specific, often self-imposed rules (Pachria 2014).

The idea that play is inherently serious is supported by reversal theory, which is a psychological theory of motivation and emotion that describes how human experience can oscillate – or reverse – between psychological states (Apter 2001). While traditional arousal theory stresses that as arousal levels increase, there is an experiential move from boredom to excitement, relaxation, and anxiety, reversal theory suggests that there are two paths depending on the *metamotivational state*: One *excitement-seeking* path between boredom and excitement and another, *anxiety-avoiding* path between relaxation and anxiety. The metamotivational states help us organize and interpret motivation. Central to reversal theory is the idea that these states both concern arousal and that whether or not this arousal is experienced as negative or positive – as anxiety or excitement – depends on how the individual interprets an experience. In other words, since anxiety and excitement are both forms of arousal, one can easily reverse into the other depending on the framing of a specific situation. In this sense, an activity that at one point is relaxing can easily change into boredom, and exciting activities can easily become anxiety-inducing (Apter 2001; Stenros 2015). For example, gameplay that would normally be experienced as relaxing when played for recreation may easily turn into boredom if played for work, and a suspenseful horror game may at a certain point turn from excitement to anxiety if the player does not master controllers. In other words, the fun factor can easily change into discomfort (Jørgensen 2016b). The anxiety-avoiding and the excitement-seeking metamotivational states are in reversal theory called *telic* and *paratelic* states (Apter 2001). Both are prevalent in gameplay.

The telic state

The *telic* metamotivational state is a serious, goal-oriented mindset (Svebak and Apter 1987). It comes into being when strategic thinking and long-term effects are in focus. This mindset values careful planning while avoiding arousal, risk, and anxiety (Stenros 2015; Svebak and Apter 1987). The telic mindset can be put in context with games in situations where the players' mindset and motivation are more calculated, and is oriented toward the game's goals and how to reach them in a strategically optimal manner. It is typically present when players direct their attention toward utilizing game mechanics in an optimal gameplay and can, for this reason, be associated with the playstyle of Bartle's *achiever* – players who are motivated by the possibility of acting on the game world (1996). The telic mindset is in this sense also characteristic of what Yee calls *achievement*, which cover motivations relating to advancement and progression, understanding mechanics, and competition (Yee 2007). The telic mindset is an instrumental approach to games, which according to Miguel Sicart calls for powergaming, in that players "make decisions based on strategies afforded by the game design, rather than on the moral meaning of their actions" (Sicart

2013, 31). Sicart's view illustrates quite precisely the experiences that the Polish student "Stan" (27) had with *This War of Mine*. He explains how he devasted when he found himself in a situation where he had to choose between robbing an elderly couple or starving his own household. In the end, he found himself playing to win:

> What happened from time to time, that… when I started I was pretty much cool as a person and I was sometimes choosing stupid decisions, but the more I played, the often I made decision, I actually noticed how to survive the game and how to think really tactically and strategically.
>
> (Individual interview, Oct 14, 2016)

"Stan's" experience shows how the telic metamotivational state may draw the player's attention toward the game mechanical aspects of the game and away from the fictional context, in line with what game researcher Anders Frank calls *gamer mode* (Frank 2012). Gamer mode is a mindset in which the player looks at the game as something that can be learned, mastered, and won. In gamer mode, the player focuses on the structure of the game – its rules, affordances, restrictions, and rhythm. These include mastering the technology, scoring points, beating timed play sessions, acquiring the right equipment, and learning the best strategies. Gamer mode allows the player to focus on the ludic aspects of a game while ignoring or disengaging with the fictional representation (Frank 2012). In this sense, the game becomes rules rather than context. Games are generally utilizing a combination of fictional and ludic elements to communicate game mechanics and the goals of the game, but gamer mode makes the fiction of the game fade into the background, and the player will focus on the more technical aspects of play.

The paratelic state

Intrinsically motivated, the *paratelic* state of mind is, in contrast to the telic, characterized by being oriented toward the present time, with an "emphasis on immediate gratification, emphasis on process, passion, spontaneity, freedom, willingness to experiment, disposition towards make-believe, and the tendency to prolong the activity if possible" (Stenros 2015, 66–67). Further, it is innate to the player and characterized by being its own goal: This goal is to maintain this mindset rather than be concerned with long-term consequences. While it can be activated in an instant, it may also change over time and also disappear spontaneously, and its presence in the moment makes it fragile. Stenros equals the paratelic metamotivational state with *playfulness*, and points out the importance of separating between *playfulness* as a mindset and *play* as an activity (Stenros 2015, 77). Although the division is purely analytical since the two are, in reality, closely intertwined, the differentiation is important because it highlights the social fact that we may sometimes engage in gameplay even when not in a playful mindset as well as how playful behavior can be performed in non-game situations (Salen and Zimmerman 2004, 303). Further, reversal theory also postulates that when people are in the excitement-seeking or paratelic metamotivational state, we experience a protective psychological frame: It is a frame that allows us to acknowledge the risks and possibilities of danger at the same time as we *feel* safe, regardless of whether or not we are actually safe (Apter 1992, 25–27). This sense of safety is what allows us to experience dangerous or uncomfortable experiences in terms of excitement rather than anxiety.

For transgressive games, the paratelic metamotivational state is of particular interest because of this protective psychological frame: It invites players to explore situations that would feel unsafe and uncomfortable outside of this mindset. This helps us understand why some people engage in BASE jumping and other playful endeavors that are actually dangerous. However, the protective frame also opens up for connecting playfulness with fictional engagement, something which is already indicated in that make-believe is a characteristic of the paratelic mindset. While appreciators of fiction are not in any real danger of the events they are witnessing or enacting, they are in a situation of make-believe where they are actively entering a mindset where they pretend to believe that this is real in the context of the staged situation (Jørgensen 2016a, 92). In other words, fiction allows us to engage in situations that would be dangerous and unsafe in real life, but knowing that we are safe makes it possible for us to endure it. The balance between the safe and unsafe is central for the paratelic metamotivational state and is also central in connecting play and fiction.

From paratelic to parapathic

Make-believe is in video games often described in terms of *immersion*, a term used to indicate an absorption into the game, a sense of feeling lost within the experience. In Yee's terminology, *immersion* concerns a player interest in discovering the gameworld, role-playing, character customization, and escapism (Yee 2007). This form of engagement that invites the player to use their imagination and enjoy the fantasy of the game is what Laura Ermi and Frans Mäyrä call *imaginative immersion* (Ermi and Mäyrä 2005). For them, this is the kind of involvement in which the player becomes absorbed in the story and fiction of the game and begins to feel empathy or identify with the game's protagonist. Imaginative immersion is important for a sense of transgression because when players become closely involved with the game's fiction, narrative, and characters, what happens in the game will feel more personal for the player and have more emotional impact. Character involvement and a well-built narrative are central to imaginative immersion and contribute to an increased sense of seriousness. This is illustrated by "Tony", who in one of the focus groups explains why he does not feel that the infamous torture scene in *GTAV* is impactful:

> But if the sequence in GTA included a character you had a relationship to, and that you had become familiar with, then I think it would have had much greater impact, but in this situation it is just some poor bastard who gets it from Trevor. (...) Because when you have a relationship, there's something... then it would be uncomfortable.
>
> (Focus group, Sept 28, 2015)

"Tony" explains that the game has done little to build an empathic relationship between the player and the tortured character. On the contrary, "Tony" is to a greater degree asked to root for the torturer, Trevor, which is one of the three characters with avatar status in the game. When the player has been given very little information to establish the victim as a *character* – a defined individual with a personality and a motivation – there is also little opportunity to make the player empathize with that character (Lankoski 2011; Smith 1995). "Tony" is immediately backed up by his fellow focus group participant, "Oscar", who argues that if the victim of torture was a character he had come to know well, this would allow for emotional impact and stress a critical perspective on torture (focus group, Sept 28, 2015).

Here the participants' experiences can be characterized as *parapathic*. Derived from reversal theory, Stenros uses the term *parapathic play* (Stenros 2015) to describe the kinds of play that is carried out not for its fun value, but because the activity feels meaningful and worthwhile on a different level. Parapathic emotions can be associated with horror entertainment and other forms of painful art. In their case studies of player experiences with distressing content in intentionally distressing larps, game scholars Heidi Hopeametsä (2008) and Markus Montola (2010) discuss gameplay that can be characterized as *positive negative experiences*. These are game experiences that are intense and distressing during play yet in retrospect somehow gratifying because they create new insights or experiences (Jørgensen 2014, 6–7). In revisiting Montola's original work, Montola and Holopainen (2012) discuss the positive negative experiences of extreme larps with reference to the paradox of painful art. The paradox postulates that even though people do not generally seek out painful experiences, they sometimes do seek out art experiences that they know will be painful such as fictional tragedies and other uncomfortable entertainment (Bartsch and Oliver 2011; Cupchik 2011; Oliver 2008; Oliver et al. 2016; Schramm and Wirth 2010; Smuts 2007; Tamborini et al. 2010; Zillman 1998), including video games (Oliver et al. 2016; Rogers et al. 2017). This kind of art and media content is appreciated because of its perceived emotional relevance in our lives.

Montola and Holopainen draw on the example of the free-form larp *Gang Rape* (Wrigstad 2007), which stages a gang rape where one player takes the role of the victim while the rest are offenders. Having played the game, the players reported strong negative reactions to the gameplay itself, suffering from physical as well as psychological reactions to the game, relating to the cognitive dissonance caused by performing an action that differs radically from their typical, or normal, activities (2012). With reference to the paradox of painful art, Montola and Holopainen argue that *Gang Rape* players are willing to endure the distress of such games because they know the novel but painful experience will give them complex, challenging stimuli that are desirable in themselves. Further, they stress that experiencing this in a fictional situation is relevant. While philosopher Aaron Smuts suggests that painful situations are easier to tackle in art and fiction because one is safe from the consequences (Smuts 2007), for Montola and Holopainen, it is more complicated. For one, the experience can be more intense than in a real-life situation due to the way stories can compress and exaggerate. Further, with reference to Joseph Carroll and Lisa Zunshine, they suggest that fiction can train us in empathy and other social skills, thereby giving a better understanding of "what we are as human beings" (2012, 27). In conclusion, the discomfort that players feel when playing such games is often experienced not as pleasurable but as rewarding, and the situation becomes manageable for the players because it takes place inside the safe setting of a fictional and playful frame.

Dealing with transgressive game content

Although the playing of video games never includes the same kind of risk that race car drivers or BASE jumpers face, we have seen that excitement-seeking video game players may have an interest in exploring the boundaries of a particular game or of their fellow players. In video games, the paratelic metamotivational state also covers the desire to perform actions and elicit behavior that one cannot do in real life. Further, the sense of safety that games and play can create, and which is further emphasized through the fictional aspects of modern video games, also allows players to endure more than they would in real-world situations. In other words, what is transgressive in other situations may not feel transgressive when experienced in a video game.

However, there are situations where the participants in our study find that the protective psychological frame threatens to break due to the high discomfort they experience when they engage with transgressive game content. In those cases, players may quit playing the game, or they may use *mitigating techniques* to keep on playing. In the following, we will present four mitigation techniques employed by the player participants and discuss how they integrate with the telic and paratelic mindset. These techniques are: (1) Activating gamer mode, (2) interpreting the discomfort as meaningful, (3) framing the transgressive content as absurd, exaggerated, and humorous, and (4) distracting oneself.

Activating gamer mode

The first mitigation technique involves an activation of *gamer mode*. As Frank's description of gamer mode suggests, entering this mindset means setting the fictional context of the game aside and focusing on the instrumental parts of gameplay. Activating gamer mode indicates that the player redirects their mindset from the paratelic to the telic metamotivational state – from an excitement-seeking to an excitement-avoiding mindset. Thus, activating gamer mode can be used to mitigate the emotional discomfort of game content by taking control over the gameplay situation and ignoring what it represents. It is a redirection of attention from content to form. This strategy was observed in gameplay journals relating to all the games in our study, although to a varying degree and with varying effect on how the game consequently was experienced. Some participants consciously activated gamer mode as a mitigation strategy. In such cases, gamer mode was often experienced as having a positive effect on the player's continued interest in the game. Other participants, however, find that gamer mode is something that they gradually adopt during the process of gameplay. We observe that this tends to be experienced as having negative effect on the game experience in our study.

A participant that actively enters gamer mode in order to mitigate the sense of transgression is the Norwegian distribution associate "Norah" (35). She describes herself as a player who often reflects on the representations of video games but realizes during the journal logging period that *GTAV* is not easily enjoyable if she approaches the fiction with a critical mind. Instead, she actively pursues gamer mode and writes in her third gameplay journal that she "didn't reflect much on stealing or shooting in today's session, I was more interested in having fun" (gameplay log, Jan 18, 2016). When asked to elaborate in the interview, she explained that rather than creating a character to play:

> I just brushed off the story and the mission, and just.... kind of went in full speed. And that was it. You could say that I let go of the story. (...) Now I just put that completely aside, and I thought that was much more fun, actually.
>
> (Interview, Mar 1, 2017)

For "Norah", consciously pursuing gamer mode is a way to mitigate or ignore what the fictional representations of *GTAV* means, and through this technique, she is able to avoid feeling disturbed by the content, but instead enjoy the game just for its ludic content. The American consumer market researcher "Sally" (26) also had a similar experience with *GTAV*, although for her it is not a deliberate reframing of the game but a mental process that happened over time. In the gameplay journal, she writes:

> As I'm getting further into the game - I've noticed that I'm caring less and less about following "real" life rules about driving, etiquette whatever...the game doesn't punish me for it and the satirical nature of the whole game makes it feel more acceptable to drive like a maniac. Kinda fun actually.
>
> (Gameplay journal, Jan 8, 2017)

Participants playing *Hatred* reported similar – intentional and unintentional – mental processes toward gamer mode. While all three respondents who completed their journals initially reported finding the game's theme and actions to be uncomfortable and even repulsive, they found that the sense of transgression wore off after a time and what remained was focus on game progression and overcoming challenges. One who actively seeks out gamer mode as a way to mitigate his discomfort is the Dutch student "Brian" (19). In his gameplay log, he writes: "I feel like I've grown numb about killing people in the game. It doesn't really matter to me anymore with the excuse in my head that it's just a game" (gameplay log, October 1, 2017). In the follow-up interview, he explains, "I just did what I had to do, in order to complete the objective. So I forgot about the whole aesthetics of the game as a whole" (Interview, October 13, 2016). Not unlike "Norah", for "Brian" entering gamer mode allows him to continue playing a game despite what he considers highly problematic representational content. Although gamer mode enables "Brian" to continue playing the game, in the interview he elaborates that "it felt wrong to feel indifferent about it". While gamer mode here mitigated the sense of transgression, it did not change gameplay into something enjoyable, nor did it stop him from reflecting on the morals of his actions.

However, while "Brian" consciously engaged in gamer mode when playing *Hatred*, the Polish game designer "Keith" (29) adopted gamer mode gradually. He states: "I felt bad for playing the game, but it loses its edge very quickly and you're able to abstract it so that the mechanics start playing the first fiddle" (gameplay log, Sept 19, 2016). Describing himself as "desensitized", entering gamer mode is not something he does consciously. Instead, over time it becomes the preferred way of engaging with the game.

The anti-war game *This War of Mine* (11 bit studios and War Child 2014) is another game in which gamer mode emerges during gameplay, not as a conscious strategy on the part of the player. Instead gamer mode is here as a result of experiences the respondents consider to be based in weak game design. "Leon" (39), a Lithuanian photographer, finds that the game's design stresses the ludic aspects over the fictional and that the game mechanics get in the way of any emotional impact that the fiction could have provided. In his first journal entry, he writes that "this game paints a picture of war that is somehow dissociated – the characters feel like Tamagotchi that will die if you do not feed them" (gameplay journal, Sept 9, 2016). According to "Leon", *This War of Mine* is balanced in favor of gamer mode, and this is something that diminishes the game experience because it trivializes an important and serious message. In this sense, his response to gamer mode in *This War of Mine* is similar to that which "Brian" experiences when playing *Hatred*.

We also see that entering gamer mode explicitly mitigates the suspense that the respondents experience when playing the horror game *Alien: Isolation* (Creative Assembly 2014). Three out of the five participants playing the game describe how the suspense is lifted once they learn the monster's movement pattern. According to "David" (27), this understanding makes the game into a puzzle that can be solved rather than an unpredictable situation of which he had no control (Interview, Nov 3, 2016). The sense of discomfort made it easier to continue the game, but in the long run, it also led to boredom and repetitiveness. For the Polish graphic designer "Mel" (26), the sense of immersion into the fictional situation was broken when she figured out the game mechanics. In the interview, she explains:

> After the sequence [that] I had to repeat so many times, I started to see these gameplay patterns, gameplay mechanics. The immersion was really broken for me in this sequence. (…) In this case, it was really clear that no matter what I do, those people will always do the same thing, in the same order.
>
> (Interview, Sept 11, 2016)

The insight into the fact that the at first seemingly unbeatable alien somehow can be figured out changed Mel's focus and allowed her to activate a telic state of mind.

However, neither "David" nor "Mel" actively seek out gamer mode in order to be able to endure discomfort; on the contrary, the telic gamer mode emerges as they gradually understand the movement patterns of the monster and how the game mechanisms work. This takes the edge off a suspenseful game experience, not only with the consequence of making the game feel less scary, but also of making the game feel less interesting.

Meaningful discomfort

The second mitigation technique concerns interpreting the transgressive content as meaningful to the gameplay situation. As discussed above, painful art can be appreciated because it is experienced as being a relevant life experience. As modern video games also are important narrative media, video games have the potential for expressing such experiences. Following the idea that imaginative immersion is related to a paratelic metamotivational state, we may say that attraction toward uncomfortable narrative experiences in a game context is excitement-seeking and that it has an important aesthetic component. For many of the participants in both the focus group and gameplay journal studies, game content that is painful, provocative, or excessive is experienced as endurable in situations where the sense of discomfort is experienced as meaningful or rewarding. These are situations in which the content was seen as meaningfully integrated into the in-game context, and it made the players reflect (Jørgensen 2018, 2016b). Below, we will see how this also seems to be the case for participants playing *This War of Mine, Beyond: Two Souls,* and *Alien: Isolation.*

In our studies, "Stan" describes meaningful discomfort in *This War of Mine.* He states that he "loves the game" for its treatment of difficult ethical situations and describes several situations that he finds to be emotionally shocking or difficult. When asked in the interview about what he likes about the game, he explains that "I pretty much like the heavy climate. Because I am a fan of heavy imagery and it makes me think a lot" (Interview, Oct 16, 2016). The game's bleak presentation of the negative consequences on civilians of war has an emotional impact on "Stan", sometimes to the degree that he feels the need to quit the game for the day. He explains:

> Because when I play heavy games, sometimes I get emotions skyrocket up or skyrocket down, down bottom. And when it's really down bottom I really want to quit the day, and go to bed and dream a lot.
>
> (Interview, Oct 16, 2016)

Although the sense of meaningfulness enabled him to continue playing the game through a number of harrowing events through seven sessions, in the end it is the game's depressive nature that made him quit. This suggests that there is a limit to how long the sense of meaningfulness may mitigate the sense of transgression in games.

While "Stan" does not explain what it is about this heavy imagery that resonates particularly well with him, a respondent who does is "Penny", a 23-year-old student from Turkey. She describes her experience with *Beyond: Two Souls* as a similar meaningfully uncomfortable game experience. She explains: "I really like the story, it's really dark, but in the way it's also quite relatable. (...) I also like the way you make decisions yourself. So, it's really makes you think about a lot of things" (Interview, November 16, 2016). She elaborates that how the game focuses on unforeseeable consequences was important for the impact that the game had on her because it made her reflect over the potential consequences of her in-game actions.

The combination of relatable and the lack of transparency of the practical and emotional consequences for the characters are also important in order to engage the Finnish student "Helen" (25). She explains, "When you are (...) making the decisions for the characters, you start to reflect yourself (...), like what would I do in this situation, what is the morally right thing to do in this situation?" (Interview, Nov 16, 2016). This is in concert with the idea that games through agency and interaction may create a sense of *complicity* in the player (Jørgensen 2016b; Sicart 2013; Smethurst and Craps 2015), that is, the feeling of responsibility for causing events in a game due to the sense of direct control over actions and an interest in keeping the avatar-protagonist alive. According to Sicart, the sense of complicity allows the player to engage with the game using moral reasoning, and "Penny" and "Helen's" experiences with *Beyond: Two Souls* also point to the idea that seeing that consequences can be more severe than expected, may be another important aspect of complicity.

A variant of the paradox of painful art is what the film scholar Noel Carroll has called the paradox of horror (1990). This paradox concerns the apparent conflict between the fact that people normally would not subject themselves to discomfort, but horror fiction remains a very popular genre. Horror fiction is not for everyone, however. There appears to be a difference between people who avoid the genre because of the high suspense that it creates and people who seek such fiction because of it, or perhaps between people who find this kind of suspense emotionally transgressive and those who do not. Playing *Alien: Isolation* in the game journal study, the Polish student "Paul" (22) is one of those who are attracted to the genre. He describes a high level of suspense, which he characterizes as pleasant:

> It's a pleasant feeling, when the adrenaline goes up, the fear of not knowing what's behind the next corner, and the thing that you can maybe push it a little bit more and finish off the game, against all of the problems and fears that you face.
>
> (Interview, Nov 1, 2016)

While "Paul" finds the game to be suspenseful, he describes this as a positive sensation. It may appear that he is attracted to the game due to the combination of the suspense that the drama introduces, with the fact that he must overcome the suspense and take control over the situation in order to make progress in the game. Contrary to other horror media where the media user can only watch as the drama unfolds on the screen, in this game, he is also responsible for resolving the situation himself. He cannot hide behind closed eyes until the Alien disappears. This provides an extra thrill but also a sense of control over the situation. For "Paul", it appears that it is the combination of these factors that puts the game outside a form of discomfort that would have made him quit.

Absurdity, exaggeration, and humor

The third mitigation technique concerns a reading of the game through a lens of absurdity, exaggeration, and humor. Psychology has long known humor to have a stress-relieving function (Martin 1996), and research on humor and social interaction has postulated that humor in certain situations may lower conflict levels (Norrick and Spitz 2008). This is also in line with Goffman's frame analysis that shows how humor can work as a key to reframe social interaction and give it a new meaning (Goffman 1974). Game scholar Christopher Paul also argues that humor can mitigate the disgust of violence in games such as *GTA* as it redirects the reaction by reframing the experience (Paul 2012). In our studies, players experienced that otherwise transgressive or overwhelming game content would be moderated in situations where this content was presented in an exaggerated, humorous, or absurd context. When the in-game representations are exaggerated, they may lead to a sense of absurdity and even humor that stops the players from seeing the situations as a serious attempt of realistic representation, thereby also putting overwhelming or excessive content into an excitement-seeking paratelic frame. This was particularly evident in relation to *GTAV* and *Hatred*. An example is when the respondents were unable to take *Hatred* seriously due to its exaggerated style and excessive violence. In one of the focus group interviews, the Norwegian skilled worker "Aron" (35) described *Hatred* as "so absurd, you can't do anything but laugh at the supposed mass murderer". Thus, he finds the game to be so excessively extreme that it becomes totally unrealistic, and impossible to take seriously (focus group interview, September 28, 2015). "Aron" also points to the game's splatter rhetoric associated with the fact that the player can kick his victims' skulls in as an example of an aesthetic that borders into the absurd. The way *Hatred* plays with splatter genre conventions removes any sense of discomfort for "Aron", where more moderate representations could have preserved it. This response suggests that exaggerated violence creates a degree of desensitization and lessened emotional impact by the outrageous acts represented in the game (Brockmyer 2015; Funk et al. 2004), but it could also be read as an example of aesthetic distance (Cupchik 2002) relating to the genre conventions known from certain genres.

Actively attempting to frame actions in a humorous way can also help mitigate the discomfort of excessive violence. In one of the focus groups, the Norwegian game designer "Mary" (25) is critical toward *GTAV*, and she did not find the humor and attempts of satire to be successful. However, she still finds that the humorous context surrounding the game's torture scene somehow mitigates her discomfort:

> What I think is really strange about this scene is that they have tried to make it humorous at some points. (...) In a way, it does make it a little less nasty because it becomes more absurd. In a way this weakens it [the discomfort] somewhat. (...) [But] I still find it gross.
>
> (Focus group interview, October 16, 2015)

"Mary" recognizes but does not accept the attempts of humor and its ability to subdue the discomfort and sanitize the violence. Here, the sense of absurdity contributed to making the scene feel less representative of actual torture. This can be seen in context with research that indicates that psychological distance may help transform negative experiences into amusing and humoristic experiences (McGraw and Warren 2010).

Distraction

The last mitigation technique we have identified concerns how the players distract themselves to be able to deal with the transgression. Distracting oneself, or cognitively and emotionally reorienting away from the transgressive game content, is a strategy that may take the player out of the immersion or flow of the game. As a mitigation technique, this is associated with a telic metamotivational state in which the participants have sought to avoid anxiety and maintain control over the ludic situation. This mitigation technique is in particular evident for the players participating in the *Alien: Isolation* (Creative Assembly 2014) game journal study. The Hungarian recent graduate "David" (27) is not a fan of the horror genre and soon found that the game's suspense level moved into discomfort. In order to be able to continue playing the game, however, he employed a range of techniques to mitigate the suspense. In the interview, he describes his mitigation techniques in closer detail:

> It was the map consulting, or looking at the items, and stuff like that. Sometimes I was just starting to chat with somebody on the phone while playing; sometimes I took a deliberative break, like a full-out break, and just looked at stuff on the Internet, while the game played in the background. So it wasn't my intention to stop the game, just... I think there was a few occasions where I even pulled up a walkthrough, actually. Because I was trying to find out what's happening, so I tried to sort of mitigating my fears by getting a peek of what's gonna happen, and how I should proceed without being in real danger. So, that was a bit of cheating there. So, I think these were the main stuff. [But] I didn't put on music, or something like that. (...) [However,] I did light up all the lights in my room when I was playing at night. So, I was trying to make it more comfortable. (...)
>
> (Interview, November 3, 2016)

Other kinds of diversions, or conscious reorientations, were observed in the live-action role-playing game that were designed and organized as part of the project (Bjørkelo and Jørgensen 2018). Here, certain participants engaged in in-character activities to ease the mood in situations that were observably uncomfortable for participants. Through giving each other support, sharing in-character stories, and joking, the players used socializing techniques used in everyday situations to mitigate an otherwise uncomfortable situation (Dormann and Biddle 2009).

From engagement to emotion

In this chapter, we have discussed how players engage with games in the light of game content that they experience as transgressive. Following the argument that games and play are inherently serious in a number of ways, we have postulated that it is a fallacy to see play as fun and safe, and we argue that this is an idealized understanding that is not in line with actual play practices, nor with how modern video games operate. While play is at the core serious because the player must take a sincere attitude toward the play activity, we have also argued that aspects relating to both the telic and the paratelic mindset contribute to the seriousness of play: The telic mindset is itself characterized by strategy and careful planning, while the paratelic mindset invites imaginative immersion, which again can be a platform for the meaningful discomfort of painful art. We have also discussed in-game situations where players experience game content as transgressive, but still manage to keep playing due to the employment of certain mitigation techniques. In the coming chapter, we are asking how players deal with transgressive game content emotionally and how this experience can be understood as an aesthetic experience.

References

11 bit studios, and War Child. 2014. *This War of Mine*. 11 bit studios.
Apter, Michael J. 1992. *The Dangerous Edge: The Psychology of Excitement*. New York: The Free Press.
———. 2001. "An Introduction to Reversal Theory." In *Motivational Styles in Everyday Life: A Guide to Reversal Theory*, 373. Washington, DC: American Psychological Association.
Bartle, Richard. 1996. "Hearts, Clubs, Diamonds, Spades. Players Who Suit MUDS." *Journal of Virtual Environments* 1 (1). https://mud.co.uk/richard/hcds. htm.
Bartsch, Anne, and Mary Beth Oliver. 2011. "Making Sense of Entertainment." *Journal of Media Psychology* 23 (1): 12–17. doi:10.1027/1864-1105/a000026.
Bioware. 2009. *Dragon Age: Origins*. Electronic Arts.
Bjørkelo, Kristian A., and Kristine Jørgensen. 2018. "The Asylum Seekers Larp: The Positive Discomfort of Transgressive Realism." In *DiGRA Nordic '18: Proceedings of 2018 International DiGRA Nordic Conference*. www.digra.org/ digital-library/publications/the-asylum-seekers-larp-the-positive-discomfort-of-transgressive-realism/.
Bosser, Anne-Gwenn, and Ryohei Nakatsu. 2006. "Hardcore Gamers and Casual Gamers Playing Online Together." In *LNCS 4161 – Entertainment Computing – ICEC 2006 Cambridge, UK.*, edited by Richard Harper, Matthias Rauterberg, and Marco Combetto, 374–77. Berlin: Springer.

Brockmyer, Jeanne Funk. 2015. "Playing Violent Video Games and Desensitization to Violence." *Child and Adolescent Psychiatric Clinics of North America* 24 (1): 65–77. doi:10.1016/j.chc.2014.08.001.

Brown, Emily, and Paul Cairns. 2004. "A Grounded Investigation of Game Immersion." In *Extended Abstracts of the 2004 Conference on Human Factors and Computing Systems – CHI '04*, 1297. New York: ACM Press. doi:10.1145/985921.986048.

Caillois, Roger. 2001. *Man, Play and Games*. Urbana: University of Illinois Press ; Wantage: University Presses Marketing.

Calleja, Gordon. 2014. "Immersion in Virtual Worlds." In *The Oxford Handbook of Virtuality*, edited by Mark Grimshaw, 254–68. Oxford and New York: Oxford University Press.

Creative Assembly. 2014. *Alien: Isolation*. Sega.

Csikszentmihaly, Mihaly. 1981. "Some Paradoxes in the Definition of Play." In *Play in Context, (A(Ssn. for the) A(Nthropological) S(Tudy of) P(Lay) Proc. Ser. ; 5 ; 1979*, edited by Alyce Taylor Cheska, 14–26. West Point, NY: Leisure.

Cupchik, Gerald C. 2002. "The Evolution of Psychical Distance As an Aesthetic Concept." *Culture & Psychology* 8 (2): 155–87. doi:10.1177/1354067X 02008002437.

———. 2011. "The Role of Feeling in the Entertainment=Emotion Formula." *Journal of Media Psychology* 23 (1): 6–11. doi:10.1027/1864-1105/a000025.

Destructive Creations. 2015. *Hatred*. Destructive Creations. www.hatredgame.com/.

Dormann, Claire, and Robert Biddle. 2009. "A Review of Humor for Computer Games: Play, Laugh and More." *Simulation & Gaming* 40 (6): 802–24. doi:10.1177/1046878109341390.

Ermi, Laura, and Frans Mäyrä. 2005. "Fundamental Components of the Gameplay Experience: Analysing Immersion." In *Proceedings of the 2005 DiGRA International Conference: Changing Views: World in Play*. Digital Games Research Association. www.digra.org/wp-content/uploads/digital-library/06276.41516.pdf.

Frank, Anders. 2012. "Gaming the Game." *Simulation & Gaming* 43 (1): 118–32. doi:10.1177/1046878111408796.

Funk, Jeanne B, Heidi Bechtoldt Baldacci, Tracie Pasold, and Jennifer Baumgardner. 2004. "Violence Exposure in Real-Life, Video Games, Television, Movies, and the Internet: Is There Desensitization?" *Journal of Adolescence* 27 (1): 23–39. doi:10.1016/J.ADOLESCENCE.2003.10.005.

Geertz, Clifford. 1973. *The Interpretation of Cultures: Selected Essays*. New York: Basic Books.

Goffman, Erving. 1974. *Frame Analysis: An Essay on the Organization of Experience*. New York: Harper Colophon Books.

Hopeametsä, Heidi. 2008. "24 Hours in a Bomb Shelter." Edited by Markus Montola and Jaakko Stenros. Playground Worlds. 2008. https://nordiclarp.org/wiki/Playground_Worlds.

Huizinga, Johan. 1955. *Homo Ludens; A Study of the Play-Element in Culture. Humanitas, Beacon Reprints in Humanities*. Boston, MA: Beacon Press.

Isbister, Katherine. 2016. *How Games Move Us: Emotion by Design*. Cambridge: The MIT Press.

Jørgensen, Kristine. 2014. "Devil's Plaything. On the Coundary Between Playful and Serious." DiGRA Nordic '14. Proceedings of the 2014 International DiGRA Nordic Conference. 2014. www.digra.org/digital-library/publications/devils-plaything-on-the-boundary-between-playful-and-serious/.

———. 2016a. "Gameworld Interfaces as Make-Believe." In *Digital Make-Believe*, edited by Phil Turner and J. Tuomas Harviainen, 89–99. Cham: Springer.

———. 2016b. "The Positive Discomfort of Spec Ops: The Line." *Game Studies: The International Journal of Computer Game Research.* 16 (2). http://gamestudies.org/1602/articles/jorgensenkristine.

———. 2018. "When Is It Enough? Uncomfortable Game Content and the Transgression of Player Taste." In *Transgression in Games and Play*, edited by Kristine Jørgensen and Faltin Karlsen, 153–167. Cambridge: MIT Press.

Juul, Jesper. 2010. *A Casual Revolution: Reinventing Video Games and Their Players.* Cambridge: MIT Press.

Karlsen, Faltin author. 2013. *A World of Excesses; Online Games and Excessive Playing.* Wey Court East: Ashgate Publishing Limited.

Lankoski, Petri. 2011. "Player Character Engagement in Computer Games." *Games and Culture* 6 (4): 291–311. doi:10.1177/1555412010391088.

Linderoth, Jonas, and Torill Elvira Mortensen. 2015. "Dark Play: The Aesthetics of Controversial Playfulness." In *The Dark Side of Game Play: Controversial Issues in Playful Environments*, edited by Torill Elvira Mortensen, Jonas Linderoth, and Ashley M. L Brown, 3–12. London: Routledge.

Malaby, Thomas M. 2007. "Beyond Play." *Games and Culture* 2 (2): 95–113. doi:10.1177/1555412007299434.

Martin, Rod A. 1996. "The Situational Humor Response Questionnaire (SHRQ) and Coping Humor Scale (CHS): A Decade of Research Findings." *Humor: International Journal of Humor Research* 9: 251–72.

Maxis. 2000. *The Sims.* Electronic Arts.

McGraw, A. Peter, and Caleb Warren. 2010. "Benign Violations." *Psychological Science* 21 (8): 1141–49. doi:10.1177/0956797610376073.

McMahan, Alison. 2003. "Immersion, Engagement and Presence: A Method for Analysing 3-D Video Games." In *The Video Game Theory Reader*, edited by Mark J. P. Wolf and Bernard Perron, 67–86. New York, London: Routledge.

Montola, Markus. 2010. "The Positive Negative Experience in Extreme Role-Playing." In *Nordic DiGRA 2010.* Stockholm: DiGRA. www.digra.org/wp-content/uploads/digital-library/10343.56524.pdf.

Montola, Markus, and Jussi Holopainen. 2012. "First Person Audience and the Art of Painful Role-Playing." In *Immersive Gameplay: Essays on Participatory Media and Role-Playing*, edited by Evan Torner and William J. White, 13–30. Jefferson: McFarland & Company.

Murray, Janet. 1997. *Hamlet on the Holodeck. The Future of Narrative in Cyberspace.* Cambridge: MIT Press.

Myers, David. 2010. *Play Redux: The Form of Computer Games. Digitalculturebooks.* Ann Arbor: University of Michigan Press. doi:10.3998/dcbooks.7933339.0001.001.

Norrick, Neil R., and Alice Spitz. 2008. "Humor as a Resource for Mitigating Conflict in Interaction." *Journal of Pragmatics* 40 (10): 1661–86. doi:org/10.1016/j.pragma.2007.12.001.

Oliver, Mary Beth. 2008. "Tender Affective States as Predictors of Entertainment Preference." *Journal of Communication* 58 (1): 40–61. doi:10.1111/j.1460-2466.2007.00373.x.

Oliver, Mary Beth, Nicholas David Bowman, Julia K. Woolley, Ryan Rogers, Brett I. Sherrick, and Mun-Young Chung. 2016. "Video Games as Meaningful Entertainment Experiences." *Psychology of Popular Media Culture* 5 (4): 390–405. doi:10.1037/ppm0000066.

Pachria. 2014. "Hardcore Wow – World of Warcraft Forums." Blizzard – Forums – New Player Help and Guides. 2014.

Pargman, Daniel, and Peter Jakobsson. 2008. "Do You Believe in Magic? Computer Games in Everday Life." *European Journal of Cultural Studies* 11 (2). doi:10.1177/1367549407088335.

Paul, Christopher A. 2012. *Wordplay and the Discourse of Video Games: Analysing Words, Design and Play.* New York, Abingdon: Routledge.

Rogers, Ryan, Julia Woolley, Brett Sherrick, Nicholas David Bowman, and Mary Beth Oliver. 2017. "Fun Versus Meaningful Video Game Experiences: A Qualitative Analysis of User Responses." *The Computer Games Journal* 6 (1–2): 63–79. doi:10.1007/s40869-016-0029-9.

Salen, Katie, and Eric Zimmerman. 2004. *Rules of Play: Game Design Fundamentals.* Cambridge: MIT Press.

Schechner, Richard. 2013. *Performance Studies: An Introduction.* 3rd ed. London: Routledge.

Schramm, Holger, and Werner Wirth. 2010. "Exploring the Paradox of Sad-Film Enjoyment: The Role of Multiple Appraisals and Meta-Appraisals." *Poetics* 38 (3): 319–35. doi:10.1016/j.poetic.2010.03.002.

Sicart, Miguel. 2013. "Moral Dilemmas in Computer Games." *Design Issues* 29 (3): 28–37. doi:10.1162/DESI_a_00219.

Smethurst, Toby, and Stef Craps. 2015. "Playing with Trauma." *Games and Culture* 10 (3): 269–90. doi:10.1177/1555412014559306.

Smith, Murray. 1995. *Engaging Characters: Fiction, Emotion, and the Cinema.* Oxford: Oxford University Press.

Smuts, Aaron. 2007. "The Paradox of Painful Art." *Journal of Aesthetic Education* 41 (3): 59–76. doi:10.1353/jae.2007.0029.

Stenros, Jaakko. 2015. "Playfulness, Play, and Games. A Constructionist Ludology Approach." Tampere: University of Tampere.

———. 2018. "Guided by Transgression: Defying Norms as an Integral Part of Play." In *Transgression in Games and Play*, edited by Kristine Jørgensen and Faltin Karlsen, 13–25. Cambridge: MIT Press.

Suits, Bernard (Bernard Herbert). 1990. *The Grasshopper: Games, Life, and Utopia.* Boston, MA: David R. Godine.

Svebak, Sven, and Michael J. Apter. 1987. "Laughter: An Empirical Test of Some Reversal Theory Hypotheses." *Scandinavian Journal of Psychology* 28 (3): 189–98. doi:10.1111/j.1467-9450.1987.tb00755.x.

Tamborini, Ron, Nicholas David Bowman, Allison Eden, and Ashley Organ. 2010. "Defining Media Enjoyment as the Satisfaction of Intrinsic Needs." *Journal of Communication* 60 (4): 758–77. doi:10.1111/j.1460-2466.2010.01513.x.

Wrigstad, Tobias. 2007. *Gang Rape.* Self-published.

Yee, Nick. 2006. "The Demographics, Motivations, and Derived Experiences of Users of Massively Multi-User Online Graphical Environments." *Presence: Teleoperators and Virtual Environments* 15 (3). doi:10.1162/pres.15.3.309.

———. 2007. "Motivations for Play in Online Games." *Cyberpsychology & Behavior* 9 (4): 772–75. doi:10.1089/cpb.2006.9.772.

Zillman, Dolf. 1998. "Does Tragic Drama Have Redeeming Value?" *Siegener Periodikum Für Internationale Litteraturwissenschaft* 16 (1): 1–11.

6 Transgressive game content and emotional response

We consider games to be *emotion machines*: They are designed as procedural systems for the main purpose to generate sensations and emotions in players. Games have always touched us and influenced our emotions, whether we feel the joy of participation or the rage of loss. They are machines due to the many bits and pieces that need to be engaged for them to work, and the players are what powers them. This is regardless of the type of game: Analogue or digital; without a player, the game does not happen. Watching or listening to a game without participants makes no sense. Watching a game after it has been played has a certain value, but not as a game. At this point it has become a recording of an event, and it is being watched for its historical value. The game itself only exists while it is being powered by the players.

The player activates the different pieces of game machinery: She picks up the dice, unfolds the board, opens the file, chooses the character, and enters the field. Each part of a well-designed game works to drive it forwards. The arena, whether it is a football field, a game board, or a computer representation, limits the choices of the players; it outlines the outer limits of the machine. The pieces are the moving bits of the machine; they are the virtual objects in a video game, the pieces of a board game, or even the actual players in a game of football. Imagine the function and the fulfillment of the function as two separate aspects of a game piece. The function of a piece depends on its limitations and affordances. The player fulfills this function while playing the piece. For instance: In football, the goalkeeper has a function to stop the ball from entering the goal. The player who is playing the goalkeeper fulfills this function: She plays the piece she is given for the game. Either way, the piece cannot be played without a player – it cannot move itself across the field, and it cannot play itself in the computer game and remain a game.

Each piece follows the schematics of the machine, its structure. This is where we can understand what procedural rhetoric has to do with games. Procedural rhetoric interprets and encodes the structure, the path along which the player moves in the process of engaging the machine which is the game.

But what does this machine produce? Does it bring us anywhere? Sometimes this machine has very desirable outcomes, such as better health, higher skills, or stress relief. These are however by-products of the game machine. The essence of the game as emotion machine is that it produces emotion. It produces happiness, anger, frustration, elation, despair, and intense relief, and it does so quicker, more predictably, and with less effort than we habitually find in the rest of our lives. They may occur elsewhere, but rarely condensed in time as in a game. The frustration of rejection and loss, the joy of achievement, the delight at acceptance, the anger at unjust treatment – it can all be present, but it is more likely to be experienced over months or even years, not in a few short hours. But games let us feel this. We experience strong emotions with other media as well. But when we play, we feel like we do this on our own. We actively experience these sensations.

Understanding games as emotion machines are a prerequisite for understanding the emotional response to games. In this chapter, we are exploring how the players in our study respond emotionally to transgressive experiences in games.

Between discomfort and enjoyment

The players in our study offer rich examples of how game experiences oscillate between discomfort and enjoyment. In Chapter 5, we saw how the player respondents activate mitigation techniques when experiencing game situations that they oppose or find uncomfortable in order to continue playing the game. In this chapter, we will take a broader look at the emotional responses of the respondents. In one of the focus groups, "Karen", "Luke", and "Shaun" discuss experiences ranging from physical discomfort they have chosen to endure in order to keep the game running in larp situations, misunderstandings that led to transgressions of personal space, through uncomfortable realizations about the gendered expectations about violence revealed through comparing play with Nathan Drake (*Uncharted* (Naughty Dog, n.d.)) versus Lara Croft (*Tomb Raider* (Core Design, Crystal Dynamics, and Eidos Montreal 1996)), to making decisions in a digital game about supporting the suicide of a game character (focus group October 09, 2015). Other respondents discuss the emotional roller coaster they are on when playing games, as the earlier mentioned example of "Norah". Her initial response when hitting pedestrians in *GTAV* was discomfort, which later vanished as she decided to "have fun" and entered gamer mode. This again changed as she later reflected on the game and decided that she was not comfortable with the fact that *GTAV* makes entertainment out of people in poverty who act violently out of desperation (Interview, March 1, 2017). What we see very clearly through these discussions is that uncomfortable play is not simply something that players avoid at all costs but is an inherent part of much gameplay, and, in certain cases, players keep returning to it. Discomfort in play is clearly an expected, even anticipated, part of the experience, and while it may be there to be overcome or solved, it is not to be avoided. The player participants describe strong emotions and stress the importance of emotion for their play.

However, there are also uncomfortable emotions that can make players quit, such as the idiosyncratic transgressivity mentioned in Chapter 3, where "Theo" talked about *Beyond: Two Souls*, stating that he will not play a game in which a child suffers (Interview, Nov 28, 2016). Another example is described in a conversation between "Neil", "Ted", and "John" (focus group November 11, 2015). "Ted" described the group play in *World of Warcraft (WoW)* (Blizzard 2004), where one group was comprised of players from a different language zone. These players decided to express their displeasure with "Ted's" play in very loud, aggressive, limited English, blaming every failure on "Ted". The discomfort that "Ted" here experienced is not designed in the game, but the affordances of the game facilitate it, in this case the anonymous grouping system in *WoW*. Using the grouping system to find random players for challenging events is an important feature, and while it can be used to connect groups comprised of strangers, it is also often used to find a last player to supplement a set. This particular instance offered a kind of discomfort "Ted" was unable to mitigate, and the only way to avoid it was to cease playing. The group play in games such as *WoW* is already tense, technically demanding, and a challenge to the players' ability to cooperate, and many players use friendship and familiar groups to mitigate these challenges. When the aggression of a group is directed at the outsider and added to the existing tension, what we get is a situation that goes beyond the kind of emotional intensity players are looking to experience through play and into the area of profound discomfort.

What we see in our studies is that transgressive gameplay can create a range of emotions. In this chapter, we will investigate these emotional responses and how they relate to cognition as well as to cultural and social norms about acceptable game content. Although our focus is on *transgression* and not emotion, transgression works through emotion. The intent of transgression in design and in art is to strip the distanced gaze from the beholder and bring in the subjective immediate reaction. Hence, to understand transgression we do need to know something about how transgressive game experiences influence our emotional state. In this chapter, we will make a distinction between *affect* and *emotion*, where we, in short, will treat *affect* as the often intense, immediate response that people have to events, while we will use *emotion* to refer to long-term and more stable sensations that people have after having made judgments about the situation. In exploring the range of emotional responses to transgressive games, part of our discussion will concern the so-called paradox of uncomfortable fiction, or painful art, which has stirred wonder in psychological research, and we will also turn our attention to the romanticist ideal of a disinterested appreciation of art.

Flow and transgressive games

The idea of games as intensifiers of emotion resonates well with one of the more popular theories applied to how games work, namely through creating a positive sense of *flow*. Flow may not be an emotional response as such, but a mental state that dominates in situations that balance perfectly between challenge and skill. Flow is the target experience for many forms of gameplay, and it becomes heavily influenced by strongly felt emotions. In game design, *flow* is considered a goal, as we will discuss in Chapter 8.

Flow is understood by the psychologist Mihaly Csikszentmihalyi as a state of deep focus where one is intensively engaged in an activity for its own sake, sometimes to the degree where the sense of time and space disappears. Flow is associated with *autotelic* activities, which "we do for [their] own sake because to experience [them] is the main goal" (Csikszentmihalyi 1997, 117). Flow is also connected to *intrinsic motivation* (Deterding et al. 2011; Deterding 2012; Karlsen 2013, 71–75; Stenros 2015, 67–68, 201–2; Sutton-Smith 1997, 7), that is, motivation driven by inner goals, as opposed to external (or extrinsic) goals. In other words, intrinsic motivation concerns behavior that stems from an individual's personal interest or satisfaction, while extrinsic motivation arises from external factors. Games and play can also be autotelic activities that emerge from intrinsic motivation; they are often used as prime examples of flow activities, but focused work and the playing of music are also examples of activities that may create a sense of flow. Flow is not, however, mainly a recipe for fun. Other examples of flow experiences are being on the front line of the Vietnam War and criminal activities (Csikszentmihalyi 2002), neither of which would be our first idea of "fun" or "leisure". What they have in common with other autotelic experiences is they demand an absolute focus, you have been trained in the actions you need to take, you have the tools at hand, and you have a chance to overcome your challenges.

The central idea of flow is how it balances challenge and skill. This balance creates the flow channel, the narrow window of opportunity for the flow experience (Csikszentmihalyi 2002). If a challenge is higher than the skill set of the person involved, emotions such as frustration and anxiety will emerge; and if the player's skills are substantially higher than the challenge level, they will feel in control and start to relax until boredom arises (Csikszentmihalyi 1997, 31; Massimini and Carli 1988, 270). In the sweet spot, people will enter the state of flow, where nothing else matters than the activity itself. Several of Csikszentmihalyi's examples are of how people use game-like challenges to achieve a more flow-like experience or at least to avoid boredom (Csikszentmihalyi 2002). Video games typically try to facilitate flow through increasing challenges as the player gains skills and occasionally with the option to adjust the challenge level depending on the player's skill level.

Boredom and anxiety in transgressive games

Flow is essential for maintaining long-term motivation to play; players generally leave games that are too boring or too challenging. Thus, there is nothing inherently transgressive in breaking flow. However, in our studies we observe that *how* flow is broken may contribute to the sense of transgression.

In our study of gameplay journals, we observed that in the cases of *Bloodborne* (From Software 2015), *Alien: Isolation* (Creative Assembly 2014), and *Hatred* (Destructive Creations 2015), getting bored from the inability to overcome a high difficulty level was a factor that made the players quit playing the game. While some of those who claimed that boredom and apathy made them quit stated that they did not simply find the genre stimulating, most were giving the game in question a serious chance before coming to a point where they simply had had enough of it and lost the motivation to play. Common for the players who named boredom as a reason was that they played the game until it did not feel stimulating anymore because they did not have any progression or because they felt the game gave them nothing new at a particular point.

The game in our journal study that best replicates the traditional flow theory is the notoriously controversial *Hatred*, which ends up as repetitive and boring for all three participants. In Chapter 5, we discussed how "Keith" first found the game repulsive until he adapted to gamer mode. Allowing himself to focus on the game mechanics, he realizes that "the game is pretty boring and controls badly" (journal, Sept 19, 2016). At this point the mechanics did not offer any challenge, and while boredom mitigated the sense of outrage, nothing mitigated the boredom. The game grew tedious for "Keith", not only because of the waning shock value, but more importantly because the controllers and game mechanics do not provide any real challenge. While the game was transgressive to "Keith" in the initial phase, the discomfort disappeared as the experience became more and more dominated by boredom.

Comparatively, boredom emerged from different aspects in the horror game *Alien: Isolation*. Four out of the five participants who played *Alien: Isolation* found it to be exciting and scary at first – one even experienced a degree of anxiety that was almost game-breaking. But what made these players actually quit playing was the experience of boredom that emerged after they familiarized themselves with game mechanics, and the plot took a turn to the less scary. According to the Hungarian recent graduate "David" (27), as soon as he got the most efficient weapon, the game became boring: "I got this flamethrower, so the Alien wasn't that much of a threat anymore, because I could just shoot some flame at him and run away" (Interview, November 3, 2016).

This boredom related to *Alien: Isolation* was not however something "David" experienced all through the game. At the start, the game was unfamiliar and he felt an immediate stress due to not having full control of the game mechanics. In terms of flow, the challenge was very high, and the mastery was low; a situation that invites a high level of tension and fear, not just of the horrors in the content but of failure. While "David's" comment at first glance matches the flow theory balance of boredom and challenge, the full interview tells a somewhat different story. The overwhelming aspect of play in *Alien: Isolation* that "David" reports is not simply connected to unfamiliar game mechanics, but also to the seeming invincibility of the alien monster. While many games allow the player a mastery over the game mechanics and therefore also safety through tools, "David's" initial response to *Alien: Isolation* was to be overwhelmed by an enemy he could not subdue. When he realized there were ways to avoid and even pacify the monster, the suspense and thrill disappeared and turned into boredom. For "David" the game was only scary, approaching transgressive, for as long as he felt a lack of control and understanding of the situation.

A central principle for flow is the balance between challenges and skills. But what happens when an experience neither provides challenge nor demands any skills? While boredom still requires that the individual executes a certain kind of skill even though the task is no longer challenging, flow researchers argue that when neither challenge nor skill is present, the experience of *apathy* may easily emerge (Csikszentmihalyi 1997, 31; Massimini and Carli 1988, 270). It is thus reasonable to assume that for "David" and "Keith", what makes them quit is apathy. Apathy is also part of the reason why many of the *Bloodborne* players quit. This is interesting because four out of the five players found the high difficulty level of this game to be extremely challenging. They experienced anxiety over not being able to overcome the challenges to progress in the game. What created apathy, however, was the monotony connected to replaying the same levels over and over again. The game is relentless in its unforgiving gameplay with little room for mistake.

While three of these respondents said that they quit the game because they got bored by repeatedly dying, the Polish student "Henry" (25) on the contrary found the tension rising and decided in the end to quit as the balance shifted to anxiety:

> Annoyed, frustrated. Every time I tried to log into the game, I was thinking to myself okay, it can't be that hard this time. I was planning the strategy, for example during the day before I played; how to manage this level. But the reality showed me differently. It was just difficult to play. I know that people spend a lot of time with that game, but after two hours of dying at one point I couldn't. (…) [I] usually don't give up

very fast, and I am not sure why I did give up. I think that it was driving me mad, and one time… Seriously, normally I am a calm person, but I was screaming.

(Interview, October 18, 2016)

"Henry's" high degree of frustration with the game was completely different from what he expected. While he had expected a hack and slash action-RPG, he got a game that for him was "unplayable". To "Henry", *Bloodborne's* transgression is to be relentless to the degree that it provokes a strong, affective response that is unusual for him. In other words, the game is transgressive because it elicits strong and unexpected emotions in "Henry". *Bloodborne* is in this case a game where the flow channel is optimized for players with high tolerance for failure and specific player competencies. Players that do not fall into this category may easily find the game to create a high level of frustration. But the respondents did not feel that the games became boring because of the lack of challenge; they were bored or apathic by repeatedly dying and experiencing no progress.

So far in our examples of flow and transgressive games, we have seen that while there is no direct link between flow and transgression, the sense of transgression does interact with and can potentially alter the flow experience. "Keith" experiences transgression in the immediate shock effect created by *Hatred*, but the sensation wore off and eventually turned to boredom as the game stopped being interesting on a gameplay level. Similarly, "David" experienced transgression through the high level of suspense of *Alien: Isolation*, but it waned when he felt in control of the situation. "Henry", on the other hand, quit after he experienced a frustration with *Bloodborne's* rising challenge that he found transgressive.

Further, it is also essential that the experience of transgression that "Keith" had with *Hatred* concerned the fictional context of the game, while "David" and "Henry" experienced a sense of transgression related to gameplay. What disturbed "Keith" was not connected to the challenge of the game, but to the fictional framing of the protagonist and avatar as a sociopathic killer. This is an example of what we discussed in Chapter 2 as *diegetic transgressivity*. However, what made "David" and "Henry" uneasy is related to lack of balance between challenge and skill. We can therefore associate "David" and "Henry's" experiences with what was referred to in Chapter 2 as *ludic transgressivity*.

Transgressive games beyond flow

The example of "Keith" shows that in certain transgressive video games, challenge and skill are not central in creating a sense of transgression because the transgressive aspects are grounded in the game's fiction. In other words, while flow concerns a game's form, the sense of transgression often stems from a game's content. In such cases, the sense of transgression may still create similar emotions as those that emerge when flow breaks. While flow is a particular kind of state that concerns the sweet spot between skill and challenge, in video games, which are characterized by a unique combination of game and fiction, flow is also closely related to other kinds of involvement, such as imaginative immersion (see Chapter 5). This means that emotions relating to anxiety, boredom, and apathy may also emerge from cases of diegetic transgressivity.

In the following, we will discuss how the player participants in our studies experience situations in which fiction was essential for their sense of transgression and thus made them stop playing. These issues are emotions that lead to a *disconnect*, which refers to a sense of disengagement relating to a lack of recognizable situations, and *antipathy*, which refers to content that breaks with one's personal sensibilities or is experienced as offensive.

Disconnect

Like Jørgensen has discussed elsewhere (Jørgensen 2018), another factor that made the respondents in the study stop playing was a sense of detachment or distancing, in the sense that they feel that the game is not able to connect with them on the level of character empathy and narrative involvement. We call this kind of detachment a *disconnect*, and would like to stress that this kind of distancing or detachment separates itself from the "disinterestedness" that Immanuel Kant claims is defining for aesthetic appreciation. As we will discuss at length in Chapter 8, Kant's disinterestedness involves contemplatively appreciating the work of art objectively and without emotion (Cashell 2009, 5), but what the player participants here are experiencing is a sense of disruption that threatens to break the ability to engage with the work. While Kieran Cashell claims that provocative art can never be disinterested because of the emotional response it evokes (2009, 8), such provocations may alienate the player and prevent full involvement with the game. In this sense, the disconnect that the player participants refer to is more closely related to the estrangement effect, introduced as *Verfremdungseffect* by Bertolt Brecht, since it concerns how the game content hinders the player from identifying with the characters and actions in game and makes the audience aware of the communicative process (Brecht 1964, 151). However, for the respondents in the study, this estrangement is independent of the intention of the game designers to create such an effect. While related to apathy in the sense that it hinders engagement and an intrinsic motivation to continue playing, the sense of disconnect separates itself from apathy by being connected to the specific feeling that one is not the target group of a particular message or the content does not address issues that the particular player may identify or engage with. In other words, it has little to do with challenges and skill.

The British student "Bridget" (21) was initially excited to play *GTAV* (Rockstar North 2013), but ended up only playing the game three times over the course of the journaling month. She described that her dislike for the stereotypes of gender and race were wearing on her, although it was the dislike for the characters and storyline that made her stop:

> Honestly, I just couldn't play it anymore. As much as I liked some of the small aspects (like the stealth missions, the character swapping and creation). I hated the storyline, I didn't like the characters and it wasn't captivating enough for me to be able to push past that.
>
> (Interview, February 9, 2016)

The inability to feel involved in the narrative and characters of a game is important for a sense of detachment. "Bridget" is echoed by "Mary":

> My problem with all GTA games is that you basically play a psychopath. But in a way he is played as a good guy. (...) And that, kind of, falls to the ground. (...) It's so ridiculous and stupid. Like they're trying to sell you this character as one you would want to play, want to identify with, while he actually is quite unsympathetic, really.
>
> (Focus group, October 16, 2015)

For both of these respondents, what made them give up on play did not concern the game mechanics or the actions the game made them perform. What they rejected, and what made the game unplayable for them, was the fiction. "Bridget" and "Mary" both stress that in order to keep engaging with the game, they need to experience a sense of connection, but their negative emotions stopped them from playing. Game narratives, rather than being irrelevant decorations on top of more or less functioning systems, have this influence on players and their playstyles. This reflects an earlier study of playstyles and moral conflicts in games, where Mortensen has documented how this kind of dissonance with the storyline and the character can have a strong impact on the player and the play experience (Mortensen 2015).

Antipathy

Related to diegetic transgressivity, another reason why the participants decided to stop playing was due to an *antipathy* relating to personal sensibilities, an issue that ties well into detachment above. Antipathy refers to the feeling of intense opposition or aversion to something. In this context, it can be related to *idiosyncratic transgressivity* (see Chapter 2) connected to personal preferences and interpretations, and it may also be connected to previous experiences and traumas. Personal sensibilities based in an individual's subjective responses to content are a complex issue that designers can never completely avoid. It is important to separate between situations where game content evokes subjective associations in the player rather than culturally grounded connotations. While the inclusion and exclusion of cultural connotations are dependent upon the designers' intent, they can never be able to avoid sensibilities connected to an individual's personal associations. In other words, designers are aware that the inclusion of excessive violence is likely to break with cultural norms, but whether a character's looks remind the player of their abusive father is a personal sensibility that designers have no control over. While designers obviously have a choice when including transgressive imagery, there is a limit to their control over player response.

In the case of this study, we have seen that antipathy can make players interpret the same video game content in widely different ways. *GTAV* is the game that best illustrates how the same cultural connotations create a variation of responses. Following Stuart Hall's theory on encoding and decoding (2006), which we have previously discussed, a media text is always formed by a specific socio-cultural context. Intended encodings of the message may or may not be shared by the audience who interpret and thus "decode" the content. Thus, misunderstandings as well as different interpretations become possible, and while acknowledging the author's power in creating a message, the theory also highlights the importance of subjective and individual interpretations such as subjective sensibilities.

While "Bridget" reported above that the disconnect to characters and story was the main reason why she stopped playing, as a black woman she also found the racial and sexual slurs problematic in *GTAV*. On the use of the "N-word", she explains:

> I am black so hearing it a few times didn't really bother me, I didn't like it but it didn't hurt, but it was used in almost every other sentence and it started to grate on me and the more I heard it the more uncomfortable I got. While of course black people can say it to each other, I'm not used to hearing it that much and so often, it was difficult as it's always been a racial slur to me rather than a term between friends/family.
>
> (Interview, February 9, 2017)

Although the sexism and racism of the game were pointed out by several of the participants in the focus group and game journal studies, there were also many who did not mention this as problematic. For many it appears that the humor and satire may have mitigated these issues, or at least it is something that has little apparent effect on their game experience. This is an example of how sensibilities are subjective and differs between individuals.

We have previously mentioned one example of a situation where the game content interfered with one of the participants' sensibilities on a more associative level in one of the respondents who played *Beyond: Two Souls* (Quantic Dream 2013). The Norwegian student "Theo" (23) had only filled in his game journal once when he wanted to quit. There was little in the journal that revealed why he wanted to stop, but in the interview, he explained that the game touched his personal sensibilities:

> Well, I think that in retrospect, what I kind of have been thinking as what I didn't like was kind of seeing children who suffer or who are under a lot of stress. It didn't occur to me right at once, but it kind of hit some personal notes which I thought, this is not okay, this is a line that I don't want to cross.
>
> (Interview, November 28, 2016)

The sensibility that exposing children for harm is unacceptable is something "Theo" shares with many people, and there is reason to believe that the game developers have included this for greater emotional impact. However, while other respondents in our study found the emotional impact to be meaningful in the gameplay context by adding empathy, this was what made "Theo" want to stop playing the game. This demonstrates how the same game content can be received quite differently for different players, and content that was made to create a deeper sense of meaning may be transgressive for some players.

Emotions at play

So far, we have seen that transgressive games may create an emotional tension that often can be in conflict with the flow experience. Also, while flow concerns game form, game content is often what creates a sense of transgression in players. To understand the emotional impact of transgressive games, we need to go beyond flow and look at how emotions are formed in dialogue with transgressive games.

One of the central characteristics for fiction is its ability to evoke emotions in its appreciators. Making the audience not only feel compassion and empathy for characters but also anguish, despair, and joy for the fictive situations on stage were paramount already for the drama of the ancient Greek. Traditionally, the art of persuasion through emotion has been the issues of the so-called *pathos rhetoric*. Despite its long history, the pathos of games is weakly explored. When the rhetoric of games is addressed, it tends to be explored through its procedural properties. Procedural rhetoric focuses on the idea that the algorithmic nature of rules and mechanics can be used to model processes (Bogost 2007, 28) and is less invested in the traditional types of arguments, such as pathos, logos, or ethos, and more in the persuasion inherent in the structure and progress of the game. However, one of the scholars who has taken the more traditional approach to rhetoric seriously in connection with games is Christopher Paul in *Wordplay and the Discourse of Video Games* (2012). He argues that the rhetoric of the game itself mitigates the potential transgression of the game content: "Humor may seem like a non-essential component of *GTA*, an ornamental flourish, but its impact on what we remember and how we perceive things has a tremendous impact on the rhetorical force of the series" (Paul 2012). What Paul points out here is how the story, style, and content-based play of the game change the experience and how the players feel about the game – it changes our emotions.

Two other important works discuss the emotional value of games, although without looking at the rhetoric. One is games and interaction design researcher Katherine Isbister's *How Games Move Us* (Isbister 2016), which is a discussion of how to design games for emotional impact. Mirroring one of our basic assumptions, Isbister argues that games are not a lesser medium when it comes to eliciting emotions, but that they work differently from traditional media in their ability to evoke experiences and emotions in players. What distinguishes games from traditional media is how they use game mechanisms to allow the players choices as well as a flow experience, which are central for the ability of games to create empathy and connection. In *Playing with Feelings: Video Games and Affect* (2018), games and new media scholar Aubrey Anable approaches games as a medium and how they affect us, focusing on games as such rather than play. Investigating the relationship between video games and affect, she argues that video games do not only engage with us on an emotional level; affect also connects the cultural, historical, and political context of games. Thus, it becomes important to consider what impact emotion and affect have on game preferences and perceptions. She claims that "[v]ideo games—as media objects, as cultural practices, and as structures of feeling—can tell us quite a bit about the collective desires, fears, and rhythms of everyday life in our precarious, networked, and procedurally generated world" (Anable 2018). Further, Anable argues that game studies in its focus on game mechanics and computation has become poorly equipped for considering how emotion and affect impact gameplay. The lack of discussions of emotion in games may also be connected to the difficulty of documentation that follows the ephemeral nature of play. Also, the reluctance to talk about emotion in games may also be connected to the ideal of maintaining a certain analytical distance from the object of study that has dominated Western thinking in both the scientific and artistic disciplines.

Emotion and rationality

In Western thinking, the ideal that there should be an analytical distance between the human subject and the object of observation is one of the more dominant paradigms. Science and academia have idealized the distanced researcher who takes an objective, sober, and un-emotional intellectual relationship to the object of study. Likewise, since Immanuel Kant presented his aesthetic theory in *Critique of Judgment* (Kant 2007), the ideal of the disinterested appreciator who only can see the true beauty of a work from an abstract, contemplative distance has been a central paradigm

(Cashell 2009). Common to both of these modes of thinking is the idea that emotion and rationality are opposites, and that approaching an object or phenomenon with emotion risks clouding one's rational judgment. However, this ideal of distance is exactly what transgressive art has been designed to disrupt. By causing affect, transgressive experiences force an emotional reaction that ruins the disinterest of aesthetic appreciation, and our paradigm of criticism fails. Transgressive aesthetics is thus by definition a form of art that is meant to create an emotional effect. As such it has often been seen as suspect – a speculative attempt of moving the audience through cheap tricks.

While we will discuss the aesthetics of disinterest in closer detail in Chapter 8, we will here discuss the value of emotion and affect in aesthetic appreciation in order to understand how it can be used and utilized in game design and criticism, and how it connects to play. We will bring together a wide range of views from philosophy, psychology, poetics, and design, in order to approach an understanding of how the game-text addresses not only the analytical mind, but also through shocking, overwhelming, or delighting the pre-analytical body and mind.

Emotions are, according to philosopher Robert C. Solomon, rather underrated in Western culture. The history and philosophy on which we build our civilization is one where emotions are mainly a distraction – to be repressed. He argues that there is a dominating idea in our civilization that emotion is "more primitive, less intelligent, more bestial, less dependable, and more dangerous than reason, and thus needs to be controlled by reason" (Solomon 2008). Solomon traces the history of the idea that emotion needs to be controlled, repressed, and criticized to Greek rationalism, which fits well with the medieval idea that emotions that would lead to temptation and sin needed to be repressed (2008). There were, seen with the medieval filter, some emotions that were desirable, and they were framed not as dangerous passions (greed, lust, envy, and pride), but as virtues (love, hope, and faith). This indicates that there was an ethics based on emotions or rather on the careful selection of emotions, where being ethical meant pursuing certain emotions known as virtues. When David Hume later looked to emotions for a construction of ethics, he turned this medieval Christian model on its head, and claimed that pride was a good emotion, while humility was the opposite (Solomon 2008). Hume still kept the distinctions between "good" or "bad" emotions, though, and did not question this dichotomy at the core of Western thought.

But emotion is not a simple good/bad dichotomy in all cultures. As an alternative to this Western understanding of emotion, there exists an Eastern tradition with a much deeper exploration of emotion. Communications scholar Zizi Papacharissi describes how Eastern philosophy "views emotion and rationality as potentially opposable but ultimately reconcilable states" (2015, 11). Cultural anthropologist Richard A. Shweder and colleagues offer further examples of the cultural meanings of emotion in their discussion of different culturally based understandings of anger (2008, 416–18). Elsewhere Mortensen has used the Buddhist term *duhkha* to describe the desire for change, an emotion for which there is no synonym in European languages and for this reason ends up outside of commonly known Western classifications (Mortensen and Navarro-Remesal 2018). Most cultures have very specific words to emotions important to them. The Eastern understanding of emotion takes a contextual perspective that better reflects how emotion is integrated into the mental processes that allow us to make sense of the world around us. Reflecting German faculty psychology and the German philosophical tradition, Papacharissi shows how the *cognitive* processes related to thinking, the *affective* processes related to emotion, and the *conative* processes related to acting and will are connected:

> Affect presents a key part of how people internalize and act on everyday experiences. In psychology, affect refers to feeling or emotion. It is thus connected to the cognitive and the conative, and can be understood as the link between how we think and how we act. However, cognitive, affective, and conative processes are interconnected and overlap. Therefore, the affective is frequently considered to be part of the cognitive, as our feelings about things may give shape to how we process information.
>
> (Papacharissi 2015)

Papacharissi stresses how the lines between these three mental processes blur: Since our desire to act – our will – also influences our thinking, the conative must also be considered part of cognition. The same is true about affect, and affect simultaneously influences both our thinking and our desire to act. This connects the three faculties of the mind, including thinking (cognition) and feeling (affect), the two that Western tradition has considered opposites, and introducing the third – that of will to action (conation) – effectively softening and blurring the dichotomy of emotion versus intellect to an interdependent triad of emotion, intellect, and willpower.

Emotion and affect

Despite the low esteem in which emotion often is held in public discourse, emotion has always had an important role in the lives of humans. From an evolutionary perspective, the ability to respond to imminent dangers has been central to our survival, and we have for this reason developed an emotional response system that allows us to respond appropriately (Eysenck and Keane 2010, 580–82; Schwab and Schwender 2011).

In the beginning of the chapter, we introduced the distinction between *affect* as an immediate and often intense emotional response, and *emotion* as the relatively stable sensation that people gain after having made a judgment of a situation. One researcher that supports our distinction between affect and emotion cultural studies is scholar Jo Labanyi. Based on the work of philosophers Teresa Brennan and Brian Massumi, Labanyi argues that *emotion* is the slow-working reaction that has had time to be processed by cognition. She argues that emotions by definition are conscious and that they also involve judgment: "[I]f I feel afraid, I am aware of feeling afraid, and I have a word to give to that emotion: 'fear'" (Labanyi 2010). According to Labanyi, cognition, which is the ability and time to become aware of, think about, and interpret what is happening, is what distinguishes emotions from affect, as affect is the reaction we can perceive when the body acts before we understand that something is happening. In Brennan's words, "affect" is what we feel, while feelings are what we feel with. Affect is the step between the physical body and our feelings and emotions (Brennan 2004, 5). Or it is the immediate response in our mind toward stimuli not yet processed by cognition, while emotion is affect that has been processed by cognition.

Not all who discuss emotion and affect agree with Massumi, Brennan, and Labanyi. With basis in Lynn Worsham's work, rhetorics scholar Julie Nelson (2016) argues that emotion and affect should not be separated, and that Massumi's – and by extension Labanyi's – distinction between emotion and affect has created an unfortunate scholarly division between the two (Nelson 2016). This disconnect has also been detected by cognitive psychology. Cognitive psychology has been attentive toward the fact that human emotion can take different forms related to whether they appear to be spontaneously elicited by a certain event or whether they are the result of interpretation and reasoning. Cognitive psychologists have also disagreed whether emotion is independent of cognition or not, but there is today an agreement that emotion and cognition in practice operate together (Power and Dalgleish 2008) and that emotion is linked to a variety of cognitive processes, some which are automatic and some which are conscious (Philippot et al. 2004). While these mental processes are complex and multi-faceted, different theories agree that emotional responses can either be immediate reactions to a situation or be based on deliberative reasoning (Eysenck and Keane 2010, 581; Philippot et al. 2004).

A number of researchers now argue that conscious or non-conscious assessment of the situation is essential to cognitive processes involving emotion (Power and Dalgleish 2008). Three basic assessment mechanisms have been identified in appraisal theory (Eysenck and Keane 2010, 573–74): *Associative processing* is automatic and rapid, and involves the activation of memories. It is the raw emotion that we register before actively having interpreted and processed an experience. *Reasoning* is a slower and more flexible process that involves deliberative thinking. It is the sensation we are left with after we make sense of the experience and what we feel about it. Cognitive psychology also identifies a third mechanism that determines the individual's current emotional state based on information gathered through the two first processes, but for our purpose, it is the difference between the *immediate associate processing* and the *slower reasoning* that is of relevance and which resonates with how we distinguish between *affect* and *emotion*.

Emotion, affect, and transgressive games

The insight from cognitive psychology that there are two mental processes – one that deals with immediate responses and another slower form of reasoning – and that the two operate together in fuzzy and complex ways demonstrates that Labanyi and Nelson are both correct in their assumptions. At the same time, we find that the direction suggested by Labanyi makes the most sense for our distinction between affect and emotion. By speaking about affect and emotion as separate concepts, we can talk about the immediate emotional responses that we have to situations while still leaving room for the fact that these may change in the mind of the player when the experience has become more thoroughly processed. It is still important to keep in mind that in reality, this is not this clear-cut; the distinctions are fuzzy, and separating precisely between affect and emotion is difficult when we talk about mental processing. We can look at something as simple as the so-called jump-scare, which is a common effect in certain genres of horror, both in movies and games, and clearly plays with the viewer or player's immediate responses – in other words – with affect, and still engage in a discussion about whether or not this is really affect – non-interpreted – or emotion – already interpreted through the expectations of genre.

For our purpose of understanding the emotional response to transgressive game content, the division between an immediate affective response and a slower-working process based on reasoning is central. First, we find that our choice of research methods in this project has been particularly fruitful for addressing this distinction. By triangulating gameplay journals that were filled in immediately after play and follow-up interviews around two weeks after the respondents had quit the game, we were able to gain insight both in their immediate affects as well as their more processed emotions relating to the specific game.

Further, distinguishing between affect and emotion gives us a basis for understanding what is happening when players, like "Norah" mentioned in the introduction to this chapter, encounter game content that brings forward one particular immediate emotional response at the moment it is encountered and another when they have had the time to process and interpret the game experience. Also, "Cole" (34), a teaching assistant from Canada, describes something similar, as he writes in his journal how gameplay can be "exciting and tense" (Jan 17, 2017), but when reflecting over the game he finds the scenarios to have uncomfortable political undertones (Interview, Feb 22, 2017). In other words, whether the game is transgressive or not for these players changes as they process the sensations.

More importantly, the fact that there are two systems that may operate simultaneously and also create conflicting feelings strengthen our understanding that what may be experienced as transgressive is fluid and flexible. It shows that what may be initially shocking or provocative may not be the same as what is seen as a profound transgression over time. Finding a game situation to be profoundly transgressive may not be based on how strong the immediate emotional response is when the game is played, but can also emerge after deliberative reasoning and interpretation of the situation. What may be immediately shocking or offensive may not be the same thing as players find to be the real controversy of a certain game. This is also demonstrated by how players in our study describe their experiences with *Hatred*: Earlier in this chapter, we discussed how "Keith" found that his emotions toward the game changed. In the interview, he further elaborates that while the unmotivated killing of civilians did have an initial shock value, this was not what actually disturbed him. Rather, what he found to be truly disturbing was the fact that killing civilians was carried out using the same game mechanics as any other shooter game:

> But after I played the game for a while, I noticed that really like, mechanically speaking, the way that the *Hatred* protagonist disposes of civilians isn't all that different from how heroes from, say *Gears of War*, would do their kind of execution animations on the enemies. So in this case I think that context is everything for that game. And that is what makes it truly disturbing initially, but later on, after the initial shock, the game just gets kind of boring, to be honest.
>
> (Interview, October 18, 2016)

While this only became clear to "Keith" after he had been able to process his reactions to the game, his sense of disturbance is further cemented as he links one of the levels in the game where the player is to perform an attack on a political rally to his own life:

> I also recently took part in few rallies myself with certain political agendas into public space. (...) I kind of found myself on the other side of barricade so to speak playing this game. And (...) it resonated with me, because recently I was in a situation, which could have gone the same way given some circumstances. Like if there was a mass murder somewhere in the crowd, right, it would be also very difficult to get out of there, and that idea of being a person in the crowd, trying to run for your life, that kind of resonated with me, because of my recent events.
>
> (Interview, October 18, 2016)

While the initial processing of shock quickly wears off, "Keith" still finds himself disturbed by the game after further reasoning. In line with cognitive psychology, his emotions regarding the game are ambivalent and partly contradictory.

The distinction between an immediate sensory response and a slower-working reflective process – between affect and emotion – is also important for understanding the ambivalent experiences that players may have toward transgressive game content. In *Parables for the Virtual*, Brian Massumi describes how German researchers discovered what we discussed in Chapter 5 as the paradox of painful art. In a study, participants were asked to rate film scenes on two scales: "Happy-sad" and "pleasant-unpleasant", and the researchers found that "[t]he 'sad' scenes were rated the most pleasant; the sadder the better" (Massumi 2002). This resonates with our findings that show that certain players found the discomfort of games such as *This War of Mine* and *Beyond: Two Souls* to be gratifying.

After exploring these findings, Massumi concludes that this is connected to the distinction between emotion and affect. Although often used as synonymous to emotion, he stresses that affect implies intensity and that the two follow different logics (Massumi 2002). While looking at transgressive aesthetics, this is vital because of the goal of this particular aesthetic. It is aiming to bypass the intellectual and analytical, distanced gaze, and elicit an immediate, subjective response. This may mean that it is not simply an emotional response but also, according to Massumi, an *affective* response. This can explain several of the results we have seen from the players and from the public, and is for this reason relevant for research on games with structure or content that is difficult to handle. The players' path from the immediate response of disgust to intellectual enjoyment of unpleasant content as well as the non-players' consistent disgust can be explained by the different processing of the initial affect, where players interpret this affect based on the rules of the game, while non-players interpret the affect based on a widely different set of experiences, mainly unconnected to what the game is expressing. On the background of this logic, one of our claims is that an aesthetic aiming at immediate and strong provocation, exemplified by transgressive aesthetics, will depend more on the context of the viewer than in other cases. Since a transgressive aesthetic often depends on shock value, we cannot be habituated to it, and when we do not have previous patterns for reaction, the framing will play a vital role in the interpretation of the initial sensation.

The emotional roller coaster of transgressive games

One of the main emotional responses that transgressions elicit is outrage. We see this in so-called *gamer rage* and the act of *rage quitting a game*, phenomena that well illustrate what happens when the flow experience is broken by challenge and frustration (White 2014, 59), but we also often see public outrage related to many of the controversies over particular kinds of game content that we discussed in Chapter 1.

Obviously, these two situations illustrate quite different emotions, in particular in terms of intensity. While the strong immediate responses of outrage and anger that players who rage quit experience can be considered examples of affect; the public outrage tends to be an emotion formed over time and fueled with political or social concern. If we accept the connection between affect and emotion as the relatively non-processed and the actively interpreted aspect of the same experience, it is clear that using strong sensations in order to touch others is a risky process. Several very successful, long-lasting games appear to rather try to drain the structure of random emotion than to add it.

Games cater to large, overwhelming emotions, so it should not be a surprise when games evoke outrage, and with outrage, controversy. Even feeling positive emotions can be a source for difficult emotions, as it can be a source for manipulation. And a good game does not only strike one emotional string and leave it at that. It takes us from anticipation through frustration to mastery and victory, and then back to loss, despair, and anger, at the levels of game structure, the fiction, and other players. Games are also very good places to be frustrated with and angry at ourselves, as *we* – the players – are the ones who fail, nobody else (Juul 2013). Accordingly, the progress of a game is as much a progress through emotions as a progress through levels, labyrinths, or achievements.

We consider this function of outrage and controversy to be part of what we can call the emotional roller coaster of the game experience. While play can be a very cerebral experience, the experiences of play are emotional. Game designer Nicole Lazzaro studied the emotional responses players expressed during play – what we would call *affect* – and isolated a list of main responses (Lazzaro 2004). These were *fear, surprise, disgust, naches/kvell* (Yiddish for pride in others), *fiero* (Italian for triumph over adversity), *schadenfreude* (German for rival misfortune), and *wonder* (Lazzaro 2004). This indicated a set of strong and intense emotional response, which was simultaneously very diverse. A wide range of emotional responses spanning from *anticipation, surprise, pleasure, understanding,* and *strength* to *poise* were also described by play researcher and medical doctor Stuart Brown (Brown and Vaughan 2010). Brown specifically describes this as a ride, evoking a carousel or roller coaster. Referencing play historian Scott Eberle, the emotional responses Brown describes are gentler and generally more positive than the emotions described by Lazzaro. This may be due to the difference in what they studied. Lazzaro looked at players engaged in gaming, often competitive, generally fast-paced, and tense. Brown, on the other hand, looked at play, frequently free form, loose, and with fewer rules and goals. Still, it is clear that play is associated with the process of feeling strong immediate responses. We do not play in order to reach a goal in the manner we engage in our work, we play in order to feel something.

Sociologist Colin Cremin discusses video games on a background of the affective theory of French intellectuals Gilles Deleuze and Felix Guattari

(Cremin 2016). On a background of their statement that what artists use to create is sensations, Cremin claims that sensations are also central for video games. In line with our theory that state that players' emotional response to video games oscillate between affect and emotion, Cremin argues that "We do not 'play' videogames as such. We intensify them. We are not gamers. We are intensifiers" (Cremin 2016). By this, he postulates that while games in themselves may create rich, affective, and emotional experiences in players, players are also instrumental in intensifying the experiences that gameplay evoke. While the players play the game, he claims, the game plays their emotions. The term *play* is here used by Cremin in a manner that indicates manipulation. "Getting played" is very different from playing or playing with as it connotes fraud, cheating, and betrayal. This means that the idea of the game playing the emotions of the player indicates a situation where the player loses agency to the game and is helpless in its grip. Such assumptions about players are based on players not understanding what they do when they play a game, which is a fallacy. The lengths to which players go in order to discuss, analyze, and criticize the games they play indicate the opposite: Engaged, devoted players are not helpless victims of games; rather, they enter into the play looking to have a very specific experience, deliberately seeking to reach a goal. As Cremin points out, the apprentice strives to become the artist rather than remaining a regressive apprentice, repeating the same tricks to inevitably win (Cremin 2016).

If what we are looking for while playing a game is intensified emotions, it may, for instance, explain why we keep playing through failure. As long as we have hope of winning, failure can be increasingly painful and uncomfortable, and we will still keep playing because we get what we are looking for. It is the moment that the failure is so overwhelming that we can no longer put it into the same context as winning, when winning is off the table and the emotions felt by the losses are no longer intensified by their opposite; this is the point where we stop playing, dejected, unable to feel for the game anymore. Something very similar, interestingly, happens if we keep winning a game – without failure or loss to offset the emotions engendered by winning it, it loses its attraction. While flow theory (Csikszentmihalyi 2000, 2002) explains this experience of disinterest and boredom as lacking the tension of challenge, Cremin's understanding of games would explain boredom as lacking intensity. Without the experience of loss, winning becomes commonplace, and the emotional arc of play flattens out. And winning and losing are only two of many different sensations we experience while playing, as Lazzaro and Brown both point out above.

Emotion and aesthetics

Transgressive aesthetics is always pushing at the emotional boundaries of profound transgression. Transgressive aesthetics continuously challenges our emotional boundaries, including those of the flow channel. It tests the boundary between the transgressive aesthetic located safely inside the flow channel, and the profound transgression transforms the player's experience of flow into anxiety.

So far in the discussion on flow and transgressive games, we have seen that overwhelming emotions can break flow and make players unwilling to engage with further with the game. For some game researchers and designers, flow has become the holy grail of game design (Isbister 2016). Flow theory is seductive to game design because it looks like all the designer needs to know is how to create that flow channel. If the challenges are balanced with the player progress, this should be easily doable. It should also apparently be an easy task to make work itself more interesting, and workers would perform much better if work *was* more like a game. Csikszentmihalyi tells us why it is not that easy:

> [I]t would be erroneous to expect that if all jobs were constructed like games, everyone would enjoy them. Even the most favorable external conditions do not guarantee that a person will be in flow. Because optimal experience depends on a subjective evaluation of what the possibilities for action are, and of one's own capacities, it happens quite often that an individual will be discontented even with a potentially great job.
>
> (2002, 154)

Flow in game design is very different from flow in the workplace and remains contested as an aesthetic ideal.

What flow does not describe is why players enjoy the unexpected, the randomness of games. Even abstract games with no random elements built into their systems, such as chess, invite a certain randomness in the scope of different strategies and tactics the players can choose from. The fact that so many games rely on systematic unexpectedness contradicts flow theory, which is very much a theory of control. Instead, it points to the potential of turning everything on its head: The possibility of putting the expected to the side and transgressing against everyday norms that we find, for instance, in the carnival. In the next two chapters, we will look at game aesthetics beyond the ideal of flow. First, we will discuss the transgressive aesthetics of video games as a carnivalesque aesthetics before discussing game aesthetics against the ideals of aesthetic appreciation and the importance of emotion and affect in transgressive aesthetics.

References

Anable, Aubrey. 2018. *Playing with Feelings: Video Games and Affect*. Kindle edition. Minneapolis: University of Minnesota Press.
Blizzard. 2004. *World of Warcraft*. Blizzard Entertainment Inc.

Bogost, Ian. 2007. *Persuasive Games : The Expressive Power of Videogames*. Cambridge: MIT Press.

Brecht, Bertolt. 1964. "On Chinese Theatre, Verfremdung and Gestus." In *Brecht on Theatre: The Development of an Aesthetic*, edited by John Willett, 149–99. London: Methuen.

Brennan, Teresa. 2004. *The Transmission of Affect*. Cornell University Press.

Brown, Stuart, and Christopher Vaughan. 2010. *Play; How It Shapes the Brain, Opens the Imagination and Invigorates the Soul*. New York: Avery.

Cashell, Kieran. 2009. *Aftershock : The Ethics of Contemporary Transgressive Art*. I.B. Tauris.

Core Design, Crystal Dynamics, and Eidos Montreal. 1996. *Tomb Raider*. Eidos Interactive and Square Enix.

Creative Assembly. 2014. *Alien: Isolation*. Sega.

Cremin, Colin. 2016. *Exploring Videogames with Deleuze and Guattari : Towards an Affective Theory of Form*. London: Routledge.

Csikszentmihalyi, Mihaly. 1997. *Finding Flow. The Psychology of Engagement with Everyday Life*. New York: Basic Books.

———. 2000. *Beyond Boredom and Anxiety*. 25th anniv. Jossey-Bass Publishers.

———. 2002. *Flow : The Classic Work on How to Achieve Happiness*. Rev. and u. London: Rider.

Destructive Creations. 2015. *Hatred*. Destructive Creations. www.hatredgame.com/.

Deterding, Sebastian. 2012. "Gamification: Designing for Motivation." *Interaction – Social Mediator*, no. July–August.

Deterding, Sebastian, Dan Dixon, Rilla Khaled, and Lennart Nacke. 2011. "From Game Design Elements to Gamefulness." In *Proceedings of the 15th International Academic MindTrek Conference on Envisioning Future Media Environments – MindTrek '11*, 9. New York: ACM Press. doi:10.1145/2181037.2181040.

Eysenck, Michael W, and Mark T. Keane. 2010. *Cognitive Psychology: A Student's Handbook*. 6th ed. Hove, New York: Psychology Press.

FromSoftware. 2015. *Bloodborne*. Sony Interactive Entertainment.

Hall, Stuart. 2006. "Encoding/Decoding." In *Media and Cultural Studies : Keyworks*, edited by Meenakshi Gigi Durham and Douglas M. Kellner, 163–172. Malden, Oxford, and Carlton: Blackwell Publishing.

Isbister, Katherine. 2016. *How Games Move Us : Emotion by Design*. Cambridge: The MIT Press.

Jørgensen, Kristine. 2018. "When Is It Enough? Uncomfortable Game Content and the Transgression of Player Taste." In *Transgressions in Games and Play*, edited by Kristine Jørgensen and Faltin Karlsen., 153–167. Cambridge: MIT Press.

Juul, Jesper. 2013. *The Art of Failure : An Essay on the Pain of Playing Video Games*. MIT Press.

Kant, Immanuel. 2007. *Critique of Judgement*. Kindle. Oxford: Oxford University Press.

Karlsen, Faltin author. 2013. *A World of Excesses; Online Games and Excessive Playing*. Wey Court East: Ashgate Publishing Limited.

Labanyi, Jo. 2010. "Doing Things: Emotion, Affect and Materiality." *Journal of Spanish Cultural Studies* 11 (3–4): 223–33. doi:10.1080/14636204.2010.538244.

Lazzaro, Nicole. 2004. "Why We Play Games: Four Keys to More Emotion Without Story." In *Game Developers Conference (GDC)*. San Jose, CA: Game Developers Association.

Massimini, Fausto, and Massimo Carli. 1988. "The Systematic Assessment of Flow in Daily Experience." In *Optimal Experience: Psychological Studies of Flow in Consciousness*, edited by Mihaly. Csikszentmihalyi and Isabela Selega Csikszentmihalyi, 266–87. Cambridge, New York, Melbourne: Cambridge University Press.

Massumi, Brian. 2002. *Parables for the Virtual : Movement, Affect, Sensation.* Durham, NC, London: Duke University Press.

Mortensen, Torill Elvira. 2015. "Keeping the Balance; Morals at the Dark Side." In *The Dark Side of Game Play: Controversial Issues in Playful Environments*, edited by Torill Elvira Mortensen, Jonas Linderoth, and Ashley M. L. Brown, 155–70. New York, London: Routledge. doi:10.4324/9781315738680.

Mortensen, Torill Elvira, and Victor Navarro-Remesal. 2018. "Asynchronous Transgressions: Suffering, Relief and Invasions in Nintendo's Miiverse and Streetpass." In *Transgression in Games and Play*, edited by Kristine Jørgensen and Faltin Karlsen, 27–44. Cambridge: MIT Press.

Naughty Dog. n.d. "Uncharted." Sony Interactive Entertainment.

Nelson, Julie D. 2016. "An Unnecessary Divorce: Integrating the Study of Affect and Emotion in New Media." *Composition Forum* 34.

Papacharissi, Zizi. 2015. *Affective Publics: Sentiment, Technology and Politics.* Oxford: Oxford University Press.

Paul, Christopher A. 2012. *Wordplay and the Discourse of Video Games: Analysing Words, Design and Play.* New York, Abingdon: Routledge.

Philippot, Pierre, Céline Baeyens, Céline Douilliez, and Benjamin Francart. 2004. "Cognitive Regulation of Emotion: Application to Clinical Disorders." In *The Regulation of Emotion*, edited by Pierre Philippot and Robert S. Feldman, 71–97. New York: Laurence Erlbaum Associates.

Power, Mick, and Tim Dalgleish. 2008. *Cognition and Emotion: From Order to Disorder.* 2nd ed. Hove, New York: Psychology Press.

Quantic Dream. 2013. *Beyond: Two Souls.* Sony Interactive Entertainment.

Rockstar North. 2013. *Grand Theft Auto V.* New York: Rockstar Games.

Schwab, Frank, and Clemens Schwender. 2011. "The Descent of Emotions in Media: Darwinian Perspectives." In *The Routledge Handbook of Emotions and Mass Media*, edited by Katrin Döveling, Christian von. Scheve, and Elly Konijn, 422. Abingdon, New York: Routledge.

Shweder, Richard A., Jonathan Haidt, Randall Horton, and Craig Joseph. 2008. "The Cultural Psychology of the Emotions: Ancient and Renewed." In *Handbook of Emotions*, edited by Michael Lewis, Jeannette M. Haviland-Jones, and Lisa Feldman Barrett, 3rd ed., 409–27. New York: Guilford Press.

Solomon, Robert C. 2008. "The Philosophy of Emotions." In *Handbook of Emotions*, edited by Michael Lewis, Jeannette M. Haviland-Jones, and Lisa Feldman Barrett, 3rd ed., 3–16. New York, London: The Guilford Press.

Stenros, Jaakko. 2015. "Playfulness, Play, and Games. A Constructionist Ludology Approach." Tampere: University of Tampere.

Sutton-Smith, Brian. 1997. *The Ambiguity of Play.* Cambridge, MA, London: Harvard University Press.

White, Matthew M. 2014. *Learn to Play: Designing Tutorials for Video Games.* Natick, MA: A K Peters/CRC Press.

Part 3

Games and transgressive aesthetics

7 The carnivalesque aesthetics of games

Games tend to portray other worlds, and the sensation of being in a different world is important for modern video games. New media scholar Lisbeth Klastrup calls this *worldness* (Klastrup 2003): The experience that an environment is not only a space, but a unique environment that obeys certain natural laws and that consists of concrete objects and living inhabitants that affect its environment. Worldness indicates a sense of having a community, of belonging, and it is this social connectedness that contributes to the sense of traversing a *world*, and not just a game (Klastrup 2003). When the player experiences a sense of worldness, the gameworld becomes close to real in the sense that emotional bonds are stronger, including the sense of transgression. These worlds tend to ask the question "what if the world worked differently" and then explore this idea to the point of giving the player the opportunity to influence some of what happens in these worlds. *Pokémon Go* (Niantic 2016) shows us a world where monsters and fantastic creatures roam, if we look at our mundane world through the lens of the mobile device. *The Witcher 3* (CD Projekt RED 2015) shows us a world where magic is real, and history never followed the path we recognize. Even sports games based on a real game with real players playing on real fields at the same time as players play with them on computers, such as *FIFA 19* (EA Vanvouver and EA Romania 2018), are "what if" worlds – what if we put these players together, how would that work? This is in a way the very spirit of the carnival, the moment when we let the world be different, and to play a game is to revisit this other reality, where we follow different rules. In this chapter, we will discuss transgressive games and aesthetics through the concepts of the carnival and the carnivalesque – the idea that transgressive games can be understood as an example of a practice where the ideal is to turn everything upside down, at least for the time being.

Carnival or revolt?

Through the decade leading up to the writing of this book, a series of events have put its stamp on the term "gamer" and the use of games. The concern of society has changed from a fear that youth caught up with games may end up doing poorly on exams or even drop out of school to game culture being a breeding ground for a dangerously aggressive, anti-social culture, where the world is understood as a game and not as reality. One recent event that caused this concern was the attack on two mosques in Christchurch, New Zealand, in March 2019. For this attack, the attacker announced that "something would happen" on a discussion site on 8chan (Bjørkelo 2019); made a reference to the well-known game stream person-ality Felix Arvid Ulf Kjellberg known as PewDiePie (Flynn 2019) as he was about to start the attack; and live-streamed it, imitating the view of a first-person shooter game. The similarities were superficial enough that the reporters pointed out that it is easy to see that this is not a game (Marsh and Mulholland 2019), but the reference was unmistakable. However, the Christchurch shooter was not the first mass murderer to reference games. The Norwegian murderer from Utøya in 2011 claimed he had used *Call of Duty: Modern Warfare 2* (Infinity Ward 2009) for target practice and *World of Warcraft* as an alibi for social isolation when preparing his terror-ist attacks (Karlsen and Jørgensen 2014, 43). These references have fueled the discussion about the dangers of games and made many ask whether games turn the players into killers. While this is an understandable ques-tion, we find this direct causality to be too simplistic. For the Christchurch attacker, there are too many benefits to inserting himself into the debate on games in this context.

Jenni Marsh and Tara Mulholland, reporters writing for CNN, delivered a compelling analysis of how including game culture in the mix ensured increased coverage, while also directing the attention away from the organ-izations driving the white supremacy movement (Marsh and Mulholland 2019). By mentioning PewDiePie, the shooter ensured that his subscribers – at the time, more than 80 million – would hear about the event, if nothing else because Kjellberg would have to publicly denounce it. By releasing a video that looked like a first-person shooter stream, the shooter ensured that it would be recognizable and relatable for a huge audience with a solid portion of the people he probably wanted to reach: Unsatisfied young men with enough resources to play games and a lot of time on their hands.

Still, the relationship between the alt-right and contemporary game cul-ture is more complex than this. Since the online, harassment-rife campaign known as #gamergate (#GG), the alt-right has been studied in relationship to gamer culture (Bezio 2018, 563; Blodgett and Salter 2018, 142; Neiwert 2017; Salter 2018, 254–55). What these studies suggest is that while gamer culture in itself is not racist – there is too much diversity among gamers to sustain that – there are some online strongholds for far right politics, where the alt-right has blossomed, and these online spaces are often adjacent to game discussion sites. This complex relationship between the alt-right and gamer culture in terms of common platforms and discourses leads to what is known as *context collapse* (Davis and Jurgenson 2014; Marwick and boyd 2011). Context collapse is what happens when multiple audiences flatten into one, and the different self-presentation strategies fail (Marwick and boyd 2011). In the relationship between gamer culture and alt-right, context collapse happens as the two cultures use the same online areas and also refer to the same culture of resistance, irony, and transgression, particularly on the imageboards 4chan and 8chan. The discussions, and quite a bit of the rhetoric and jokes, spill over and mix. David Neiwert's discussion of the "Birth of the Alt Right" (Neiwert 2017) draws direct parallels between the so-called troll logic and the contrary view of reality that internet trolls often represent, and the contrariness of conspiracy theories (Phillips 2015, 24). Troll logic is the idea that if you are sufficiently ill-informed or naive as to be caught up in a troll's net or swallow their virtual bait, you deserve what happens to you, whether it's a relatively mild reveal of your ignorance or a more serious event (Neiwert 2017). According to troll logic, if you make yourself vulnerable to their trolling, you have only yourself to blame if you experience unpleasant repercussions. A moving target, online trolling is a spectrum of behaviors moving from jokes and pranks to harassment.

The online spaces where these different audiences meet is also the homeland of *memes*, which we most commonly encounter as humorous images with a caption, spread virally. Memes are defined as what evolutionary biologist Richard Dawkins calls "small cultural units of transmission", which spread through copying or imitation (Varis and Blommaert 2018, 36; Shifman 2013, 362). Cultural studies researcher Pia Varis and sociolinguist Jan Blommaert underline the multimodality of the signs – or memes in this case – and argue that they include not only copying but re-contextualization as they gain new meaning when they are encountered in a new context, connected to new modalities or texts, and hence will be read as new signs. This re-contextualization of the units of transmission – most frequently pictures – leads to a constantly repeated context collapse, and the memes are continuous examples of how close to each other different cultures live online and how easy it is to have your entire point of view uprooted and turned around. New media researcher Limor Shifman calls memes a conceptual troublemaker and discusses how re-contextualization can turn the original meaning of an image around to the almost opposite meaning of the original meme (Shifman 2013). Memes are examples of how meaning can be played with and subverted, and it is essential for this play that the online spaces where they are designed and spread are considered safe havens of free speech: They are liberated from the social norms of regular society through anonymity or, as Whitney Phillips claims, hidden behind the "mask of trolling". When donning this intentionally unperceivable mask, the troll ensures that the victim believes that what the troll says is serious and reacts accordingly, or the trolling is failed (Phillips 2015, 33). This is a one-sided carnival.

When we think of carnivals today, we tend to think of either the fun of dressing up with friends or the traditions of Rio de Janeiro. Neither image prepares us for the idea that carnival may be something threatening, dangerous, and even revolutionary. There is however a close connection between social upheaval and the carnival. Historian Bob Scribner describes the carnival of the Reformation. Starting in Wittenberg in 1520, students staged a carnival procession, re-enacting in public and on a larger scale Martin Luther's burning of the papal bull that condemned him (Scribner 1978, 304). This was the beginning of several German, carnival-type, anti-papal events. The events increasingly mocked the Catholic Church, leading to processions where relics and holy objects were included in secular celebrations. Several of the incidents are being described as results of "youthful high spirits" (Scribner 1978), a recognizable description of the antics of modern-day trolls (Phillips 2015).

The trolls of the Reformation were celebrating a very real social change that became the social norm in Germany and several of the northern European nations. That does not mean they brought it about. There is an ongoing debate whether the Reformation was brought about by the influence of Martin Luther's vision, a general malcontent with the corruption of the Catholic Church, or the pressure of secular rulers (Berentsen and Lawrence 2019). While the Reformation was not brought on by carnivals, the carnivals were still threatening and uncomfortable, as they demonstrated and made visible the presence of real change with their celebrations of the overturned power structures. Another problem that was seen among the carnival revelers of the Reformation was the breach of the boundary between the carnival and the mundane world. When the carnivalistic acts were interpreted out of context, they lead to tragic events, such as accidental deaths, as people defended themselves from perceived demons (Scribner 1978).

If we want to understand what is happening in game culture and in the cultures surrounding it, the contexts it tends to collapse into, we must understand the pleasure and even importance of the carnivalesque aspects of the transgressive pleasures that games lead to. Some of these carnivals are acts of exuberance and celebration, while some are acts of revolt, a challenge to the existing norms and structures of power. We want to discuss how to understand the alternative worlds that games play with in order to support a better understanding of how games are carnivalesque and act as companions to transgressive aesthetics.

The digital carnival of games

What is an example of carnival in games? Game scholar Tomasz Z. Majkowski uses *Assassin's Creed II* as an example (Majkowski 2018). The game is a carnival within a carnival, in which the player dons not only the mask of the avatar, but also the avatar's avatar: The player takes the role of Desmond Miles, a modern-day man who replays the memories of his ancestor Ezio Auditore to solve a historic mystery. Ezio himself is an assassin, trained in the skills of stealth and deception, and gameplay therefore also involves disguising as a civilian by blending in among them. The game is in itself thus also a carnival in the sense that it allows for transgressions: As an assassin, it is Ezio's duty to kill. The game constantly subverts expected behavior and roles: Climbing rooftops rather than streets is often the better way to traverse the cities, and characters such as the brothel-operating nun and the heretic pope are commonplace (Majkowski 2018, 197).

This kind of stepping beyond the regular experiences of life is the rule of video games, not the exception. In Chapter 5, we mentioned *The Sims*, a game that does not at first glance invite transgression, but in which certain players torture their characters (Consalvo 2006; Flanagan 2003; Wirman and Jones 2018). This demonstrates how players take the opportunity to make the mundane strange, different, and transgressive as they use the rules of the game to create horrible, and unrealistic, scenarios. This takes us back to "Norah" and her change of attitude toward *GTAV*: Although she feels bad for running over pedestrians, in the end she gives up her rational self and finds that "it's fun to find the nicest Porsche and crash it until its unrecognizable" (gameplay log, January 18, 2016). And masked as the avatar in the game, she can break all that she likes.

Bakhtin and the carnivalesque in *Grand Theft Auto*

Considering that a main characteristic of transgressive game aesthetics is its *carnivalesque* nature, we need to address one of the main theories on the carnival. Philosopher and literary theorist Mikhail Bakhtin's description of the carnival is an important lens through which we may understand not only the cultural context of transgressions evident in game culture, but also the transgressive aesthetic of games. The carnival as a cultural institution serves to uncover and make visible the unspoken agreements, norms, and hierarchies that make our stratified society run smoothly. As a temporary setting for subverting normalcy and transgressing the boundaries of ordinary life, the carnival, as Mikhail Bakhtin points out, "is life drawn out of its *usual* rut, it is to some extent 'life turned inside out,' 'the reverse side of the world'" (Bakhtin 1999, loc. 3330). The carnival is the setting where the beggar temporarily can be crowned king, and the king can be decrowned. Bakhtin explains how the carnival reveals the power structures of society by mapping the relationships of individuals to hierarchies. The outrage and eccentricity of carnival, of the regular and expected transgression of existing boundaries, reveal the otherwise invisible hegemonic norms and make them explicit (Bakhtin 1999). In order to reverse, oppose, and poke fun at the status quo, one needs to map, understand, and reveal it. As we have seen, video games allow players to temporarily play with identities and don the "mask" of an avatar, and they invite players to engage in activities that are otherwise restricted. Further, the ritualistic nature of the carnival is as dependent on rules as are games.

However, while carnivalism is often transgressive, transgression is not automatically carnivalesque. Bakhtin underlines the dualism of carnivalism: The crowning of a carnival king always means a decrowning will follow. During the carnival, order is supplanted with chaos for a short period of time, and then order will be imposed again. Given time, this in itself becomes a matter of order, as the carnival returns at the same time, in the same manner, with the same expectations. Every carnivalistic transgression is temporary and will pass. By being framed by ritual, routine, and order, the chaos of carnival is mitigated by its boundaries. The chaos is real, but it is not lasting (Bakhtin 1999). By being restricted, framed, and limited, the transgressions that happened during the time of the carnival ceased being profound, as they would have been at any other time of the year, and became aesthetic. Through this limited, framed, and restricted nature of carnival and its transgressive aesthetic, we can recognize the transgressive aesthetic of games, as their nature is also limited, carefully set aside from the norm and from mundane life.

The carnivalesque nature of the *GTA* franchise is a recurring topic in cultural studies scholar Nate Garrelts's edited collection *The Meaning and Culture of Grand Theft Auto*, which celebrates the supposedly liberating power of *GTA*. The *GTA* series is infamous for revealing and inviting the players to engage in this topsy-turvy world of the carnival. New media scholar Dennis Redmond argues that *GTA* through its comic relief created an escape from the hegemony in an era of political regression (Redmond 2006, loc. 1959). In another essay in the same anthology, writer and scholar David Annandale argues that the detailed world creation of *GTA* makes it "so excessive as to be encyclopedic" (2006, loc. 1677). In the *GTA* games, the player can engage in the fiction of actions that are not only frowned upon but that would have strong consequences in real-world contexts, and the franchise delivers this with a strong sense of humor, exaggeration, and absurdity. Killing other criminals, police, or bystanders; stealing and ruining cars; and inviting fights – while these have in-game consequences, the moment the player turns off the computer, the opposite world ends, and the only consequence is the passage of time. Annandale's understanding of the carnivalesque nature of *GTA* leans heavily on the humorous aspect of it, on satire and parody, both vital in Bakhtin's analysis.

However, while the *GTA* franchise currently allows the white middle class an escape into the world of crime, like Bakhtin's carnival, it does stop short of truly switching around the modes of power, where the beggar is made into a *true* king. Reflecting our initial description of the game in Chapter 3, professor of comparative ethnic studies David Leonard points out that while the *GTA* franchise may seem liberating, it maintains several of the stereotypes of race, poverty, and crime, thus reinforcing dominant ideologies (Leonard 2006, loc. 1137). Leonard refers to several players who reject the idea that *GTA*'s images of blackness are racist. Rather, these players find the representations to be realistic on the grounds that showing the criminals in the *GTA* franchise as anything but black would be ridiculous. Also one of our respondents finds the representations to be unproblematic.

"Sally" (26) enjoys the parodic and satiric elements of the game, and appreciates how it takes certain situations into the absurd. She states:

> The game seems to be fairly equally opportunity in what gets lampooned. Hipsters, capitalism, the ultra-wealthy, everyone gets the treatment which I found very interesting.
>
> (Email interview, March 7, 2017)

For these players, *GTA* is a liberating and carnivalesque medium, but a part of Leonard's implicit argument is that dominant ideologies sometimes may be hidden from those not directly targeted by them. While black Americans are more likely than white to be incarcerated in the US (Carson 2016), the reason for this is much more complex than a direct correlation between crime rate and prison population. In this manner, ethnicity and crime becomes one of the fields where *GTA* loses and rejects its carnivalistic potential, adhering instead to the white middle-class worldview, titillating the players with an innocent glimpse of being on the other side rather than truly transgressing on their white-dominated normativity by shifting the balance of power. And as such, the series becomes an example of what Pötzsch calls *hegemonic transgressivity* (see Chapter 3): It appears to challenge the established norms, but instead reproduces existing power relations (Pötzsch 2018). And, he points out, *GTA* is thus transgressive in Jenks's understanding of the concept as something that works to reaffirm the boundaries that it is crossing by simply challenging them (Jenks 2003, 2).

If we take a look at this debate with point of departure in our game journal data, we see that the racial profiling of *GTAV* to some of our player participants is transgressive to the point of being unacceptable. We have earlier discussed the general sense of unease that "Norah" (35) and "Cole" (34) express with regards to how *GTAV* appears to make poverty and misery into entertainment, but more explicit statements come from the interview with "Bridget" (21), a British student and woman of color. She finds the game to have a high degree of sexual and racial slur and is disappointed to see the game reinforces stereotypical representations. She explains:

> I knew that you could play as a black character in GTAV and was really excited, hoping that he'd be a really cool character, but instead he fell to racial stereotypes.
>
> (Individual interview, February 9, 2017)

Later she explains how she feels about how the game represents the social world:

> I feel like it plays a lot on stereotypes and that while I'm sure that people like the characters in the game do exist, it would have been great to see them push stereotypes. Having said that I know that people will

do a lot to make money, and the characters attitudes towards money is probably pretty accurate in society. As well as their treatment/attitude towards women is pretty common in today's society.

(Individual interview, February 9, 2017)

In the end, "Bridget" finds that *GTAV* is not a liberating rebellion against the establishment, but that it reinforced the stereotypes common in society. As "Bridget" represents a minority, it may be easier for her to discern the structural issues that black Americans face and thus also identify how the game reinforces established stereotypes. For her, the game is thus transgressive in its inability to challenge the establishment.

Menippean satire and the freedom of the plot

We are left with the question as to whether games can be carnivalesque or they are just all playing around with the same apparent provocation. To try to understand whether the surface rebellion of *GTA* is a matter of the particular form and content of this one franchise, or it is a matter of how all games are structured, concluding that games can never be truly transgressive in the sense of portraying a radically different world, we want to look at the Menippean satire, one of the main features of carnivalesque genres.

Bakhtin underlines that carnival is a spectacle, not a genre or an art form, specifically not a literary phenomenon, but a ritualistic pageantry (Bakhtin 1999). However, we can still identify genres that are closely related to the carnival and which, in Bakhtin's expression, are *carnivalesque*. Leaning heavily on satire, the *GTA* franchise is an example of the carnivalesque, a main point in Garrelts's collection of essays on *GTA*. But satire is not something unique to the *GTA* franchise. We might claim that the majority of digital games are satires, particularly if we lean on Bakhtin's description of the Menippean satires or *menippea*. This understanding of satire goes beyond the obvious parodying of popular culture, and it may position large swaths of game fictions, as well as game structures and media forms, firmly within this genre.

Originating from the classic Greek satire, *menippea* was a unique literary mode that combined verse and prose in service of presenting an ideological narrative (Majkowski 2018). Bakhtin revitalized the term in his research on Russian author Fyodor Dostoyevsky and connected it to his own concept of the carnivalesque. For Bakhtin, the menippea is a satiric genre that brings the values of the carnival into narratives (Bakhtin 1999) through techniques such as the use humor and contrast; play with the fantastic, mystical, and religious; and the inclusion of scandalous, inappropriate, and taboo topics and abnormal states of mind. While the purpose is to provoke and violate the accepted, the menippea "questions established truths in new, unexpected ways, either to validate them as universal or ridicule them as false" (Majkowski 2018, 191). These characteristics are often found in games, and we will in the following discuss how video games as a medium address Bakhtin's 14 characteristics of the Menippean satire (Bakhtin 1999).

Menippea as fun and serious

According to Bakhtin, menippea is both fun and serious – it contains comic elements but it also works as social commentary. Like the carnival, this is a mixture that allows menippea to partly challenge the establishment but still remain located safely inside the frames of a joke. This allows menippea to address transgressive topics and social and cultural taboos. This resonates well with the argument that "it is only a game" that is often postulated when games are criticized in public discourse.

The first characteristic of menippea identified by Bakhtin is that it leans heavily on the comic, but the laughter may be strongly reduced. *Reduced laughter* in this context means laughter that "does not ring out" in the sense that it is not expressed directly but remains traceable in the text itself (Bakhtin 1999, 178). It is an expression of the position of the author, which invites a style where heroes can be simple and one-sided, while the "great dialogue" of the work remains unresolved and open. In other words, while there may be a humorous tone to the menippea, this may be subtle and sometimes hidden.

Video games often feature episodes that in themselves provoke laughter, both directly expressed and reduced. A typical example of expressed laughter is the expression "LOL", from "laughing out loud", which is a common written and spoken response to events and discussions about games. As discussed above, the *GTA* franchise is a series that have been characterized as satire and for using humor and the absurd to present a criticism of modern American society (Annandale 2006, loc. 1677). Further, the playful exploration of a game's rules and simulated worlds often lead to exaggerated and excessive situations that tap into the absurd, and thus add an implicitly humorous aspect to gameplay. "Cole" (34) provides an example of this when describing a *GTA5* car chase in his gameplay journal. Losing control over the car, he finds the car flying through the air before landing safely on the side of the road: "When I took to the air, I started laughing because I was pretty sure I had failed the mission, but when I managed to land perfectly intact, I started laughing harder" (gameplay journal, January 14, 2017). Situations like this are often understood as a weakness in the simulation, an incident that makes us stop accepting the simulation. Ian Bogost calls this phenomenon *simulation fever* (Bogost 2008, 106–7). However, such situations are characteristic for video games and stress one of the Menippean aspects of video games.

However, while the example above illustrates expressed laughter, video games also often contain reduced laughter. An example is the sense of being in on the grand joke by the designers or an implicit understanding of what the game is actually about that the fictional characters do not understand.

This War of Mine (11 bit studios and War Child 2014) is an example of this kind of reduced laughter. A player who has read about the game in advance is aware that playing the game is going to be emotionally harrowing and a tragedy, but by knowing this, the player simultaneously is in on this joke made by the designers and participates in this reduced laughter – the quiet joy of a horrible experience. A different example of reduced laughter can be found in *Hatred* (Destructive Creations 2015). According to "Keith" (29), the game's protagonist sounds like "a cartoony supervillain, which makes the game funny in a probably unplanned way". He elaborates in his gameplay journal:

> The dialogue was just kind of pathetic in its attempt to be dark. It was really hard for me to understand what impression they were trying to make with it. Were the developers inspired by actual quotes from spree killers, or did they just take whatever sounded the most dark and controversial? Hard to say, but the effect is an unexpected moment of humor, however dark it is. It's not funny per se, but it's almost of the "so bad it's good" variety.
>
> (Gameplay journal, September 30, 2016)

While the exaggerated characteristics of *Hatred* were widely discussed among the participants, the parodic elements that "Keith" identifies were also discussed explicitly in two of the focus groups (September 28, 2016, and November 11, 2016). This also shows an example of how transgressions may be mitigated by the use of humor, which we discussed in Chapter 5.

Another characteristic of menippea is "its concern with current and topical issues" (Bakhtin 1999, 118) and that it echoes or comments on the topics of its time. For this reason, Bakhtin calls menippea the "journalistic" genre of antiquity. In relation to video games, it reflects how we can see that games are deeply embedded in popular culture, which keeps making them focal points for fierce discussions, at times flaring up to cultural wars. One example is the #gamergate actions (Mortensen 2018), which now are discussed as a prelude or test case to the activism around Donald Trump's presidency through the active participation of central agents (Cross 2017; Lees 2016). While this does not demonstrate the journalistic content of one particular game, it demonstrates how games and game culture reflects the hot topics of their time. Also the so-called games for change segment of serious games, exemplified by Gonzalo Frasca's *September the 12* (Frasca 2003), is an example of the "journalistic" aspects of menippea. In our selection, there are also a number of games that can be considered social commentary: Not only *GTAV* but also *Spec Ops: The Line*, *This War of Mine*, and *Life is Strange*, and *Hatred*, as we discuss in Chapter 6 when "Keith" describes how the protagonist's attack on a political rally makes the otherwise exaggerated game experience suddenly very real. "Mary"

(25) describes how she finds *Spec Ops: The Line* to be a commentary on current war politics:

> For instance, USA just accidentally bombed a Doctor Without Borders hospital, right. So the whole situation here is based on many similar situations that have taken place in active warfare. And... it's uncomfortable because it is correct, I think. The presentation moved you and gives you an icky sensation because you know these things do happen.
>
> (Focus group, October 16, 2015)

With its ability to put focus on some of the problematic sides of war and also make players associate it with current events, *Spec Ops: The Line* corresponds to the menippea's engagement with current affairs.

To sum up, while there is often a humorous tone to the menippea, it is also able to address serious topics. In video games, this is actualized in the fallacy of play – the idea that games and play are only fun and nonserious and not an appropriate arena for serious matters. Looking at games as a Menippean genre, this comic characteristic of menippea stresses the fact that games are indeed nonserious, although the concern with current issues also demonstrates the fact that games are not only playing around with serious topics, but that they are also a medium for the subtle communication of critical matters.

Menippea as fantastic and extraordinary

Several of the characteristics of menippea that Bakhtin identifies concern in some way the fantastic and the extraordinary, ranging from how menippea allows us new and unfamiliar points of view to how it may include the supernatural and the abnormal. The use of the fantastic is one of the main characteristics of games, as they lean heavily on science fiction and fantasy. Philosopher and literary theorist Tzvetan Todorov defines the *fantastic* as the duration of the uncertainty of whether something impossible can exist (1975, 25). In other words, when we experience something as impossible but remain wondering about whether it actually could exist, we are in the domain of the fantastic. And once we answer the question, we are either within the uncanny or the marvelous – two ends of a scale of the fantastic (Todorov 1975). Todorov's scale of the fantastic reaches from the uncanny to the marvelous, which we also address in Chapter 8. *The uncanny* in the context of games can both refer to the "supernatural explained", as Todorov defines it (Todorov 1975), and the "uncanny valley", the point at which virtual representations become so life-like that it is uncomfortable, as hypothesized by Japanese robotics professor Masahiro Mori in the 1970s (Mori, MacDorman, and Kageki 2012). *The marvelous* is the "supernatural accepted" (Todorov 1975). The scale between these extremes demonstrates the importance of contrast in the menippea, and they also demonstrate why the fantastic is such an important genre for games. Games, adhering to the genre descriptions of the menippea, embrace the negative emotion that Massumi points to as desirable (Massumi 2002), letting it out as we play with the uncanny, the almost-real-but-disturbing we particularly see in horror games, at the same time as it lets us jump into the marvelous, different, and spectacularly unrealistic. The different ends of the scale of the fantastic let us experience the full weight of emotion, whether we prefer to play in the uncanny valley of disgust, shock, and fear or in the wonderland of the marvelous with joy, delight, humor, and beauty. The popularity of games indicates that we apparently *want* to play both in the uncanny valley and at the amazing peaks. What both ends of the spectrum have in common is that they make the players keenly experience emotions. While all the games in our sample deal with the fantastic in one way or another, *Bloodborne* and *Alien: Isolation* are the games that most faithfully follow the traditional understanding of the fantastic. The inclusion of monsters in the form of aliens and zombie-like creatures as well as robots is tapping into sensations of uncanniness as well as of awe, stressed by several of our game journal participants. "David" describes his experience with *Alien: Isolation* as one that spans the spectrum from the marvelous to the uncanny, from the terrifying threat of meeting the seemingly undefeatable alien monster to the uncanny encounters with malfunctioning support androids that at the end of the day is the feature that gives him most discomfort (Interview, November 3, 2016).

While the fantastic may most truthfully be encountered in the horror genre, for Bakhtin the most important characteristic of menippea is an unrestrained use of the fantastic that creates extraordinary situations in order to test and explore philosophical ideas (Bakhtin 1999). This can sometimes manifest itself in travels to faraway and unfamiliar lands. These can be *social utopias* (Bakhtin 1999): *Life is Strange* poses as an example by being set in Arcadia Bay, a fictional place that is quite literally named after a mythological utopia. The worlds we meet in video games tend to be unfamiliar to us in the sense that they function according to their own logic, often based on game mechanics (Jørgensen 2013). As mentioned in the introduction to this chapter, games have an inherent "worldness" which defines them. In a gameworld, it may be true – as in *Super Mario Bros.* – that plumbers need to jump chasms and collect mushrooms in order to reach the castle where a princess is kept prisoner (Nintendo Research & Development 4 1985).

In the menippea, however, using extraordinary situations and unfamiliar settings are often associated with exploring philosophical ideas. The idea of possible worlds and what could have been if the world had taken a somewhat different turn is a part of this. In video games, this tends to go hand in hand with the two characteristics of menippea: The concern for the ultimate philosophical questions that provoke the decisive actions of a person (Bakhtin 1999, 115) and *threshold dialogues* or *heavenly gates discourses*, which concerns existential questions or decisions that lead the protagonist beyond the threshold that lead to other realms, such as the underworld or heaven (Bakhtin 1999, 116). "Nathan" (37), an unemployed Norwegian, describes how *Bloodborne* is able to make him feel as a visitor in a different world by his statement that "you are just a tourist in hell" (gameplay journal, October 10, 2016). The game's twisted, gothic reality and the vague environmental storytelling (Jenkins 2004) that only hints at the avatar's motivation makes "Nathan" also question the avatar's identity as savior of the realm.

Another defining characteristic of the medium is how video games often force the players into decisive actions. In order to maintain game progress, players are put in a position from which they will have to choose life or death not just for non-playing characters but also for their own character and often also entire universes and species. The structure and technology of digital games also opens up for extended use of the choices leading to other realms, which may in some cases be directly to heaven or hell, but may also be other alternative parts of the game universe, depending on the rest of the fiction. *Beyond: Two Souls* and *Life is Strange* are both games in our sample that feature explicit player choices through dialogue trees, and they also invite the player to face ultimate questions with regards to suicide, euthanasia, birth, and death. *Life is Strange* goes even further in playing with decisions, as it features the manipulation of time as a central game mechanic. The Norwegian student "Luke" (29) talks about how the player is put into extraordinary positions when they must make decisions on matters of life and death:

> In Life is Strange, there are at least two really awful things: You can save a friend from committing suicide, and you can let your girlfriend live or kill her in what is almost a case of mercy killing. And these are two things that you cannot rewind afterwards.
>
> (Focus group, October 9, 2015)

Both these situations concern events that are absolute: In the suicide scene, the player can either talk their friend out of suicide or not, depending on their dialogue choices and previous actions concerning this friend, but regardless of the outcome, this is an event that cannot be rewound. Unlike most other video game deaths, this is a potential death that is given weight in the narrative climax. The euthanasia episode is one that takes place in an alternate timeline that explores what would have transpired if the protagonist had been using their power to rewind time to save a secondary character's life earlier in the game. In this sense, the episode puts decisive actions with major ethical implications inside a possible world scenario, thereby tapping into three of the fantastic and extraordinary aspects of the menippea at the same time.

Life is Strange's play with time also taps into menippea's characteristic of being liberated from the restrictions of history and memoir, particularly because the memory of all other game characters but the players' avatar is altered in the process of winding back time. This characteristic stresses that the freedom of the plot is absolute, as menippea is not restricted by any form of realism, but allows for historical and philosophical invention and the intermingling of historical and fictional characters in the same narrative (Bakhtin 1999, 114). Being liberated from history and time is also a dominating feature for most video games, where the players may save games and load previous saves in order to perform better. A particularly illustrating example is the *Assassin's Creed* series, which inserts a non-historical character into world history and then plays around with the facts concerning historical characters that may come in contact with the main character of the game (Majkowski 2018).

The freedom from memory and history is also closely connected to what Bakhtin calls the *experimental fantasticality* of the menippea. Experimental fantasticality allows the player an unusual point of view that radically changes the perspective of the observed phenomena (Bakhtin 1999, 116). This relates to how the use of alternate worlds invites alternate viewpoints and new experiences. Games allow us to temporarily take on a fictional identity and explore unfamiliar gameworlds with skills and abilities that we would never gain in the real world. However, it is important to point out that video games are frequently criticized for not being able to offer new perspectives as the point of view tends to be that of a white male, but the games that transgress against the norms and expectations of game culture tend to challenge this facility. Offering the perspective of a female teenager, *Life is Strange* is thus an example of this. Further, *Spec Ops: The Line* allows players to see the world through post-traumatic stress syndrome, and *Hatred* invites the player to take the perspective of a mass murderer. *This War of Mine* lets the player see war through the eyes of civilians, all different and unusual viewpoints for the majority of players. For the Norwegian student "Neil" (25), new experiences are essential to his game preferences, and he describes himself as "the mountaineer who always looks for a new mountain, to gain a new experience" (focus group, November 11, 2015).

By providing insight into the damaged minds of their protagonists, *Hatred* and *Spec Ops: The Line* are also illustrative examples of menippea's tendency to include moral-psychological experimentation of unusual, abnormal states of mind (Bakhtin 1999, 116). In *Spec Ops: The Line*, the players alignment with the protagonists and his inability to fully process the harrowing memories of his past works as a narrative drive and turning point, and is central for how the game creates meaningful discomfort (see Chapter 5) in the player. According to "Oscar" (35), a Norwegian engineer:

> After a while you start to realize that the person you are playing is actually mentally disturbed. So the information you have in order to make choices during the game is not actual information.
>
> (Focus group, September 28, 2015)

Digital role-playing games that are experienced as transgressive may ask the player to use ethical reflection in the problem-solving process (Sicart

2013, 2009), forcing them to consider other mind-sets and perspectives than they otherwise would have employed. This is also a central aspect of games that create meaningful discomfort (see Chapter 5) in the player. Playing with the state of mind, either of the player character or of other characters that the player must support or overcome, is also a vital part of the horror genre.

Another aspect related to the fantastic and the extraordinary is menippea's combination of the fantastic, the mystical and religious, with crude slum naturalism. In menippea, the truth is searched for and found in the parts of society with the lowest status – the slums, brothels, and den of thieves – where insightful wisdom and words of magic often are found among the most vulgar and evil characters (Bakhtin 1999, 115). This is paralleled in the player's traversal through the dark and filthy streets of *Bloodborne*, and "Nathan" (37) further explains how the best of advice seems to come from the least likely of messengers as a machine-shooting madman warns about entering a certain district (gameplay journal, October 3, 2016). Although these characteristics may be transgressive due to the subversion of aesthetic ideals, including fantastic elements may also be transgressive because they invite exploration of the boundaries of the imagination.

Menippea as the ultimate transgressive genre

Menippea can be understood as the ultimate transgressive genre by encompassing several understandings of transgression. First, menippea contains scandal scenes, inappropriate behavior, speeches, and performances, violations of the generally accepted (Bakhtin 1999, 117). It thus spans social taboos and public controversies. This resonates with the attraction of video games toward the socially unacceptable. The degree of violence in almost all games – even children's games – is still prevalent. Video games offer a simulated world where the player can carry out actions that go beyond that which is possible in the real world, thereby creating a space for exploring immoral, taboo, and criminal acts. In the less provocative games, the unacceptable is played out by the antagonist, and it is the player's duty to overcome it in order to restore balance and order. In the more provocative games, it is the player character that breaks the norms and goes outside the acceptable, either in brave defiance or with reckless abandon. In *Dragon Age: Origins*, the player must do unspeakable acts of blood magic in order to save the son of a noble; in contrast, in *GTAV*, there is a side mission in which the player subjects an innocent to torture. In certain instances, the public image of video games as ultraviolent is explicitly exploited for the purpose of attracting attention. The Polish software engineer "Danny" (22) describes his experiences with *Hatred* in this way:

> I was expecting to be shocked. I thought the things that they showed in the trailer, that's just the beginning. But well, it is pretty much it. After

the first level, the game has literally nothing more to show. Nothing to show.

(Individual interview, October 7, 2016)

Hatred's inclusion of extreme violence is in "Danny's" view more than anything else a spectacle, a speculative way of gaining attention through provoking common sensibilities.

Menippea also deals directly with the transgressive through its use of sharp contrasts: Virtue and sin, glory and loss, are often found in the same character or context, exemplified by the fall of the emperor and the noble bandit. This is transgressive in so far that it concerns the subversion of roles, surprising twists, and emotional manipulation. According to Bakhtin, "[t]he menippea loves to play with abrupt transitions and shifts, ups and downs, rises and falls, unexpected comings together of distant and disunited things, mésalliances of all sorts" (Bakhtin 1999, 118). The narrative of a hero moving from rags to riches is a typical example prevalent in games. Also the contrast between the representation of the player character as a virtuous and likeable hero, which nevertheless kills everything in their path without much consideration is a clear example of this. An example is Trevor, one of the three protagonists in *GTAV*, an ex-con and excitement-seeking sociopath. Although some of the player participants have no sympathy for the character, others find certain redeeming features in him:

> Trevor is the comic moment, due to everything he says, the things he does. A normal person would never do these things. (…) He is comedy, simple as that. He is a violent psychopath, but you learn through the story that he has, there are good things in him, you just have to search for it.
>
> ("Tony" (36), focus group interview, September 28, 2015)

Other examples are the subversion of the hero role, as we discussed above in the cases of *Spec Ops: The Line* and *Bloodborne*. Other games that subvert the trope of the heroic game protagonist are *Shadow of the Colossus* (Team ICO 2005) and *Far Cry 5* (Ubisoft Montreal 2018).

Last, menippea can also be considered transgressive in the sense that it challenges established genres (Majkowski 2019). Menippea is typically a mixture of genres, inserted speeches, prose, and poetry, and is characterized by its multi-styled and multi-voiced nature (Bakhtin 1999, 118). Video games are by definition a mixture of established media, and the different media and the popular cultural mesh that games tend to be part of are so much a part of the medium that they can be hard to distinguish and recognize. The video game as medium combines game mechanics with the cinematic as well as with text. Role-playing games such as the *Mass Effect* series allow the player to hone their tactical skills in combat, and combine this with cinematic cutscenes as well as with written texts to be encountered as books or emails in the gameworld. Also, most video games today do not follow the conventions of one game genre only; instead, they combine the best of several genres into one. For instance, *Horizon: Zero Dawn* (Guerrilla Games 2017) combines open world exploration with the 3D climbing puzzles and acrobatic action gameplay. In our sample, *Spec Ops: The Line* combines traditional shooter mechanics with the narrative of Joseph Conrad's literary classic *Heart of Darkness* (Conrad 1899). An example of how this may be experienced as transgressive is given by "Jane" (38), who, as discussed in Chapter 5, was frustrated by how *This War of Mine* melds a serious war game with resource management simulation, turning a profound problem into a resource management game (Individual interview, October 29, 2016). "Jane's" reaction shows how the mixture of genres sometimes can be a transgression. While it stylistically may be unproblematic, its explicit failure to fulfill expectations may be confusing. This shows that sometimes transgression can spring out of the fact that situations may prove to be something other than what they pretend to be.

Menippea, intent and transgression

There are also games where, while we can pinpoint some aspects of menippea, the connection is not a major feature of the attraction to the games. The wildly popular sports games, such as the *FIFA* franchise (EA Vancouver and EA Romania 2018), may be used by players to create humorous or transgressive situations, such as playing the representation of the young star Mbappe as an unstoppable player (Bristow 2018) or letting unlikely, low-rated video game characters perform the spectacular overhead kicks of football superstar Ronaldo (Yin-Poole 2018), but they are aiming to represent not a different, fantastic world but a simulation of this world, with a bit more agency given to the players than they would have while simply watching the game. In this case, the satire that occasionally does happen is not a design goal, but more likely a flaw, such as with the unstoppable feature of Mbappe, or a result of how players want to play the game, as with the overhead kick. While the game definitely comments on current affairs, such cases offer a utopian universe in which all players can do overhead kicks, and involuntary offer moral dilemmas, such as whether or not it is acceptable to play a character that cannot be stopped, but such features are not the main design goals of the game. A *FIFA* game "brings The World's Game to life, letting you play with the biggest leagues, clubs, and players in world football, all with incredible detail and realism" (Electronic Arts 2019). This indicates that the intent of the game is not satire, but realism and simulation. Whether this is possible is another matter.

On the one hand, the discussion of the Menippean satire shows that video games can hardly avoid the menippea and, for this reason, are irrevocably part of the carnivalesque tradition as Bakhtin describes it. Through adopting Menippean qualities, video games are by nature subversive, inviting the player to temporarily take on new perspectives in a topsy-turvy utopian – or dystopian – world. The rebellious undercurrents of the carnival are also still intact in video games, reflected not only in the content of games, but also in gaming culture. The idea that games are at heart a subculture only for a certain group of insiders and that they require a certain kind of literacy not easily acquired is a part of this. On the other hand, not all games aim at being Menippean satires, but go to great length to offer different representations. While we can't really analyze intent while studying the text of a game, we can look at how a game either deliberately uses the elements of satire or falls into it at random through design flaws, like with *FIFA*.

Neither do we claim that all Menippean satire is transgressive. While satire lends itself to transgression, as it is in itself a contrary genre that plays with the stupidity of humanity, scorn, and ridicule (Merriam-Webster Dictionary 2019), if it is the general consensus that what is being mocked is deserving of mockery, the satire is not transgressive. However, as we saw at the start of this chapter, many games come from and are being targeted at a demographic segment already saturated in a culture where political and cultural opposition; mockery; and transgressive acts, ideas, statements, and claims are the norm rather than the exceptions. And in this reality, many, if not most, games with a narrative or obviously fictional element, will become deliberate Menippean satires, with a strong underlying acceptance of the importance of the topsy-turvy world of the carnivalesque.

The importance of transgressions

In his work about video game culture as a toxic meritocracy, game researcher Christopher Paul writes about what he calls the jerks of gaming. In this context, he underlines the connection "between the reality we perceive and the symbol systems we use to describe it" (Paul 2018, 63). Paul describes the toxic culture of gaming through a discussion of the webcomic *Penny Arcade* (Krahulik and Holkins 2019). The comic was criticized for transgressive statements, for instance the infamous "dickwolves" comic (2010), a satire on the structure of quests in RPGs. The comic was criticized for making fun of rape victims, and the controversy peaked as *Penny Arcade* created dickwolf merchandise. At a conference, illustrator Mike Krahulik said that they should have let the merchandise stay on the store rather than discontinue it, even if the merchandise were intended to insult the rape victims that protested. This was applauded by the audience (Paul 2018). Paul argues that inside of a toxic game culture, removing a reference to rape once it had been made would be more problematic and more norm-breaking than leaving it in.

Our claim here is not that games should not be transgressive. Rather, we believe in the power of games to challenge through transgressive aesthetics, and we claim that insight into the toxic side of game culture demonstrates why transgressions are important. However, the transgressive aesthetics of games is not a one-way street: Game enthusiasts who accept games that break other players' sensibilities must also accept the potential existence of games that may provoke them. It is ironic when game enthusiasts who defend the right of games to offend themselves become offended by certain kinds of game content or criticism. As game culture becomes more diverse and as a consequence also more politicized, game enthusiasts can in the future expect to more often encounter game content that they find transgressive. Creating games that challenge the players' cultural complacency as well as their expectations may offer a way to provoke discussion among groups that are otherwise too risk-adverse to engage with interaction in other cultural strata than their own. Games and the culture that surrounds them belong to a part of our online culture that appears to keep a deliberate distance from the mainstream. This exclusion tends to lead it into the contextual vicinity of other topics – for instance, racism and misogyny with game criticism – making a contextual collapse possible. By taking game aesthetics seriously and acknowledging the transgressive power of games, we can make game subcultures more distinct. By not confusing contextually close subcultures, we may avoid contextual collapse.

While this indicates that more games in the future may provoke common sensibilities, this also means that it is possible to transgress as an opposition to oppression and social injustice. Game scholars Kishonna Gray and David Leonard demonstrate how games can be transgressive and carnivalesque, and still be what they call "woke" – conscious of the social injustices in contemporary culture (Gray and Leonard 2018, 13). Their book is a collection of counter-narratives, demonstrations of how players cannot just have access to transgressive games, but also can play games that deal with other types of transgressions, such as *Hair Nah*, which allows an avatar to smack away white hands trying to touch a black person's hair (Momo Pixel, n.d.). Touching black hair is here a demonstration of different life experiences and cultures meeting. Here the conflict between a white person's curiosity and a black woman's annoyance with being the target of this curiosity makes this game a demonstration of how games can address real-life transgressions. And this game does transgress, stepping straight into the discourse of race in the US, as the designer Momo Pixel experienced. Although she claims that she designed this for herself, it is born from her own frustration with transgressions (Payne 2018). It is a transgressive response to a transgression.

Aesthetic transgressions are often efficient tools to highlight topics that may be hard to talk about. We already know that transgressive aesthetics can be planned, as we see in the carefully designed art pieces that fold into a movement of transgressive art, art which is supposed to stir us, and to dispel the disinterest which comes with Kant's understanding of the conditions of aesthetic judgment: "The delight which determines the judgement of taste is independent of all interest" (Kant 1790). *Independent* is, by Kant and following critics, understood as disconnected, and the critics' gaze needs to be a disinterested gaze, specifically one that is not moved by emotion. Kieran Cashell describes this credo of aesthetic appreciation, and continues by demonstrating the role of transgressive art in relation to the dominant, anti-sentimental understanding of aesthetics:

> Yet it is precisely this concept that much important contemporary artistic practice actively tries to sabotage by engaging with the 'extra-aesthetic' contexts of the very emotional, sexual and especially moral life-worlds prescriptively disengaged by the dogma of disinterestedness.
>
> (Cashell 2009, loc. 313–15)

Transgressive art, when it is deliberate, is designed to negate the trained and nurtured intellectual, analytical distance and make us feel. It is an aesthetic of emotion and affect. But in order to reach this point, it needs to step around the trained and educated aesthetic responses of distance and cool appreciation, and reach for an appreciation that has room for different, perhaps more immediate, strategies of judgment.

References

11 bit studios, and War Child. 2014. *This War of Mine*. 11 bit studios.

Annandale, David. 2006. "The Subversive Carnival of Grand Theft Auto: San Andreas." In *The Meaning and Culture of Grand Theft Auto: Critical Essays*, edited by Nate Garrelts, Kindle, 88–103. Jefferson, NC: McFarland & Company Inc.

Bakhtin, Mikhail. 1999. *Problems of Dostoevsky's Poetics*. Minneapolis, London: University of Minnesota Press.

Berentsen, William H., and G. Duggan Lawrence. 2019. "Germany – The Reformation." *Encyclopædia Britannica*. Encyclopædia Britannica, Inc. www.britannica.com/place/Germany/The-Reformation.

Bezio, Kristin MS. 2018. "Ctrl-Alt-Del: GamerGate as a Precursor to the Rise of the Alt-Right." *Leadership* 14 (5): 556–66. doi:10.1177/1742715018793744.

Bioware. 2007. *Mass Effect*. Microsoft Game Studios.

Bjørkelo, Kristian A. 2019. "Er Det Ein Samanheng Mellom Drapa i Christchurch Og Spelkulturen?" *Fri Tanke*, March 2019.

Blodgett, Bridget, and Anastasia Salter. 2018. "Ghostbusters Is for Boys: Understanding Geek Masculinity's Role in the Alt-Right." *Communication, Culture and Critique* 11 (1): 133–46. doi:10.1093/ccc/tcx003.

Bogost, Ian. 2008. *Unit Operations: An Approach to Videogame Criticism*. Cambridge: MIT Press.

Bristow, Thomas. 2018. "FIFA 19: 5 Gameplay Mistakes and Hilarious Moments Users Have Already Spotted." Mirror. September 27, 2018. www.mirror.co.uk/sport/football/news/fifa-19-5-gameplay-mistakes-13320546.

Carson, E. Ann. 2016. "Bureau of Justice Statistics Sentenced Population." www.bjs.gov/content/pub/pdf/p16_sum.pdf.

Cashell, Kieran. 2009. *Aftershock : The Ethics of Contemporary Transgressive Art*. I.B. Tauris.

CD Projekt RED. 2015. *The Witcher 3: Wild Hunt*. CD Projekt.

Conrad, Joseph. 1899. *Heart of Darkness*. London and Edinburgh: William Blackwood and Sons.

Consalvo, Mia. 2006. "From Dollhouse to Metaverse: What Happened When The Sims Went Online." In *The Players' Realm: Studies on the Culture of Video Games and Gaming*, edited by J. Patrick Williams and Jonas Heide-Smith, 203–221. Jefferson, NC: McFarland & Company.

Cross, Katherine. 2017. "We Warned You about Milo and You're Still Not Listening." *The Establishment – Medium*, October 9, 2017.

Davis, Jenny L., and Nathan Jurgenson. 2014. "Context Collapse: Theorizing Context Collusions and Collisions." *Information, Communication & Society* 17 (4): 476–85. doi:10.1080/1369118X.2014.888458.

Destructive Creations. 2015. *Hatred*. Destructive Creations. www.hatredgame.com/.

EA Vancouver, and EA Romania. 2018. *FIFA 19*. EA Sports.

Electronic Arts. 2019. "FIFA Video Games – Official EA Site." EA Games. 2019.

Flanagan, Mary. 2003. "Simple & Personal: Domestic Space & The Sims." In *MelbourneDAC 2003*. Melbourne.

Flynn, Meagan. 2019. "'I Didn't Want Hate to Win': PewDiePie Ends 'subscribe' Meme after Christchurch Shooter's Shout-Out." *The Washington Post*, April 29, 2019. www.washingtonpost.com/nation/2019/04/29/i-didnt-want-hate-win-pewdiepie-ends-subscribe-meme-after-christchurch-shooters-shout-out/?utm_term=.f328ffbb14d2.

Frasca, Gonzalo. 2003. "September 12th: A Toy World." Newsgames.com.

Gray, Kishonna L., and David J. Leonard. 2018. *Woke Gaming: Digital Challenges to Oppression and Social Injustice*. Seattle: University of Washington Press.

Guerrilla Games. 2017. *Horizon: Zero Dawn*. Sony Interactive Entertainment.

Infinity Ward. 2009. *Call of Duty: Modern Warfare 2*. Activision.

Jenkins, Henry. 2004. "Game Design as Narrative Architecture." In *First Person: New Media as Story, Performance, and Game*, edited by Noah Wardrip-Fruin and Pat Harrigan, 118–30. Cambridge: MIT Press.

Jenks, Chris. 2003. *Transgressions*. London: Routledge.

Jørgensen, Kristine. 2013. *Gameworld Interfaces*. Cambridge: The MIT Press. doi:10.7551/mitpress/9780262026864.001.0001.

Kant, Immanuel. 1790. *Critique of Judgement*. Kindle. Oxford: Oxford University Press.

Karlsen, Faltin, and Kristine Jørgensen. 2014. "Mediepanikk Eller Medieskepsis? – En Analyse Av Dataspilldebatten Etter 22. Juli." *Norsk Medietidsskrift* 21 (1): 42–61.

Klastrup, Lisbeth. 2003. *Towards a Poetics of Virtual Worlds – Multi-User Textuality and the Emergence of Story*. Copenhagen: IT University of Copenhagen.

Krahulik, Mike, and Jerry Holkins. 2010. "The Sixth Slave." Penny Arcade. 2010. www.penny-arcade.com/comic.

———. 2019. "Penny Arcade." Penny Arcade. 2019. www.penny-arcade.com/comic.

Lees, Matt. 2016. "What Gamergate Should Have Taught Us about the 'Alt-Right.'" *The Guardian*, December 1, 2016. www.theguardian.com/technology/2016/dec/01/gamergate-alt-right-hate-trump.

Leonard, David. 2006. "Virtual Gangstas, Coming to a Suburban House near You: Demonization, Commodification, and Policing Blackness." In *The Meaning and*

Culture of Grand Theft Auto: Critical Essays, edited by Nate Garrelts, 49–69, Kindle. Jefferson, NC: McFarland & Company, inc.

Majkowski, Tomasz. 2018. "The Renaissance Ass. Ezio Auditore and Digital Menippea." In *Transgression in Games and Play*, edited by Kristine Jørgensen and Faltin Karlsen, 189–206. Cambridge: MIT Press.

Marsh, Jenny, and Tara Mulholland. 2019. "How the Christchurch Terrorist Attack Was Made for Social Media." *CNN Business*, March 16, 2019. https://edition.cnn.com/2019/03/15/tech/christchurch-internet-radicalization-intl/index.html.

Marwick, Alice E., and danah boyd. 2011. "I Tweet Honestly, I Tweet Passionately: Twitter Users, Context Collapse, and the Imagined Audience." *New Media & Society* 13 (1): 114–33. doi:10.1177/1461444810365313.

Massumi, Brian. 2002. *Parables for the Virtual: Movement, Affect, Sensation.* Durham, London: Duke University Press.

Merriam-Webster Dictionary. 2019. "Satire | Definition of Satire." *Merriam-Webster Dictionary*. Merriam-Webster. www.merriam-webster.com/dictionary/satire.

Momo Pixel. n.d. *Hair Nah*. Momo Pixel.

Mori, Masahiro, Karl F. MacDorman, and Norri Kageki. 2012. "The Uncanny Valley." *IEEE Robotics and Automation Magazine* 19 (2): 98–100. doi:10.1109/MRA.2012.2192811.

Mortensen, Torill Elvira. 2018. "Anger, Fear, and Games: The Long Event of #GamerGate." *Games and Culture* 13 (8). doi:10.1177/1555412016640408.

Neiwert, David. 2017. "Birth of the Alt Right." *The Public Eye*, March 2017.

Niantic. 2016. *Pokémon Go*. Niantic.

Nintendo Research & Development 4. 1985. "Super Mario Bros." Nintendo.

Paul, Christopher A. 2018. *The Toxic Meritocracy of Video Games: Why Gaming Culture Is the Worst*. Minneapolis: University of Minnesota Press.

Payne, Teryn. 2018. "Momo Pixel 'Hair Nah' Video Game Interview." *Teen Vogue*, January 5, 2018. www.teenvogue.com/story/momo-pixel-hair-nah-video-game-interview.

Phillips, Whitney. 2015. *This Is Why We Can't Have Nice Things; Mapping the Relationship between Online Trolling and Mainstream Culture*. Cambridge: The MIT Press.

Pötzsch, Holger. 2018. "Forms and Practices of Transgressivity in Videogames: Aesthetics, Play, and Politics." In *Transgression in Games and Play*, edited by Kristine Jørgensen and Faltin Karlsen, 45–61. Cambridge: MIT Press.

Redmond, Dennis. 2006. "Grand Theft Video: Running and Gunning for the U.S. Empire." In *The Meaning and Culture of Grand Theft Auto: Critical Essays*, edited by Nate Garrelts, Kindle, 104–114. McFarland and Company, inc.

Salter, Michael. 2018. "From Geek Masculinity to Gamergate: The Technological Rationality of Online Abuse." *Crime, Media, Culture: An International Journal* 14 (2): 247–64. doi:10.1177/1741659017690893.

Scribner, Bob. 1978. "Reformation, Carnival and the World Turned Upside-Down." *Social History* 3 (3): 303–29. doi:10.1080/03071027808567430.

Shifman, Limor. 2013. "Memes in a Digital World: Reconciling with a Conceptual Troublemaker." *Journal of Computer-Mediated Communication* 18 (3): 362–77. doi:10.1111/jcc4.12013.

Sicart, Miguel. 2009. *The Ethics of Computer Games*. Cambridge: MIT Press.

———. 2013. *Beyond Choices*. Cambridge: MIT Press.

Team ICO. 2005. *Shadow of the Colossus*. Sony Computer Entertainment.

Todorov, Tzvetan. 1975. *The Fantastic: A Structural Approach to a Literary Genre*. Ithaca, NY: Cornell University Press.

Ubisoft Montreal. 2018. *Far Cry 5*. Ubisoft.

Varis, Piia, and Jan Blommaert. 2018. "Conviviality and Collectives on Social Media: Virality, Memes, and New Social Structures." *Multilingual Margins: A Journal of Multilingualism from the Periphery* 2 (1): 31. doi:10.14426/mm.v2i1.55.

Wirman, Hanna, and Rhys Jones. 2018. "Let's Play Performance as Transgressive Play." In *Transgression in Games and Play*, edited by Kristine Jørgensen and Faltin Karlsen, 99–113. Cambridge: MIT Press.

Yin-Poole, Wesley. 2018. "FIFA 19 Review – the Spectacular, Troubling Video Game Modern Football Deserves." Eurogamer. September 19, 2018. www.eurogamer.net/articles/2018-09-19-fifa-19-review-the-spectacular-troubling-video-game-modern-football-deserves.

8 Game aesthetics and the sublime

If we look at games as emotion machines and assume that their main purpose is not to be won or lost, but to be felt, we need to consider the point of view from which we appreciate and analyze them. In the introduction to this book, we stated that aesthetics is not something that exists objectively in an artwork, but it emerges as a result of a value judgment of a work and therefore depends on the relationship between the perceiver and the work. While aesthetic philosophy has a long tradition of debating the role and value of emotions in the appreciators' response to aesthetic works, we look at transgressive aesthetics, where we consider feelings to be vital for aesthetic appreciation.

In this chapter, we are looking at how we can study the emotional aspect of games through aesthetic theory. Specifically, we will illuminate how transgressive game aesthetics can be understood as a contrast to flow through the concepts of kitsch and avant-garde, before moving on to discussing the relationship between transgressive game aesthetic and the sublime. Our central argument in this chapter is that transgressive game aesthetics indeed is dependent upon emotional response.

Designing for emotions and flow

Game designers are well aware of the connection of emotion and games, and have developed strategies for designing for emotion (Freeman 2004; Freeman and David 2004). Katherine Isbister's work, introduced in Chapter 8, explores the argument that games are made up of meaningful choices, which leads us into the idea of *flow* as the ideal of game design. Echoing *Civilization* designer Sid Meier's claim that a game is a series of interesting choices (Alexander 2012; Isbister 2016), Isbister states that *meaningful choices* indicate a sense of mastery and responsibility for one's own choices and their outcomes, experiences that resonate strongly with Csikszentmihalyi's emphasis on the meaning-making in the experience of flow (Csikszentmihalyi 2002). For us, the most important aspect of Isbister's discussion is in how choice leads to involvement and mental activity. This is one of the core properties of a game: It needs to offer choice of some kind, and these choices are meaningful because they create emotion.

As we discussed in Chapter 6, one of the most frequently cited theories when game designers discuss how to create good games is Csikszentmihalyi's theory of flow (Csikszentmihalyi 2002). Isbister holds flow theory up as the main tool for designers to design engaging games. She claims that "[f]low theory has been a boon to the game design and research communities", and that this approach has moved the discourse into how emotions can be affected by design (Isbister 2016, 5).

While flow theory, as theorized by Csikszentmihalyi, is a description not of the field of ultimate game play but of the zone of ultimate autotelic experience in life in general, it offers designers a model for the winning condition of game design: If a designer can manage to keep the players in the flow zone for a long time, it is a well-designed game. It is in many ways the opposite of what Isbister discusses – rather than being a way to relate play with emotion, it describes an emotional balance to avoid feeling anxiety and boredom, two overwhelming emotions connected to the demands of living with routine work. While playfulness can foster flow, flow does not necessarily foster playfulness. The terms are not synonymous (Stenros 2015, 65).

Kitsch and the avant-garde in game aesthetics

However, the claim that flow is a good thing for game design has its critics. Game scholar and designer Brian Schrank sees flow as something suspect because of the way it is used to control the player's emotions (Schrank 2014, 34). Schrank claims that flow controls the player in the same way as how the central perspective of Renaissance painting and architecture controls the viewer. Where Isbister uses Renaissance art as an analogy for new ventures in game design and for how video games experience a burst in new genres and emotional territory (Isbister 2016, xvii), Schrank's comparison to the Renaissance when talking about the flow aspect of games describes it as an aesthetic style that restricts its audience more than it liberates or empowers.

The difference is rooted in the use of the term. *Renaissance* is often used as synonymous for renewal and rejuvenation, but we tend to forget that it also means a comeback or a return to something old, in the sense that the Renaissance appropriated the aesthetic of the Greek and Romans of the Antique. Considering that video games have never previously been as sophisticated nor is there something previously forgotten that we have re-learned about how to design them, it is difficult to see today's advances in game design as a return to former glory. Rather than talking about the Renaissance as a *renewal* of game design, Schrank speaks of Renaissance as an artistic direction and a specific game design aesthetic (Schrank 2014, 32). He justifies this with the illusion of immersion that the central perspective strived to create, as it was reintroduced during the Renaissance period to Western art. According to Schrank, a well-executed Renaissance painting fixed the viewer in one position in relation to the canvas, at which point the image could be experienced in the best way. In the same manner, flow as a design paradigm fixes the player in one position in relation to the game, leading the player along carefully regulated paths.

Schrank goes one step further, though, and claims that what is created by flow is not the perfect, artistic illusion, a Renaissance art work, but *kitsch*:

> Solution space is a way of quantifying the possibilities of play and rendering them tangible within a computational system. No matter how large or complex the system of a game is, if it is designed to transform the player into its ideal subject who can perform their part perfectly, then the game is a form of contemporary kitsch – the antithesis of formal avant-garde art.
>
> (Schrank 2014, 36)

Kitsch is when a work of art is mediocre or banal; it has become a stereotype (Poggioli 1981, 80). Kitsch is, according to Schrank, a term for easily consumable media and characterizes a standardized aesthetic to which the audience know how to respond. Kitsch games thus offer universal literacy and predict and cause emotion on cue. This resonates with Colin Cremin's double understanding of the player either as an apprentice striving to become an artist, learning from the process, or the player as a regressive apprentice, aiming only to repeat the same tricks that lead to the same results (Cremin 2016).

In opposition to kitsch games, Schrank positions avant-garde games, and he claims the main value of these games is that they weaken or break up flow (Schrank 2014, 7). He continues in his description of what can make games avant-garde in pointing out how limited the current explorations of what video games can do really is, talking about how it can be explored as something sensual or material, how they relate to economy and politics, and how they can be different from the current idea by being more changeable (Schrank 2014). They are distinguished from mainstream games by how they demonstrate diversity of gameplay and break apart how we think about game design and game play (Schrank 2014). This is consistent with Schrank's understanding of avant-garde art in general, as art that disrupts the illusion of coherence.

The avant-garde is generally thought of not as a fixed design trend but as a movement. In its conception, it was closely connected to political revolt and expresses something new – that which is just invented (Poggioli 1981). Rather than a movement away from a careful rendering of reality, the avant-garde is a movement away from the established and fixed. Schrank defines avant-garde as a specific movement of art, one where the hegemony of the painting as a perfect window is broken. In avant-garde, according to

Schrank, the image is fragmented, the perspective disrupted, and the illusion ripped aside. This is a very specific understanding of the avant-garde, where it becomes fixed to a specific genre of visual art.

Literary scholar Renato Poggioli expands on the connection between the avant-garde and kitsch (Poggioli 1981). The two aspects rely on each other, as avant-garde can only exist as long as there is an established tradition – the stereotype; and the stereotype is created from successful new inventions – from a successful avant-garde. With this in mind, the avant-garde in games is not be understood as one specific direction where it is possible to list certain aesthetic features; on the contrary, once avant-garde games become a particular genre that needs to follow a specific format, they have by definition become kitsch. As Schrank states in his concluding chapter, "The avant-garde leads or protests the current state of games, and it does so in many ways, just as it historically led or protested mainstream art and culture in many ways" (Schrank 2014, 182). The avant-garde does not follow the rules, even its own. It breaks them.

Ludic dysphoria

The works of Isbister and Schrank give us an opportunity to look at two very different game design paradigms, both of which point toward positioning *emotion* as the main goal of gameplay. Isbister's point of departure is how designers can control the reactions and bodies of the players through emotion-bound design, while Schrank's is how players can be jolted out of their comfort zone in order to become aware of their emotions beyond the controlled experience. Both of these positions, however, aim at aesthetics of experienced emotion.

In Chapter 5, we discussed play that is carried out not because it is fun, but because it is gratifying on other levels as parapathic game experiences. We will now introduce the related idea of *ludic dysphoria*, a trend of designing games that are deliberately uncomfortable and jarring. In psychology, dysphoria refers to a disconnect in emotion connected to a profound state of dissatisfaction and discomfort characterized by anxiety and restlessness (Purse 2019). Ludic dysphoria is the disconnect players feel when they encounter games that are truly disruptive. They are avant-garde because they break fundamentally with our idea of what a game is and should be. If we follow Poggioli's understanding of the avant-garde, ludic dysphoric games will – if they become established as genres or because their game mechanics become widespread – sooner or later be described, defined, and framed, at which point they become kitsch, and the avant-garde will have moved on to new inventions. Ludic dysphoric games are transgressive because of the strong and often conflicting emotions they evoke. In Chapter 2, we discussed *That Dragon, Cancer*, which disturbed players as well as critics because it thematized childhood cancer, using few traditional game mechanics and thereby also raising the question whether it was a game or not. Similarly, the much debated story-game *Depression Quest* (Quinn, Lindsey, and Schankler 2013) also raised controversy over whether or not depression was something that made a suitable topic for play (Parkin 2014). *Depression Quest* and *That Dragon, Cancer* can also be seen as avant-garde in that they introduced something truly novel into the gaming world and thereby also created ludic dysphoria in a large group of players who neither expected nor wanted a form of innovation in games that included stripped-down mechanics for the sake of a transgressive form of realism (Bjørkelo 2018).

A different example of ludic dysphoria is the previously mentioned *The Artwork Formerly Known as PainStation*. *PainStation* is a piece of interactive art that is also a game. The point of the game is to get a high score by keeping your hand on the *pain execution unit* – a panel that delivers pain to the player. Each player can hurt the other through gameplay, and no matter the score, the player to first lift a hand from the game will lose. *PainStation* was both an art success and a more commercial success, and the designers had to make a new version to avoid some of the liabilities that came with having designed a popular game that could potentially harm others. While this is not exactly a mainstream game, it does prove that there is not an automatic connection between pleasurable emotion and game pleasure. Like with Massumi's example of the paradox of painful art from Chapter 6, *PainStation* is popular because it makes such a huge impression through a distinctly unpleasant sensation. The physical and emotional upset is, in many ways, as enjoyable as a pleasing or soothing experience. As a work of art, *PainStation* falls neatly into a tradition of transgressive art. *PainStation* also carries a double dose of transgression; the player will feel pain, which to most people is quite transgressive, even in an aesthetic context, and they will cause pain, which we have learned from an early age is morally wrong. The player is both the transgressee and the transgressor.

What *The Artwork Formerly Known as PainStation* – named thus because *PainStation* violated the copyright of *PlayStation* – indicates is that intense experiences, even if they are painful and they cause pain, are pleasurable in themselves, given the correct context. It is, literally, painful art in a physical sense, not just art that is highly uncomfortable in an aesthetic or psychological sense, like parapathic play. This is the opposite of a tradition of aesthetics emphasizing that what we access has to be immediately considered pleasing, and it also indicates that the shock of emotion in itself can be a quality in a work of expression, which goes in the face of the traditions of disinterested aesthetic evaluation.

This painful type of disruptive, unpleasant excitement is the opposite of flow, which puts it within Schrank's definition of avant-garde games (Schrank 2014), and makes them examples of ludic dysphoria. *PainStation* is also an example of is how transgressive aesthetics can sometimes emerge from game mechanics – game form – alone. *Depression Quest* and *That Dragon, Cancer* both show examples of how the ludic dysphoria and hence also the sense of transgression spring out of a combination of form and content, but this is hardly avant-garde as such games are becoming frequent. However, of these three examples, *PainStation* may be the only truly avant-garde game because of its ability to create truly innovative game mechanics without the support of fiction.

Overcoming disinterest

We have established that transgressive aesthetics in games challenge and create conflicting and often strong emotion in the player. Here we will discuss how transgressive game aesthetics challenge and break with *disinterest*.

In Chapter 6, we introduced Immanuel Kant's concept of disinterest, which to him was the ideal way of appreciating an artwork: A distanced and contemplative mode of rational reception that is disengaged from any emotional response (Cashell 2009, 5). For Kant, disinterest is necessary to be able to truthfully perceive beauty; otherwise the perceiver may consider other aspects than the actual beauty of the object itself, such as the political correctness of the message or the artwork's potential economic value.

Disinterest has become closely connected with objectivity (Bratkowski 2014; Bullough 1912; Levine 2001) to the point that it is hard to distinguish between disinterest as a tool to judge beauty and objectivity in a matter of political discourse. This understanding of disinterest suggests that using art for activist or argumentative purposes is at odds with any "true" appreciation of art, because of its aim to create an emotional response. In this sense, it is a dismissal of pathos rhetoric. In our discussion, we do not argue against disinterest because we believe a work of art should be judged based on political position or cultural immersion, but because we consider the emotional investment in and entanglement with the object an important part of the aesthetic experience. In order to clarify our argument, we will look more closely at disinterest. In our point of view, to claim that objectivity and disinterest overlap would be to simplify the matter too much. Instead, we want to look at the Kantian idea of disinterest.

According to philosopher James Shelley (2015), Kant's *disinterest* indicates a disengagement from desire. To illustrate this, Shelley distinguishes between the judgment of morally good actions and the judgment of beauty. To judge the morality of an action relates to the desire or lack of desire to perform the action. To judge an object beautiful is free of this desire for any particular performance. Cashell illustrates the difference with an example of a picture of a nude: For an aesthetic appreciation of the nude, it is essential that the observer disengages with any erotic desire. Not before we can "consider the naked body as an abstract design that stimulates a kind of pleasure completely unlike the visceral thrill of erotic desire" can we begin to contemplate it from a disinterested perspective (Cashell 2009, 5).

Disinterest, as Kant describes it, indicates that we have no interest in the outcome apart from the intellectual stimulus that the artwork gives us.

When we claim objectivity, this often concerns the political or economic independence from parties that might desire to influence us. Literary theorist Satya Mohanty attempts to distinguish objectivity from disinterest. He claims that objectivity exists because what we try to make a judgment about is already dependent on society and culture. Our aesthetic values are always relational and grounded in our lives, and we do not deny our aesthetic values objectivity because we cannot claim that they are universal (Mohanty 2001, 823). To Mohanty, objectivity is not disinterest – quite the opposite: Objectivity is a state of reflexivity where we do not try to apply the rules of the science of the extrahuman (physics, chemistry, etc.) but accept that we are all human, we are influenced by our humanity, and that is the same for all of us. We are not detached from the judgment, we are accepting of the potential bias of it, and we understand how being human influences a decision.

The disinterest of Kant is even more closely connected to the artwork. It is a matter of recognizing beauty not because we have no interest in the outcome of the judgment, but despite it. Disinterest does not mean that the appreciator cannot say that they like an artwork, but it concerns the dispassionate and sober, if not descriptive then surely analytical, approach to the artwork. The object itself forces the judgment of beauty, and in this logic, if the judgment is made in a way that does not serve our interests – acknowledging that the painting of another artist is more beautiful, for instance – it is apparently a more disinterested claim. This is a matter of judgment unaligned with what we today understand as bias – an unbiased judgment of taste, if this is possible. In order to disinterestedly judge the quality of a game, then what we feel about it is not unimportant.

The sublime

There is, however, according to Kant, one point where our rational judgment will eventually fail in the face of the sensations we experience. This is when we experience the *sublime*, which is the sensation that may emerge when we encounter natural or designed phenomena that are so overwhelming that it makes us realize our intellectual limitations. We argue that understanding the sublime is essential for understanding transgressive aesthetics in games. To understand the concept of the sublime as an aesthetic experience, it is important to stress that it does not only emerge from absolute and indescribable beauty but may also emerge from the awesome, terrifying, and incomprehensibly monstrous. This connects it to the transgressive in media and the arts, and hence also in games. We understand the sublime as an aesthetic experience that contributes to making transgressive situations not only endurable, but sometimes also desirable for media audiences, including game players.

The sublime is a concept with a long history in Western thought and is assumed to have been introduced by the Greek author and teacher Longinus in the third century AD. The concept was absent from popular discourse for a long stretch of time, only to have re-entered European thought through two separate translations after 1530 (Lang 2015, loc. 45–46). Kant separates between two forms of the sublime. The *dynamically sublime* is an almost spiritual experience of awe and terror associated with the uncontrollable powers of nature. The *mathematically sublime*, on the other hand, is the experience of something that is intellectually difficult to grasp, such as the incomprehensible nature of the magnitude of the infiniteness of the universe (Kant 1790, 78, 84–85, 91–92). An important aspect of the sublime is that even when it strikes us with awe and terror, it is experienced as something positive; it is something that "lifts us up" in its sensation of being "larger than life". The idea of the sublime has had a large impact on how to understand and talk about overwhelming emotions in the judgment of art. Although the sublime is often associated with an ultimate and overwhelming beauty, it is elusive and does not inherently reside in the phenomenon experienced as sublime. The sublime distinguishes itself from the beautiful exactly through the failure of our human judgment to grasp it. Beautiful, according to Kant, lends itself to our faculties of observation, while

> the feeling of the sublime, may appear, indeed, in point of form to contravene the ends of our power of judgment, to be ill-adapted to our faculty of presentation, and to do violence, as it were, to the imagination, and yet it is judged all the more sublime on that account.
>
> (Kant 1790, 76)

In the following paragraphs, we will discuss transgressive aesthetics in games through the lens of the sublime. We will first explain the concept of the sublime and its roots in European Romanticism before we move on to discussing how the sublime has been used as a framework for understanding monstrous aesthetics. We will then present the ludic sublime and discuss how transgressive aesthetics in games relates to this specific notion of the sublime.

European Romanticism

The sublime became connected to the Romantic movement of art through the paintings of J. M. W. Turner (Llewellyn and Riding 2013), which gave philosopher Edmund Burke a visual expression to his concept of the sublime. Burke's concept is tightly interwoven with the emotional responses of the observer, closely connected to ideas of pain, danger, and the terrible, which he claims is a source of the sublime (Burke 1757). Burke understood the sublime as something born of a combination of pain and pleasure, and of these, pain was the stronger feeling. To Burke pain and pleasure are not opposites, but independent. Lack of pleasure does not lead to pain, nor does lack of pain lead to pleasure, but the two can exist simultaneously, and the sublime resides in this coalition. According to this definition, painful art should be able to facilitate the sublime.

The main aspect of the sublime is the sense of being overwhelmed. In order to illustrate how we understand this sense of being absolutely overwhelmed by nature, we will take advantage of our heritage and turn to the dramatic nature of Norway. In Romantic art, we see a turn to wild and untamed nature. This was the period when Norwegian artists turned to their own homeland for motives, and the ragged, wild, and harsh landscapes otherwise considered ugly and crude were suddenly sublime. As the movement that started with Turner's interpretations of Burke reached Norway through the academies in Germany, artists such as J. C. Dahl, Hans Gude, and Adolf Tiedemand painted clouds, mountains, and pagan peasant traditions. Until this period, if the Norwegian landscape was painted at all, it was as something cultivated, idyllic, and tame, as close to the ideal hills of Tuscany as possible. But when the painter J. C. Dahl, a local of Bergen, Norway, traveled to Italy for the obligatory education in art, he ended up painting the erupting Mount Vesuvius, a typical topic for an artist focusing on the overwhelming and terrifying, the sublime (Lederballe 2017). At his return to the Norwegian landscape, he brought this sense of the sublime with him, and he tried to capture the overwhelming rather than the cultivated (Dahl 1842). What we see in Turner, Dahl, and other Romantic painters is the freedom to appreciate another type of feeling, the feeling of being terrified and overwhelmed rather than charmed. And they expressed it by painting the storm, the wild mountains, and the flowing waters. This permitted the renewal of an art, which was, at that point, pretty close to perfect in simulating the world and expressing beauty through oil and canvas. And so, the yearning to express the undisciplined and shocking renewed an art form that had, through versions of the Renaissance, been returning to the ideals of antiquity for generations, and artists expressed the shocking and overwhelming, or rather the sublime. When an artwork is able to tap into the sublime, this is a way to aestheticize the overwhelming and make it endurable in all its awe.

The uncanny, the abject, and the monstrous as sublime

The link between the sublime and the transgressive is particularly evident in Gothic literature and aesthetics. Literature professor Fred Botting points to how Gothic literature deals with overwhelming emotions relating to transgression, horror, and the unnatural (Botting 2005, 4–6). Gothic aesthetics involves fantastical but also norm-breaking topics that are terrifying, yet a source of pleasure. It concerns a mixture of terror and horror that transgresses rationality and human reason (Koçsoy 2018). Relating the sublime to the monstrous, philosopher Stephen Asma uses monsters in popular culture to show how important it is to understand the emotional connection to aesthetic appreciation and how horror works at a non-cognitive level

(Asma 2009, 192). With point of departure in Asma's work, game scholar Jaroslav Švelch identifies the idea that monsters overwhelm our senses and fill the perceiver with awe and terror as "the sublime thesis", which Švelch describes as the "normative yardstick for measuring monstrosity" (2018). Two of the important ways that video games deal with monstrous aesthetics is through the *abject* and the *uncanny*. While both may engage with the sublime, we will argue that in video game contexts they often counter this sensation. For this reason, they are examples of the paradox of transgression in games.

With the amount of blood splatter and gore in video games, it would be reasonable to expect that *the abject* would be an important aspect of video game transgressions. Philosopher Julia Kristeva's description of the abject relates to the boundaries between the body and its decay, and the rejection of the abject is a rejection of the self (Kristeva 1982). However, Švelch argues that the abject is *not* like the monstrous in games. While Kristeva states that the abject indicates the monstrous facing me, in video games, I face the monstrous. Governed by an algorithmic logic, game monsters are objects that can be controlled rather than invincible sources of terror (Švelch 2013, 195). For this reason, as the respondents of *Alien: Isolation* demonstrated, monsters are only transgressive until the player has figured out how they work and how to beat them. According to "Nathan", "[t]he whole horror sensation is lost in a kind of power fantasy" (Interview, December 2, 2016). As objects of the player's power fantasy, monsters are not sublime because of their incomprehensibility and invincibility. If any sense of the sublime emerges, this comes as an initial response to the abject representation of the monster and is likely to wane as the player solves the puzzle of how to beat it. Alternatively, the sublime may emerge from the player's sense of power and mastery, illustrated by the strong emotional relief that the Polish student "Paul" (22) described when he finally was able to beat a *Bloodborne* boss (Interview, November 1, 2016).

Further, gore in games is also not the same as the gore of the abject. Rather than the physical rejection of gore that Kristeva describes (Kristeva 1982), in video games, gore is playful, and it often does not look anything like bodily fluids, but can have other colors or totally different shapes (Kocurek 2015, 83). Blood and gore is typically far from realistic and often also sanitized (Pötzsch 2017). Further, although using red splatter is common, game gore is not the self being dissolved, but the monster. We face the monstrous and fight it.

However, although the monstrous in games is there to be faced, and the blood and splatter tend to be very far removed from the physically repulsive fluids of the body, we still find traces of the abject in video game aesthetics. The transgression of the abject is by definition at a level of uncontrollable disgust. Kristeva underlines how the body reacts with physical rejection, throwing up as a way to distance itself from the decay of living (Kristeva 1982). A game that made the players throw up would be a profoundly transgressive game, although we could say that games of vertigo, what Roger Caillois calls *ilinx* (2001), are designed to play with nausea and sickness. The discomfort of ilinx is, however, nausea caused by being physiologically unsettled, while the abject unsettles you psychologically.

Moving on to *the uncanny*, in relation to computer games it most commonly refers to when something ends up in the uncanny valley. The *uncanny valley* effect, hypothesized by Japanese robotics professor Masahiro Mori in the 1970s (Mori, MacDorman, and Kageki 2012), is something games both strive to avoid and to achieve, depending on the desired interpretation of the game. In the original article, the uncanny valley describes the moment when a robot stops being interestingly anthropomorphic and human-like, and starts being uncomfortably human-like, best described as "creepy". We enjoy anthropomorphism: When objects or animals gain human traits (Guthrie 2008). But the uncanny valley is marked by a dip in positive response to this approximation of humanity: When non-humans are too human-like, people do not respond positively to the human-like representation until those representations become almost indifferentiable from humans. The uncanny valley indicates the point where we stop being charmed by the imitation of humanity and start feeling it in a very different and mainly negative way. When playing *Alien: Isolation*, "David" uses the term uncanny to describe how he found the android workers be more frightening than the alien (gameplay journal, October 5, 2016). In his journal, he explained that while mechanical behavior and their red eyes were part of it, his anticipation that there might be something wrong with them was an important part of this sensation (Interview, November 3, 2016).

The sense of the uncanny is a frequent feature in the Gothic sublime, represented, for instance, by Frankenstein's monster. This experience is regularly encountered in game design as graphically impressive games easily can slip into the uncanny valley when human bodies stop being obvious imitations but still do not seem perfectly human. This is a problem that represents a limitation for contemporary game developers (Madigan 2013). Thus, the uncanny also demonstrates the paradox of transgression in games in a specific way. While the uncanny may evoke a sense of the sublime when we are overwhelmed by the fact that these almost human beings are the product of human technology, the disgust may become profound when the effects of the uncanny valley become too strong.

Our conclusion here is that the monstrous in games is rarely truly monstrous. While monsters themselves are in-game resources to be controlled, the abject tends to be sanitized and can only be traced in the bodily responses of vertigo games. Further, the uncanny is, in modern video games, the result of technological limitations and rarely something that makes the player awestruck. This demonstrates the paradox of transgression in games: When transgressions take place in a playful context, they change as they become play elements. Even in situations when their representation remains abject and repulsive, they are playthings. Our question at this point is whether there still can be a ludic sublime or whether the sublime is an experience not compatible with playfulness? If not even monsters and classical horrors are able to create awe and terror in us, is it still possible to experience the sublime in video games? And if yes, does it lift the genre of digital play toward a new experience?

Technology and the sublime

The ludic sublime must be seen in context with discussions of the sublime relating to the digital and the technological sublime. There are two conflicting trains of thought around digital media and the sublime. One is quite enthusiastic and can be associated with the American tradition relating to the what professor of American history David Nye calls *technological sublime* (Nye 2004; Shinkle 2012). The second train of thought concerns the banality of technology and games, illustrated through cultural theorist Sienne Ngai's idea of *stuplimity* (Ngai 2000; Shinkle 2012).

The *technological sublime* relates to the formation of an American modernity, and incorporates Kant's mathematical and dynamical sublime in its acknowledgment of the overwhelming impression of human achievement relating to phenomena such as design and engineering. The technological sublime was first formulated by architectural historian Richard A. Etlin as the *architectural sublime*, which is a genre of architecture that aims at awing the spectator through mass, weight, and the defiance of gravity for the purpose of creating awe-inspiring experiences with references to the cosmos (Etlin 2012). Etlin brings examples of this mixture of human achievement with awe and terror from antiquity and onwards. Examples are the Pantheon in Rome and the Mausoleum in Ravenna, both demonstrating technical skill achieving apparently impossible feats that in themselves also may be as overwhelming as the powers of nature.

The idea of the technological sublime is also preserved in sociology professor Vincent Mosco's book *The Digital Sublime* (2004), which focuses on the ideas and ideals of the information revolution. Mosco speaks about how ideas of the sublime can be traced in the visions of how digital technology was expected to revolutionize society, but also about how banal it turned out to be (Mosco 2004). Art history scholar Eugénie Shinkle follows the same direction of thought in her discussion on the sublime in video games. She argues that technology has been granted a status as both sublime and banal due to its ambivalent position in contemporary culture, and that we see a merger of these two counterparts in cultural phenomena that combine entertainment and technology. On this backdrop, Shinkle asks whether video games are the source of "stuplimity or flow", based on the assumption that flow is the ultimate experience of video games (Shinkle 2012, 99–100). *Stuplimity* is a term she borrows from Sianne Ngai, and refers to "an amalgam of two 'paralyzing' affects – shock and boredom – that

'confront us with the limitations of our capacity of responding in general'"
(Ngai 2000). Stuplimity is specifically not sublime; it is the antithesis to
the sublime. Where the sublime lifts us upwards toward the divine, stuplimity pulls us downwards toward denseness (Ngai 2000). Stuplimity is
a combination of aesthetic awe with boredom, and may for this reason be
understood in the context of Schrank's understanding of flow in terms of
an uninteresting and banal aesthetic experience.

While we cannot argue against the idea that commercial games are artifacts designed to be consumed, the treatment of the game experience as one
of passive consumption implied in stuplimity is problematic. In the more
than 30 years of studies of digital games, the main conclusion that most of
the scholars who engage with the material agree on is that players are not
passive consumers in a mystic trance. Not even scholars like Isbister, who
finds flow to be one of the main goals of gameplay, consider it to be passive
consumption. Shinkle's criticism of flow as a passive state does to a certain
extent align itself with Schrank's, but where Shinkle sees its disruption as
a dissipation of the self, as a loss of agency, and the experience of a jarring
affect as a negative experience, Schrank sees the jarring experience of disruption as a goal in itself (Schrank 2014). Failing, as Juul points out (2013),
is a vital part of play.

These understandings of the sublime and the banal in alliance in a digital context are based on the users being paralyzed, and in the case of the
ludic sublime, paralyzed by the process of play. The technology is too overwhelming, and the user becomes embroiled in the nit-picking of traversing
it – caught up in the banalities of use rather than inspired and uplifted
by the intricacy, complexity, and vast dimensions of human engineering
and creativity. Shinkle describes gameplay as repetitious, constantly inter-
rupted, and without a narrative variation. This, she claims, is typical of
stuplimity. In contrast to the technological sublime, which celebrates the
power of design and engineering, games are being used not to control nature, but to simulate it. If there is a way to redeem games, Shinkle sees it as
coming from the experience that she connects with flow. While flow is simultaneously a state of release and control, Shinkle still does not see it as a
matter of immersion into the sublime, but into the beautiful. Where games
approach the sublime is in what she calls failure events, which are failures of the interface such as bugs and glitches. Failure events may disturb
the flow experience and rupture the bonds between player and technology,
thus bringing about a loss of control, meaning, and the "sense of a post-
human, technologically enabled self" (Shinkle 2012, 103). Here the sublime emerges due to the player's inability to comprehend the inner workings
of the game. This resonates with Schrank's understanding of avant-garde
games as games that disrupt the experience of play, and both clearly share
a preference for an aesthetic that breaks flow. What Shinkle sees in games
is an empty presentation of an intelligence that humans cannot interact
with, which resists meaning-making from the users, reducing the play from

affective, engaging experience to plain consumption, leading to "nothing more elevating than frustration" (Shinkle 2012, 104).

The ludic sublime

In this description of the sublime in technology and video games, Shinkle, Schrank, and Ngai agree that the sublime is not to be found in the experience of flow, but in the moments when it all collapses – in the disruption of the experience.

This understanding of the sublime in video games stands in stark contrast to game researcher Daniel Vella's viewpoint. Inspired by game scholar Paul Martin's analysis of the sublime in *The Elder Scrolls IV: Oblivion* (Bethesda Game Studios 2006), Vella introduces the concept of the *ludic sublime* (Vella 2015). While Shinkle, Mosco, and Martin find that the sense of the sublime in the digital in general and games in particular is limited, Vella offers the view of a different experience – that of the continuous insecurity that games are designed to supply.

According to Vella, the ludic sublime relies on the moments of mystery when the boundaries of the game are unclear and its limitations are blurred. It is a result of how a video game can never be seen in its entirety, due to their black box nature in which much of the game's procedures are hidden from the player. While the sublime may emerge from *mystery*, *mastery* will make the sublime collapse. For Vella, this does not mean that the sublime cannot exist in video games, even though mastery is a central element in many gameplay experiences. To him, gameplay concerns an alteration between mystery and mastery. The sense of the sublime is always fleeting and transient, and the experience would by definition not be sublime if it were a constant feeling that was able to withstand mastery. In the end, since games are designed with an implicit uncertainty, mastery will do away with the mystery after all (Vella 2015).

We appreciate Vella's approach to offer more room for the aesthetic player experience in a tradition that has focused on the procedurality of games. His concept of the ludic sublime demonstrates that video games indeed can offer sublime experiences and that these may be specifically associated with the ludic aspects of video games. At the same time, his description of the ludic sublime appears too instrumental to be in line with the core characteristics of the sublime as the overwhelming sensation of awe that emerges from the incomprehensible. Vella states that the ludic sublime emerges in the player's awareness of the gap between their experiences with the game and their understanding of the game as a system and the underlying game object. One of his examples is indistinct boundaries: Situations where the player wonders what parts of the landscape represented in front of them can be explored or how to reach a treasure that is visible but in an inaccessible area. Other examples concern unclear causes and effects, unidentified entities, and ergodic irony – the fact that the player does not know what they are missing when they are choosing a certain path (Vella 2015). Such events are indeed essential to video games, as Vella argues, but they do not create sublime experiences *by default*. Even though we may wonder about the boundaries of a game, this may tickle our curiosity and interest – but it rarely creates emotions of overwhelming awe.

We believe that this obscurity in Vella's description of the concept is connected to the fact that his understanding of the ludic sublime is so closely associated with Kant's mathematically sublime. As noted earlier in this chapter, the mathematically sublime concerns the sensation of awe relating to what is intellectually difficult to grasp, such as the marvels of engineering and design; this obviously is a good fit for games, which are indeed designed artifacts. However, we believe that when we make sense of the sublime in video games, we also need to take into consideration Kant's idea of the dynamically sublime, which concerns reverence not for the designed, but for the overwhelming and almost spiritual experience one can have when meeting the forces of nature. This experience appears to be downplayed in Vella's description of the ludic sublime.

While the mathematically sublime is characteristic for game situations where we are struck by the complexities of the game rules and the infinite strategic opportunities that may emerge, video game situations are not limited to such experiences. As we discussed in Chapter 2, video game experiences are also very much anchored in the representative aspects of games, relating to features such as audiovisual style, narrative, and worldness, and sublime experiences can also spring out of these features. The sense of being in a world and taking in its grandeur, such as a player often does when traversing the vast beautiful landscapes of open-world games such as *The Elder Scrolls V: Skyrim* (Bethesda Game Studios 2011), may in itself create a feeling of the sublime that may be independent of the fact that this landscape is designed: In other words, sometimes it is the nature of the land of Skyrim – not the human agency behind it – that is breathtaking. Of course, this is an analytical distinction, and as Vella admittedly implies but does not argue for, in many situations it is likely that the sublime emerges from an *amalgamation* of ludic and representational elements. While it is the landscape of Skyrim that at first may strike awe in the player, it may also inspire the player to start reflecting with wonder over the technical and creative skills involved in creating this marvelous sight.

Our data is admittedly scarce on explicit descriptions of sublime experiences in games, possibly due to a lack of vocabulary for talking about such experiences. However, the descriptions where the player participants do have of strong emotions relating to games suggest that players indeed have something that comes close to sublime experiences relating to video games. While these experiences sometimes are related clearly to the mechanical aspects of games and sometimes to the representational aspects, often, the experiences appear to spring out of the two in combination. For instance, when the Belgian IT consultant "Kris" (26) reports on how he experienced assisting a non-playing character giving birth in *Beyond: Two Souls,* he writes in his gameplay journal:

> It was so beautiful to assist her in giving birth. Even though it is only a game I feel I'm part of something really precious. I'm thinking of having children myself, and perhaps this is why this event made the greatest impression on me.
>
> (Journal, September 27, 2016)

Although the game mechanics are simple in the game and gameplay is not challenging, this scene becomes very important for "Kris". From his personal description, it is obvious that it is the representation of childbirth that becomes almost overwhelming. At the same time, he stresses the fact that participation is important to him. This indicates that the sublime is not only a ludic feature, but often depends on the combination of game mechanics and representation.

If we are to consider games as sublime: As terrifying and awe-inspiring, and not just massive databases whose virtual trails players traverse more or less at random, we need to understand games as a practice of tension and relief. This takes us back to our understanding of play, which positions play in a continuous tension, always at risk of failing. The failure Shinkle describes as a break of flow is not a catastrophic failure, but a failure that is at the very core of play. In games, the possibility of falling, of failing, and of losing the progress that has been made by a number of small steps is at a prerequisite for sublime experiences. Like climbing a mountain, playing a game is a process of mundane, banal actions, each of which can lead to our failure, but also to a surprising height. Climbing a mountain for the view that dwarves our bodies and overwhelms us with the awe of nature is a process of thousands of small steps, each of which can be a misstep, and most hikes before that moment are simply long hours of miserable trudging leading us nowhere but back home (hopefully) in time for dinner. As briefly mentioned above, "Paul" provides an illustrative game example. He explains how finally being able to overcome a challenge that in itself may have felt overwhelming will create an even stronger sensation of relief:

> The feeling I acquired while playing games like Dark Souls, or Bloodborne. These are the games that make you fail, but even the fiftieth failure, when you finally succeed, is the moment that you feel refreshed, that you feel actually alive, that you finally surpassed that one challenge that made you fail time after time after time. It's this feeling when you actually finish it, when you accomplish it and surpass that challenge you couldn't surpass before.
>
> (Interview, November 1, 2016)

With this in mind, it is not insignificant that the game Vella has chosen to illustrate the ludic sublime is *Dark Souls* (From Software 2011). *Dark Souls* is currently one of the most treacherous mountains of gaming, where a misstep has larger consequences than in most other games, as the process itself is so demanding that players hardly find any pleasure in the play (Starkey 2016). The repetition that Shinkle claims turns play into consumption is a vital part of the process; it is what creates a stake. Like the harsh, unforgiving beauty of a steep, overwhelming mountain, the mastery of *Dark Souls* is an experience for those who are willing to spend a lot of time learning how to walk, climb, and endure. However, this challenges Vella's argument that mastery cancels the sublime experience connected to mystery. Instead the emotional high connected to the relief suggests that even though mastery often appears to be incompatible with the ludic sublime, the sublime can also be a product of mastery in video games.

Thus, to experience the ludic sublime, the player has to expend a deliberate effort. This is a non-trivial effort in the vein of Aarseth's ergodic texts (1997), but it is more than that. Playing and enjoying a game is as much about choosing to take each step comprising the journey as it is about getting there. While the choices within a game are restricted by rules, design, and fiction, they are still choices, making the play process a deliberate experience of what the player feels along the path. Further, by choosing to spend their leisure time playing rather than watching a movie or reading, the players are choosing to expend an effort in order to transverse the experience. And if they end up feeling overwhelmed, charged with adrenaline, and eager to keep going despite the failures along the road, it is something awesome, something grand. It is the ludic sublime.

The ludic sublime and transgressive games

Transgressive games are transgressive because they create overwhelming emotions in players. This does not mean that to feel strongly is transgressive; neither does it mean that transgressive aesthetics is always sublime. But it does imply that transgressive experiences tend to create strong emotions and that sublime experiences indeed may be emotionally transgressive. A transgressive aesthetic is one that takes us out of our emotional comfort zone, although it might not be provocative as such. Ludic dysphoria is an example of this. Seen in the light of our discussion of emotions and affect in Chapter 6, it is clear to us that the sublime is first and foremost an *affective* response, although we believe that the mathematically sublime indeed also can emerge from reflection.

We have seen the paradox of transgression at work when game context mitigates the discomfort and turns it into an aesthetic experience. In certain cases, the paradox of transgression runs the risk of obstructing any sublime experiences, but as our expansion of the ludic sublime has shown, this is not always the case. So how can we better understand the ludic sublime in relation to transgressive aesthetics? First, we agree with Vella that an important aspect of the ludic sublime relates to the sense of lack of total mastery. Vella leans on the black box, or the obscured nature of games, in stressing that a game is designed to surprise, even after the player feels that they master it. The ludic sublime in this understanding depends on how a player never can be entirely certain about what the game has in store – it is connected to the practice of the unexpected. This is a sensation that takes the player out of the comfort zone, and as such, it can at times be transgressive as it contains significant risk toward what you have worked to obtain: That sense of being in control.

The second step toward connecting the ludic sublime to transgression is exactly risk. Games are defined by containing a certain tension, mainly created by the risk of failing (Caillois 2001, 17; Huizinga 2000, 11). Risk underlines our limitations and shows us how we fail. As we have seen, the sublime reduces the individual and underlines how small we are. A game does the same, by letting us fail, over and over again. And transgressive games have higher risk than others. If it is not a risk of failing, it is a risk of feeling jarred out of our sense of comfort because we have experiences that put us in unexpected position or invite us to perform acts we see as painfully beyond our moral code.

Third, games show us how small we are in relation to the game by removing agency. This is counter-intuitive if we think about games as expressing the ludic sublime by being boundless, but it is a way to reduce the player – or to transgress upon their agency. The rules and affordances of a video game do not only permit actions, they also reduce options. And this sense of having only a very few tools by which to avoid failure again underlines how small we are, how little we can do. An experience in which the game forces – or even cheats – the player into acting contrary to their interests is found in *Spec Ops: The Line*, where the player, without their knowledge, becomes complicit in the killing of civilians (Jørgensen 2016). Another example is found in situations when the player decides to activate gamer mode as a mitigation technique against transgressive representations, as we discussed in Chapter 5. In the language of aesthetic appreciation, gamer mode becomes a disinterested technique of play that permits the reflexive, self-aware play that draws back from emotional absorption and re-active play, and instead understands both the appreciation for the game and the player's playing of it. This sense of facing something that forces you to change, to choose a mitigation technique rather than staying within your individual comfort zone, is a strong reminder of how you have given yourself over to another force.

We have expanded Vella's original understanding of the ludic sublime in two ways: We have argued that in order to understand the ludic sublime in digital gameworlds, we need to acknowledge that the experience of the sublime may not only emerge from the game's ludic aspects, but also from representational aspects – in other words, the ludic sublime must be considered an amalgamation of the two. We have also shown that while the sublime may be connected to mastery, it is important to also look at the role of failure and limitations. With this expansion of the ludic sublime, we see that while not all transgressive games necessarily are sublime, the ludic sublime can be more easily experienced when the games in question are designed for a wide range of emotional upheaval, the roller coaster of emotion we find that games express. Transgression is something most profoundly felt rather than argued, and as such, the ludic sublime will be a relevant tool through which to understand the transgressive aesthetic of games.

References

Aarseth, Espen J. 1997. *Cybertext : Perspectives on Ergodic Literature*. Baltimore, MD: Johns Hopkins University Press.

Alexander, Leigh. 2012. "GDC 2012: Sid Meier on How to See Games as Sets of Interesting Decisions." *Gamasutra*, March 7, 2012. www.gamasutra.com/view/news/164869/GDC_2012_Sid_Meier_on_how_to_see_games_as_sets_of_interesting_decisions.php.

Asma, Stephen T. 2009. *On Monsters : An Unnatural History of Our Worst Fears*. Oxford: Oxford University Press.

Bethesda Game Studios. 2006. *The Elder Scrolls IV: Oblivion*. Bethesda Softworks, 2K Games.

———. 2011. *The Elder Scrolls V: Skyrim*. Bethesda Softworks LLC.

Bjørkelo, Kristian A. 2018. "Transgressive Realism in This War of Mine." In *Transgressions in Games and Play*, edited by Kristine Jørgensen and Faltin Karlsen, 169–185. Cambridge: MIT Press.

Botting, Fred. 2005. *Gothic*. London, New York: Routledge.

Bratkowski, Tad. 2014. "The Aesthetic Experience of Video Games: A Pluralistic Approach." *Dissertations*. http://opensiuc.lib.siu.edu/dissertations/799.

Bullough, Edward. 1912. "'Psychical Distance' as a Factor in Art and an Aesthetic Principle." *British Journal of Psychology, 1904–1920* 5 (2): 87–118. doi:10.1111/j.2044-8295.1912.tb00057.x.

Burke, Edmund. 1757. *A Philosophical Inquiry into the Origin of Our Ideas of the Sublime and Beautiful*. Kindle Edition. Overland Park, KS: Digireads Publishing, Neeland Media LCC.

Caillois, Roger. 2001. *Man, Play and Games*. Urbana: University of Illinois Press; Wantage : University Presses Marketing.

Cashell, Kieran. 2009. *Aftershock : The Ethics of Contemporary Transgressive Art*. I.B. Tauris.

Cremin, Colin. 2016. *Exploring Videogames with Deleuze and Guattari : Towards an Affective Theory of Form*. London: Routledge.

Csikszentmihalyi, Mihaly. 2002. *Flow : The Classic Work on How to Achieve Happiness*. Rev. ed. London: Rider.

Dahl, Johan Christian. 1842. "Fra Stalheim."

Etlin, Richard A. 2012. "Architecture and the Sublime." In *The Sublime: From Antiquity to the Present*, edited by Timothy M. Costelloe, Kindle, 304. Cambridge: Cambridge University Press.

Freeman, David. 2004. *Creating Emotion in Games: The Craft and Art of Emotioneering*. New Riders.

Freeman, David, and David. 2004. "Creating Emotion in Games." *Computers in Entertainment* 2 (3): 15. doi:10.1145/1027154.1027179.

FromSoftware. 2011. *Dark Souls.* Namco Bandai Games.

Guthrie, Stewart E. 2008. "Anthropomorphism." *Encyclopædia Britannica.* Encyclopædia Britannica, Inc. www.britannica.com/topic/anthropomorphism.

Huizinga, Johan. 2000. *Homo Ludens; a Study of the Play-Element in Culture. Sociology of Culture; v. 3.* London: Routledge.

Isbister, Katherine. 2016. *How Games Move Us: Emotion by Design.* Cambridge: The MIT Press.

Jørgensen, Kristine. 2016. "The Positive Discomfort of Spec Ops: The Line." *Game Studies: The International Journal of Computer Game Research.* 16 (2). http://gamestudies.org/1602/articles/jorgensenkristine.

Juul, Jesper. 2013. *The Art of Failure: An Essay on the Pain of Playing Video Games.* MIT Press.

Kant, Immanuel. 1790. *Critique of Judgement.* Kindle. Oxford: Oxford University Press.

Koçsoy, F. Gül. 2018. "The Transgressive Sublime in Edgar Allan Poe's 'The Tell-Tale Heart' and 'The Imp of the Perverse.'" *The Journal of International Social Research* 11 (58): 142–47.

Kocurek, Carly A. 2015. "Who Hearkens to the Monster's Scream? Death, Violence and the Veil of the Monstrous in Video Games." *Visual Studies* 30 (1): 79–89. doi:10.1080/1472586X.2015.996402.

Kristeva, Julia. 1982. *Powers of Horror; An Essay on Abjection.* New York: Columbia University Press. www.csus.edu/indiv/o/obriene/art206/readings/kristeva-powers of horror%5B1%5D.pdf.

Lang, Andrew. 2015. "Introduction." In *On the Sublime,* edited by Longinus, Kindle edition. Philadelphia, New York: Gottfried & Fritz.

Lederballe, Thomas. 2017. "Johan Christian Dahl: Eruption of the Volcano Vesuvius." *Explore the Arts/Highlights.* Copenhagen: National Gallery of Denmark. March 22, 2017. www.smk.dk/en/explore-the-art/highlights/johan-christian-dahl-eruption-of-the-volcano-vesuvius/.

Levine, George Lewis. 2001. "Saving Disinterest: Aesthetics, Contingency, and Mixed Conditions." *New Literary History* 32 (4): 907–31. doi:10.1353/nlh.2001.0054.

Llewellyn, Nigel, and Christine Riding, eds. 2013. "The Romantic Sublime." In *The Art of the Sublime.* Tate Research Publication. www.tate.org.uk/art/research-publications/the-sublime/the-romantic-sublime-r1109221.

Mohanty, Satya P. 2001. "Can Our Values Be Objective? On Ethics, Aesthetics, and Progressive Politics." *New Literary History* 32 (4): 803–33. doi:10.2307/20057697.

Morawe, Volker, and Tilman Reiff. 2001. "The Artwork Formerly Known as PainStation." Cologne. www.painstation.de/history.html.

Mori, Masahiro, Karl F. MacDorman, and Norri Kageki. 2012. "The Uncanny Valley." *IEEE Robotics and Automation Magazine* 19 (2): 98–100. doi:10.1109/MRA.2012.2192811.

Mosco, Vincent. 2004. *The Digital Sublime : Myth, Power, and Cyberspace.* MIT Press.

Ngai, Sianne. 2000. "Stuplimity: Shock and Boredom in Twentieth-Century Aesthetics." *Postmodern Culture* 10 (2). doi:10.1353/pmc.2000.0013.

Nye, David. 2004. *America as Second Creation: Technology and Narratives of New Beginnings*. Cambridge: The MIT Press.

Parkin, Simon. 2014. "Zoe Quinn's Depression Quest." *The New Yorker*, September 9, 2014. www.newyorker.com/tech/elements/zoe-quinns-depression-quest.

Poggioli, Renato. 1981. *The Theory of the Avant-Garde*. Cambridge, MA: Belknap Press of Harvard University Press.

Pötzsch, Holger. 2017. "Selective Realism: Filtering Experiences of War and Violence in First- and Third-Person Shooters." *Games and Culture* 12 (2): 156–78.

Purse, Marcia. 2019. "Dysphoric Mania in Bipolar Disorder." Very Well Mind. 2019. www.verywellmind.com/what-is-dysphoria-378817.

Quinn, Zoe, Patrick Lindsey, and Isaac Schankler. 2013. *Depression Quest: An Interactive (Non)Fiction About Living with Depression*. Zoe Quinn. www.depressionquest.com/.

Schrank, Brian. 2014. *Avant-Garde Videogames: Playing with Technoculture*. Cambridge: MIT Press.

Shelley, James. 2015. "The Concept of the Aesthetic." Edited by Edward N. Zalta. *The Stanford Encyclopedia of Philosophy*. https://plato.stanford.edu/archives/win2015/entries/aesthetic-concept/.

Shinkle, Eugénie. 2012. "Videogames and the Digital Sublime." In *Digital Cultures and the Politics of Emotion*, 94–108. London: Palgrave Macmillan UK. doi:10.1057/9780230391345_6.

Starkey, Daniel. 2016. "Dark Souls III Is Brutally Hard, But You'll Keep Playing Anyway." *Wired*, April 2016. www.wired.com/2016/04/dark-souls-iii-review/.

Stenros, Jaakko. 2015. "Playfulness, Play, and Games: A Constructionist Ludology Approach." May. http://tampub.uta.fi/handle/10024/96986.

Švelch, Jaroslav. 2013. "Monsters by the Numbers: Controlling Monstrosity in Video Games." In *Monster Culture in the 21st Century*, edited by Marina Levina and Diem-My T. Bui, 193–208. New York: Bloomsbury Academic.

———. 2018. "Encoding Monsters: 'Ontology of the Enemy' and Containment of the Unknown in Role-Playing Games." In *Values in Games – 2018 Philosophy of Computer Games Conference*. https://gameconference.itu.dk/papers/09-svelch-encodingmonsters.pdf.

Vella, Daniel. 2015. "No Mastery Without Mystery: Dark Souls and the Ludic Sublime." *Game Studies, the International Journal Computer Game Research* 15 (1). http://gamestudies.org/1501/articles/vella.

Conclusions

A theory of the paradox of transgression in games

Play is paradoxical: It is disengaged from real-life constraints, but still has social consequences (Csikszentmihaly 1981). This paradox has been the backbone of this book. Play can be split into the safe and the unsafe: Both are important aspects of the definition of play as well as games and are vital for play to function. Play exists in the balance between the safe and the unsafe, between risk and control, a balance each player needs to construct in order to find their own playful zone.

This book has focused on the unsafe area. However, since the unsafe is dependent upon the contrast to the safe, much of our debates has concerned this distinction. The balance between the safe and the unsafe is what characterizes the paradox of transgression in games: The idea that when we accept the aesthetic framing of a transgression, it stops being profoundly transgressive.

In this final chapter, we will look at how the paradox of transgression stands in this balance between the safe and the unsafe. We will first draw the lines between our main findings and arguments, looking at how the safe and unsafe work together in the transgressive aesthetics of games. We will look at how transgressive aesthetics is a balance between disinterest and the sublime, and how players deal with this balance through mitigation techniques. We have dedicated the final part of the conclusion to our theory of the aesthetics of transgressive games. In studying aesthetic transgressions, we approached a clearer understanding of what makes games interesting, potentially even parts of what makes games good and meaningful, and we will discuss that as we return to the understanding of the inner working of games as emotion machines.

The paradox of transgression

Like play, transgression is paradoxical. The idea of what is unacceptable, inappropriate, and taboo is strongly rooted in culture, but, at the same time, such ideas are easily mitigated at a personal level. On a background of already fluid norms it is no surprise that transgressions are moving targets; what is perhaps most surprising is the techniques of mitigation we have seen throughout the work with this volume, on how there is, after all, a pattern to the paradox of transgression that explains what happens when players meet a challenging, provoking, or disquieting situation where their boundaries are overstepped or broken.

The aesthetic domain – in which we also localize play – stands in a special position with regards to transgression. Central to our argument is the distinction between transgressive aesthetics and profound transgression, which postulates that while aesthetic framings tend to mitigate transgression and increase our threshold for tolerance, there are situations where boundaries are overstepped and the experience becomes a profound transgression – one that we can no longer endure. In this context, the paradox of transgressive aesthetics in games – and also in other aesthetic contexts – is that if one is willing to engage with the content, it can no longer be experienced as a profound transgression, because profound transgressions *by definition* break with what we are willing to endure.

This does not mean that talking about transgressive content in games is meaningless; on the contrary, our studies have demonstrated that not only are there individual differences and preferences, but what a player experiences as being in accord with their sensibilities at some point during gameplay may change over time. Also, what is first experienced as distasteful may over time be experienced as okay within the aesthetic context of the work.

The safe, the unsafe, and the fallacy of play

When we say "safe" in this context, it is a relative safety. Even games happening with expert coaches in specially designed arenas and with safety gear have their share of problems. Rather, what we mean by safe is that play offers an arena in which uncomfortable topics and situations can be explored without facing the actual consequences of such situations. However, games and play are not safe in the meaning of inconsequential or unimportant; on the contrary, it is consequential and meaningful and can sometimes be highly uncomfortable. Video games are objects that communicate meaning through process; image; sound; bodily response and interaction; text; social, political, and economic context; social interaction; and fictional and representative value. To grasp them all fully is a complex process demanding the interplay of a wide range of disciplines, which is why the field of game studies is rapidly diversifying. This contrast between *safe* and *unsafe* is illustrated by the opposing halves of our figure, to be presented later in this concluding chapter.

The fallacy of play is why we consider games to be worth studying at all. The fallacy of play is the erroneous idea that play and games can only concern that which is fun, safe, and non-serious. Our research and discussions in this book confirm that the idea of play as uncomplicated, fun, and without danger or conflict is a fallacy. When we argue against the fallacy of play, this is not an argument against the idea that games often are fun, non-serious, and taking place in a safe environment. Rather, we argue that games and play *also* can be frustrating, boring, serious, and unsafe, and that this aspect often tends to be ignored in public and popular discourse of games or rejected as a flaw in the design or a problem that needs to be fixed. We believe that it is a feature of games that they can be emotionally unsafe and that they indeed can tackle not only dark and distasteful topics, but are also well suitable for exploring uncomfortable topics on the verge of transgressing our sensibilities or challenging our ideology or conviction.

The fallacy of play underlines the inherent, and often paradoxical, tension that lies within play. Playing, whether it means structured gameplay or free-form play, relies on the safety that comes with knowing that it is possible to stop playing. This means that it is possible to explore something unsafe in a safe manner. Play offers us a set of tools with which to handle the unsafe. We have rules, a specific setting, or arena, and different types of signals. Children change their voices, as do adults when playing with children, and we even understand play signals across species, as we play with pets, and they play with us. This creates a setting in which it is possible to explore something dangerous, challenging, and otherwise unsafe. If play was only inconsequential fun, it would quickly become boring, because it would lack tension.

Gameplay and transgression

The unique feature of games compared to other electronic or physical media is that they demand a response that goes beyond the interpretative interaction of reader-response theory (Iser 1978). In play, the interaction involves an actual response to the procedures of the game system in the form of a continuous input, which triggers a new set of events that the player again needs to react to. Even the most linear of games, with few real options to their storyline, demand this trigger, setting them apart from most other media. For transgressions in games, this has two important implications connected to the player's relationship to transgression and to the emotions that are evoked when dealing with transgression in games.

Transgressor or transgressee?

First, the ludic involvement means that players can be targets of transgressions, and they can also be the sources of transgressions (Mortensen and Navarro-Remesal 2018) – they can be *transgressees* or *transgressors*. As *transgressees*, players are not simply observing transgressive aesthetics as they would in the art gallery or the movie theatre: They may themselves be the victim of a transgressive action directed toward them. Sometimes, it is the game and its design that transgress against the player; however, in multi-player situations, transgressions are carried out not by some distant artist removed in time and space from the transgressive situation but by real human individuals against other individuals in real time. And importantly, games put players in a position in which they can respond to transgressions directly and within the frames of the aesthetic context. This also takes us on to the player's role as *transgressor*, as gameplay invites the player to carry out transgressive actions. In Chapters 3 and 5, we described how *Beyond: Two Souls* do this both by first putting the protagonist Jodie into a difficult, potentially transgressive situation, and then allowing the player to take actions that spin the situation out of control.

This demonstrates how the player is not just the user of the game but a vital part of its procedurality, to the degree that the game does not exist until the player plays it. As such, it is hard to distinguish between the potential transgressivity of the game and the transgressions performed by the players as this may blur from the player's perspective since it sometimes may be hard to know when a player is transgressing or being transgressed against. The strong procedurality of video games, where each action triggers more options, gives a strong sense of being the actor in the experience. However, the number of options is always limited to what the platforms afford the player, and so, the system can transgress against a player by leaving few options.

Emotion

Second, the involvement on the part of the player in the game situation also means that the emotional link has the potential to become much stronger compared to other media, both because of the player's sense of complicity and because of their ability to take emotion into action. Here we see that the emotional response is strengthened by the need for a physical response, and it becomes possible to play, literally, with the contrast between what you feel and what you do, creating paradoxical, ambivalent, and often transgressive experiences. This is the background for our argument that the main risk to players in video gameplay is to their emotions.

In popular discussions about games, the dramatic effects of negative actions performed by people who also play games grab the attention and blur the view of the important fact that strong emotional responses are a vital part of the enjoyment of games. Despite the evidence of enjoyment, relaxation, and happiness described in ethnographic studies of gamers and game culture (Mortensen 2004, 2008, 2010; Pearce 2008, 2009; Taylor 2003, 2006), there is little research on the positive emotions created by games. However, in Chapter 6, we demonstrated that being emotionally moved by the game was important to the players' engagement with the games. Our claim is that video games do not specifically foster negative emotions. Rather, games offer a wide variety of emotional experiences to the player. Mastering a complicated challenge leads to a sense of accomplishment. Saving somebody weaker and caring for them lead to compassion – failing to save them to sadness and even grief. Playing around with slapstick cultural references and breaking virtual rules lead to laughter, sometimes with glee, sometimes with outright happiness. In this study, we wanted to specifically challenge our players through play that we expected to evoke negative emotions, since society rarely considers strong feelings of happiness to be transgressive. What we found was that while the games did invite feelings of anger and drama, this was not necessarily reported to be negative for the players. On the contrary, our findings support the research into the paradox of painful art that suggests that certain kinds of uncomfortable entertainment indeed may be meaningful for those engaging with it (Bartsch and Oliver 2011; Hopeametsä 2008; Montola 2010; Montola and Holopainen 2012; Oliver et al. 2016; Smuts 2007). We have also demonstrated that if the experience became too negative for the players, they mitigated them through techniques of aesthetic disinterest. The reports from our players and the studies of players' descriptions of what they value in their play experiences all indicate that even negative feelings in the game are being processed as positive feelings. The main experience of play is one of strong emotion, supporting our claim that games are emotion machines, designed to make the player feel. The ultimate experience of play is not only to play for fun, but to play for the strength and variety of experiences, creating strong highs and lows. Important, however, is our analytical division between the immediate affect and a more reflexive emotion, and our argument is that what may be initially transgressive may not continue to be so after some time of reflection and that situations that initially may have been experienced as trivial sometimes turn out to be problematic once the player has been given time to reflect on them.

The ludic sublime

The strong highs and lows of the emotional impact of play are what leads us to the ludic sublime. We position the ludic sublime as a potential for understanding game enjoyment as an experience that is intensely emotional, but not rising from either side of the form/content composition of video games. The sublime is rather a momentary experience of something overwhelming that can be born both out of a ludic experience as a form of wonder and awe based in the system and structure of the game, but also from a sense of the carnivalesque – the freedom to explore beyond traditions, norms, rules, and law, which is carried by the fictive component of video games.

When video games are sublime, they can be either sublime in the traditional aesthetic sense that Burke and Kant describe, or they can be what Vella calls the ludic sublime. Video games can overwhelm us because of intriguing character development and storytelling that make us fall in love with characters (Waern 2010), because of the fantastic landscapes that we experience when we have climbed to the scenic places in an open world game and are engrossed in the sensation that this is larger than life. But as Vella argues, they can also overwhelm us through their rules and mechanics, as when we suddenly realize the potentials of a game's rules. Also sensations such as the feeling of relief when finally overcoming a challenge can be a source for the sublime. Thus, the sublime can be created either by the content or by the form of a game. More importantly, the sublime can sometimes also be found in a transgressive aesthetic, and when these are combined players may find that the otherwise unbearable discomfort now becomes an aestheticized and therefore bearable.

In most video game experiences that allow us to sense the sublime, it can be hard to tell whether the experience is sublime in the traditional sense or the ludic sense, and in most cases the difference is not relevant. It is the video game experience as a whole that creates the overwhelming sensation: The combination of how we interact with the game and where that takes us will in most situations create a sense of the sublime. More often than not, the sublime comes into being because it is our gameplay that allows us to come to a place where we can experience the sublime: We have explored vast areas and climbed seemingly impossible spaces until we suddenly and accidentally come across a beautiful waterfall by sundown that leaves us breathless and certain that God must be a game designer. For the sublime to come into being, there is no necessary distinction between form and content in games. The sublime emerges as an aesthetic response in the relationship between game and player.

Games are however defined by the effort you need to make in order to engage with them. If using them was trivial, they would lose one of their most defining aspects. But despite the popularity of video games, this effort is also one of the things that keeps people from experiencing them. As Bogost states: "[P]laying a game is a chore. (...) To enjoy them, you have to play them. And playing them requires exerting the effort to operate them" (2019). The effort to play is however the entire point of play, and exactly why popular, often apparently trivial, games can support sublime experiences. As we stated in Chapter 8, our understanding of the ludic sublime is based on three factors: The overwhelming sense of never seeing the end of the game; the effort you need to put into any game in general and large, complex video games in particular; and the emotional highs and lows you experience while making your way through the game. This means that while a game may be underwhelming to a casual glance or after a disengaged play-through, it can from the perspective of the engaged, engrossed player be a captivating and sublime experience. The sublime is a glimpse of something bigger, which is not present in the artwork alone, but in the relationship between the perceiver and the work. Likewise, the ludic sublime is revealed in the deed, not in the observation.

Mitigation

The need for mitigation techniques makes it clear that players are being transgressed against in games, but the fact that mitigation techniques are employed also underlines that transgressions in games may not be a problem. Mitigation techniques are an indication that games are indeed understood as an aesthetic experience relating to play, one that can be controlled.

Our study uncovered four main mitigation techniques. The four mitigation techniques can be understood as a meta perspective in that they involve taking an analytical standpoint in which players would take a step back, consider the game as a game and as fiction, and interpret their experience, and can for this reason be considered as a type of a disinterested aesthetic appreciation of the game. One such mitigation technique was framing the transgressive game content in terms of humor, absurdity, and exaggeration. Another was distracting oneself by leaving the game momentarily or changing the mood in the room of play. Third was interpreting the transgressive game content as a form of meaningful discomfort that provided deeper understanding of what they had been part of. This was a delayed, reflexive understanding of what the game had actually communicated, and it was, in our material, almost completely dependent on transgressive content.

The fourth and perhaps the most prominent mitigation technique was entering gamer mode, which allows players to ignore the representational aspects of a game and treat the experience as a game to be mastered (Frank 2012). In the case of gamer mode, this disinterested approach can also be said to be a type of metagaming – gaming with the knowledge of how gaming works rather than with what the game is supposedly about. Metagaming is using game external information and strategic analysis for the purpose of mastering the game, and depends thus on stepping back from the experience and looking beyond it rather than at it. But metagaming can also be a subversive (Donaldson 2016), perhaps even transgressive, technique in itself. It is not unheard of that metagames become complicated strategies pursued for their own sake, such as the many types of torture play in *The Sims* (Maxis Software 2000). This torture play practice (Sihvonen 2011, 7) is notable because it looks like transgressive metagaming. As a subversive counter-play against the strict rules of *The Sims*, which is designed for a very specific normality, torture play is a way to use the system of normality in ways that uncovers the flaws in tightly designed and enforced structures. As a dystopic preview of life in a totalitarian regime enforcing Western everyday life, torture play is often a comic relief (Comedy Central n.d.; Hernandez 2015) from the day-to-day repetitions *The Sims* is designed to play out. When a player chooses to use a subversive – perhaps even to some, transgressive – method as a play strategy, this may also be a kind of mitigation practice. Some games have a strong social imperative, which leans heavily on including the player's social network in the gameplay. This means that play for some may feel more forced, and they need to look for creative expressions in finding alternative ways to play the game – leading to subversive and surprising play.

Opposition and balance

One reason we encounter the fallacy of play, or the idea that games are nothing but inconsequential fun, is that games contain an inner tension that keeps being reinforced. Because of the fallacy of play, it has rarely been considered that games can be sublime or that the transgressions of games can have a deeper meaning besides pure provocation or being a negative influence on players. This means that those who study games on the surface level fairly quickly can find the kind of play that confirms the idea that there is no deeper meaning created in the process and no intense experiences for the players. But this is because this experience is consistently being balanced by the counterpart. The sublime experience, for instance, is by definition delicate, and goes away when players start to analyze the situation. The aesthetic disinterest inviting a proactive play style, opposes the immersive and often reactive engagement that can lead to the ludic sublime. In the same way, emotional or affective experiences are kept in check by the flow, either through design or through player choices. A lot of the grinding – repetitive play-work – in games invites flow, a repetitive task with occasional challenges, where the player looks for a perfect balance within the flow channel as described in Chapter 6. This is a large part of play and acts as the backdrop for the more intense, sometimes overly challenging, encounters that lead to the stronger highs and lows of emotions.

We find that the real opposition contained in the fallacy of play is between the sublime and disinterest. Play, whether it is playing a game or playing with a friend, is not something that happens in a disinterested fashion. However, there are play practices that are disinterested in the manner of aesthetic disinterest. When play is heavily invested with intellectual analysis, and it is driven mainly by the desire for theorycrafting – the practice of using statistics and mathematics to understand the black box of the game's code (Wenz 2013) – it is a practice based on an interest in the idea of the game rather than the emotional experience of the game. As we discuss in Chapter 8, the disinterested judgment of a game is a position of reflexivity, of intense interest in the idea of the game while being aware of one's position as a player and of what experiences that the game affords. This is opposed to a sublime experience of the game, as submitting to the ludic sublime means to let the game overwhelm and engulf you. The experience of the ludic sublime means to accept that it may not be possible to understand every aspect of the game, and that, in itself, is a wonderful, overwhelming experience.

Comparatively, both disinterest and flow are easier to study and understand because they are more easily expressed. The deeply immersive experiences that border on the pre-cognitive affective responses are harder for the player to speak analytically about, and as such become harder to study. At the point where it is easy to talk about what happens in a very complicated passage of the game, the player has repeated that particular fight so many times that it is no longer immersive. This may not at all be conscious, as many game moves that become automated with repetition and winning strategies can be hard to describe, but they are either embodied to the point that they can be repeated or broken down into pieces of information that can be analyzed. This is the point at which the conversation about how games are experienced meet the public, which leads to the common belief that the game experience is not one of deep engagement, but one of intellectual metaplay or automatic repetition, played mainly because it is an inconsequential way to kill time. In short, we tend to end up studying and confirming the fallacy of play.

Toward an aesthetic theory of transgressive games

This book has addressed player experiences with transgressive game aesthetics from three angles. First, we explored what it is that makes games transgressive. We discussed how form and content each or in combination may contribute to an understanding of games as transgressive. We also investigated what transgressive games transgress against, separating between whether they transgress on a game internal or on a game external level. Second, we looked at what our empirical data says about the player experiences with such games. Distinguishing between gameplay experiences that are uncomfortable but tolerable because they take place in an aesthetic context and gameplay experiences that are unplayable because they cross the players' sensibilities, we have looked at how players treat transgressive gameplay experiences. When do players stop playing, and what mitigation techniques do they use to continue playing even when the game is rubbing them the wrong way? Third, we explored transgressive aesthetics in the context of video games, linking it to the classical debates of disinterest and the sublime, arguing that the interest in transgressive aesthetics in games can be connected to the sublime (Figure 9.1).

In the following, we will bring these discussions together in an aesthetic theory of transgressive games, as summarized in the model below. The model is necessarily a simplification of a complex reality, but has the strength of illustrating the most important relationships that define the experience with transgressive games. The model visualizes the paradox of transgression in games, stressing how a transgressive experience can oscillate between profound and aesthetic in one and the same game. On the macro level, the model is separated into three axes that roughly correspond to the three parts of the book described above and more carefully in the introduction:

1 *The aesthetic axis* concerns the discussions relating to disinterest and the sublime as one of opposition, illustrating how Kant and Burke's ideal of a disinterested appreciation of art falls into the emotionally and experientially safe side, while the sublime is experienced as emotionally unsafe as it is connected to the overwhelming and the uncertain. As disinterest and the sublime are characterized as two qualitatively

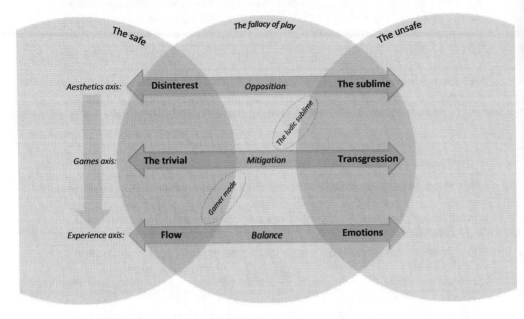

Figure 9.1 A theory of the paradox of transgression in games.

different ways of appreciating art, we see the relationship between the two as one of *opposition*. From the aesthetic axis, an arrow leads down past the game axis toward the experience axis, signaling that transgressive games are an aesthetic experience that comes into being between the player and the game, and which embraces the full experience.

2   *The game axis* concerns the discussions relating to transgressive games, spanning from how certain games can be experienced as relatively trivial and safe in terms of the topics they represent, while others are experienced as transgressive and emotionally unsafe. These two end points should be understood as a continuum, and a given game experience can be located on any point between these extremes. More important is the relationship between the two end points, which is one of *mitigation*: When a game is experienced as transgressive, players often employ different mitigation techniques in order to deal with the transgression and continue playing the game. Mitigation techniques are a negotiation between the safe and the unsafe, and thus work to negotiate the player's emotions relating to the game and are central to the dynamic process that fuels the paradox of transgression in games: Mitigation techniques enable players to redirect their orientation and focus their attention away from the transgression and toward other elements of the game. Mitigation techniques allow players to reframe and recontextualize the transgressions of a game and allow them to play even though they find that a game is challenging their sensibilities or convictions.

3 *The experience axis* concerns the player psychology activated in the interaction with transgressive games, spanning from the safe and focused sense of flow to more varying and stronger emotional responses. Flow theory postulates that an emotional balance is central for the flow experience to be upheld, and in the same way we argue that there must be a balance between the flow channel and emotional responses in order to tackle transgression in games. We have seen that emotions that spring out of a reflective process rather than the immediate affective response to transgressive games are decisive for whether a player decides to stop playing a game or not.

Three central concepts are also characteristic for the model: To access *gamer mode* is a mitigation technique that allows the player to refocus their attention away from the transgressive content of a video game and emphasize its ludic characteristics. Gamer mode interacts with the flow channel and is best activated in the flow state. When gamer mode is activated, the game experience feels safe and enables players to keep on playing the game. Also, another central concept is the *ludic sublime*, which is a way to appreciate the game through wonder, astonishment, and esteem for the game as a designed artifact. While this is a mode of appreciation that allows us to engage with the game as an amazing and sometimes almost incomprehensible construct, the ludic sublime can indeed be understood as a mitigation technique, but opposite to gamer mode, this is something that allows the game experience to remain something at the boundary between the unsafe and the dangerous.

These two concepts are well positioned to explain *the fallacy of play* – the erroneous idea that play is safe and trivial. While gamer mode indeed allows the player to position transgressive game experiences as safe, the ludic sublime demonstrates how many game experiences are precisely not something safe. Video games are emotionally risky. It is this emotional risk that is at the center of our claim that games are, to a much larger extent than other cultural expressions, designed to make us feel. They are machines of emotion. That does not mean that games create more emotion than other media, but when considered as machines, they are procedurally designed to maintain processes that do produce emotion, and it is the player's role to initiate and lead that process. Considered as emotion machines, games are not perpetuum mobiles that keep running once started or even an automaton that runs until an objective has been reached, but a vehicle that needs steering and constant input in order to not come to a halt or dramatically fail. As we have argued, *form* is at least as important as content, and perhaps more so. Instead what sets games apart from other media is not that they evoke emotion, because that is a vital aspect of all communication modalities. What sets them apart is the machine metaphor.

If we step a little closer to these emotions, we can start making assumptions about what emotions are created as a result of which part of the game. Most games, but digital games in particular, can be split in a structural and a representational level. The representational level is where the fiction, narratives, and visual and auditory aspects live. The structural level is where the limitations and affordances live – the rules, game-pieces, and boards; the things that make this a game and not just a story. While game mechanics may be formally associated with the structural level, they are in practice the connecting feature between these two worlds. From what we have seen of how players respond to the structure and representation in games, we can assume that there are different emotions that are activated. From the representational level consisting of the music, images, or texts, emotions stirred by the fictional level emerge, such as empathy, disgust, or romance – these are the emotions central to the layer that we experience as the story of the game. From the structural level victory, loss, accomplishment, or frustration with the complexity of the game emerge. Of course, some emotions overlap; we can be afraid of failing, and we can be afraid of the zombie we know is lurking, but we still know that these are not exactly the same emotions.

And it is this type of distinction between feelings that create the paradox of transgressive aesthetics in games. We play in order to feel, but we also need to control our feelings while we play. It leads the player into a loop of metareflection, where the aim is to become overwhelmed but still remain in control. In order for this to be experienced as real, the player needs to occasionally lose control – to step over the boundaries and be moved more strongly than desired. But it is not the final loss of control that is meaningful; it is the repeated loss of control, followed with the repeated regaining of control. Games let us feel, even when we fear to feel.

References

Bartsch, Anne, and Mary Beth Oliver. 2011. "Making Sense of Entertainment." *Journal of Media Psychology* 23 (1): 12–17. doi:10.1027/1864-1105/a000026.

Bogost, Ian. 2019. "Don't Play Untitled Goose Game – The Atlantic." *The Atlantic*, October 22, 2019. www.theatlantic.com/technology/archive/2019/10/dont-play-the-goose-game/600472/.

Comedy Central. n.d. "These Elaborate 'The Sims' Torture Chambers Will Awaken Your Inner Psycho." Comedy Central. Accessed October 25, 2019. www.comedycentral.co.uk/news/these-elaborate-the-sims-torture-chambers-will-awaken-your-inner-psycho.

Csikszentmihaly, Mihaly. 1981. "Some Paradoxes in the Definition of Play." In *Play in Context, (A(Ssn. for the) A(Nthropological) S(Tudy of) P(Lay) Proc. Ser.; 5; 1979*, edited by Alyce Taylor Cheska, 14–26. West Point, NY: Leisure.

Donaldson, Scott. 2016. "Metagaming and Subversive Play in League of Legends." In *Proceedings of 1st International Joint Conference of DiGRA and FDG*. Digital Games Research Association (DIGRA). www.digra.org/wp-content/uploads/digital-library/paper_95.pdf.

Frank, Anders. 2012. "Gaming the Game." *Simulation & Gaming* 43 (1): 118–32. doi:10.1177/1046878111408796.

Hernandez, Patricia. 2015. "The Sims Players Confess Their Most Evil Deeds." *Kotaku*, March 31, 2015. https://kotaku.com/the-sims-players-confess-their-most-evil-deeds-1694855714.

Hopeametsä, Heidi. 2008. "24 Hours in a Bomb Shelter." Edited by Markus Montola and Jaakko Stenros. Playground Worlds. 2008. https://nordiclarp.org/wiki/Playground_Worlds.

Iser, Wolfgang. 1978. *The Act of Reading: A Theory of Aesthetic Response*. London: Routledge and Kegan Paul.

Maxis Software, Inc. 2000. *The Sims*. Edited by Will Wright. *The Sims*. Electronic Arts, Inc.

Montola, Markus. 2010. "The Positive Negative Experience in Extreme Role-Playing." In *Nordic DiGRA 2010*. Stockholm: DiGRA. www.digra.org/wp-content/uploads/digital-library/10343.56524.pdf.

Montola, Markus, and Jussi Holopainen. 2012. "First Person Audience and the Art of Painful Role-Playing." In *Immersive Gameplay: Essays on Participatory Media and Role-Playing*, edited by Evan Torner and William J. White, 13–30. Jefferson: McFarland & Company.

Mortensen, Torill Elvira. 2004. "Flow, Seduction and Mutual Pleasure." In *Other Players*, edited by Miguel Sicart. IT university of Copenhagen: IT University of Copenhagen.

———. 2008. "Humans Playing World of Warcraft: Or Deviant Strategies?" In *Digital Culture, Play, and Identity: A World of Warcraft Reader*, edited by Hilde G. Corneliussen and Jill Walker Rettberg, 203–225. Cambridge: The MIT Press.

———. 2010. "The Player as Hedonist: The Problem of Enjoyment." *Journal of Gaming and Virtual Worlds* 2 (2): 105–13. doi:10.1386/jgvw.2.2.105_1.

Mortensen, Torill Elvira, and Victor Navarro-Remesal. 2018. "Asynchronous Transgressions: Suffering, Relief and Invasions in Nintendo's Miiverse and Streetpass." In *Transgression in Games and Play*, edited by Kristine Jørgensen and Faltin Karlsen, 26–44. Cambridge, MA: MIT Press.

Oliver, Mary Beth, Nicholas David Bowman, Julia K. Woolley, Ryan Rogers, Brett I. Sherrick, and Mun-Young Chung. 2016. "Video Games as Meaningful Entertainment Experiences." *Psychology of Popular Media Culture* 5 (4): 390–405. doi:10.1037/ppm0000066.

Pearce, Celia. 2008. "The Truth About Baby Boomer Gamers: A Study of Over-Forty Computer Game Players." *Games and Culture* 3 (2): 142–174. doi:10.1177/1555412008314132.

———. 2009. *Communities of Play: Emergent Cultures in Multiplayer Games and Virtual Worlds*. Cambridge, London: MIT Press.

Sihvonen, Tanja. 2011. *Players Unleashed; Modding The Sims and the Culture of Gaming*. Amsterdam: Amsterdam University Press.

Smuts, Aaron. 2007. "The Paradox of Painful Art." *Journal of Aesthetic Education* 41 (3): 59–76. doi:10.1353/jae.2007.0029.

Taylor, T L. 2003. "Multiple Pleasures. Women and Online Gaming." *Convergence* 9 (1): 21–46. doi:10.1177/135485650300900103.

———. 2006. *Play between Worlds: Exploring Online Game Culture*. Cambridge: MIT Press.

Wenz, Karin. 2013. "THEORYCRAFTING: Knowledge Production and Surveillance." *Information Communication and Society* 16 (2): 178–93. doi:10.1080/1369118X.2012.738695.

Index